Belonging in an Adopted World

Race, Identity, and Transnational Adoption

Barbara Yngvesson

The University of Chicago Press Chicago and London

Barbara Yngvesson is professor of anthropology at Hampshire College, the author or
coauthor of two previous volumes, and an
associate editor at *American Anthropologist.*

The University of Chicago Press,
Chicago 60637
The University of Chicago Press, Ltd., London
© 2010 by The University of Chicago
All rights reserved. Published 2010
Printed in the United States of America

19 18 17 16 15 14 13 12 11 10   1 2 3 4 5

ISBN-13: 978-0-226-96446-1 (cloth)
ISBN-13: 978-0-226-96447-8 (paper)
ISBN-10: 0-226-96446-9 (cloth)
ISBN-10: 0-226-96447-7 (paper)

Library of Congress
Cataloging-in-Publication Data

Belonging in an adopted world :
race, identity, and transnational adoption /
Barbara Yngvesson.
p.   cm. — (The Chicago series in law
and society)
Includes bibliographical references and index.
ISBN-13: 978-0-226-96446-1 (cloth : alk. paper)
ISBN-10: 0-226-96446-9 (cloth : alk. paper)
ISBN-13: 978-0-226-96447-8 (pbk. : alk. paper)
ISBN-10: 0-226-96447-7 (pbk. : alk. paper)
1. Intercountry adoption. 2. Interracial adoption. 3. Interethnic adoption. 4. Intercountry
adoption—Law and legislation. 5. Intercountry adoption—Sweden. 6. Intercountry
adoption—India. I. Yngvesson, Barbara, 1941–
II. Series: Chicago series in law and society.
HV875.5.B44 2010
362.734—dc22
                                    2009029586

Belonging in an Adopted World

The Chicago Series in Law and Society
Edited by John M. Conley and Lynn Mather

Also in the series:

Invitation to Law and Society: An Introduction to the Study of Real Law
by Kitty Calavita

*Making Rights Real: Activists, Bureaucrats, and the Creation of
the Legalistic State*
by Charles R. Epp

Lawyers on the Right: Professionalizing the Conservative Coalition
by Ann Southworth

Arguing with Tradition: The Language of Law in Hopi Tribal Court
by Justin B. Richland

Speaking of Crime: The Language of Criminal Justice
by Lawrence M. Solan and Peter M. Tiersma

*Human Rights and Gender Violence: Translating International Law
into Social Justice*
by Sally Engle Merry

Just Words, Second Edition: Law, Language, and Power
by John M. Conley and William M. O'Barr

Distorting the Law: Politics, Media, and the Litigation Crisis
by William Haltom and Michael McCann

Justice in the Balkans: Prosecuting War Crimes in the Hague Tribunal
by John Hagan

*Rights of Inclusion: Law and Identity in the Life Stories of Americans
with Disabilities*
by David M. Engel and Frank W. Munger

*The Internationalization of Palace Wars: Lawyers, Economists, and the
Contest to Transform Latin American States*
by Yves Dezalay and Bryant G. Garth

*Free to Die for Their Country: The Story of the Japanese American Draft
Resisters in World War II*
by Eric L. Muller

Additional series titles follow index.

For my son, Finn

and

In memory of my mother, Julia Belton

Contents

Acknowledgments

I am deeply indebted to the individuals and organizations whose generosity made this work possible. Many of the people mentioned here provided me with hours of taped interviews over a period of years and graciously allowed me to take part in workshops, conferences, and a range of meetings involving adoption organizations and children's homes, representatives of receiving and sending nations, and the concerns of transnational adoptees. I could not have carried out the research without their interest and engagement; however, they do not endorse this project or the analysis I present here.

I am especially indebted to Adoption Centre (AC) in Stockholm, Sweden, which provided the ethnographic starting point for my research, and to Gunilla Andersson, Annika Grünewald, Ann-Charlotte Gudmundsson, Eva Hedén, Monica Lind, Birgitta Löwstedt, and Elisabet Sandberg, who responded to my questions and in some cases spent weeks in my company visiting children's homes in Bolivia, Chile, Colombia, Ecuador, and India. Annika, Gunilla, and Monica opened their homes to me, as well as providing invaluable information and support. I am grateful to Elisabet Sandberg, administrative director of AC during the first period of my research, who shared her extensive knowledge of Swedish and international adoption law with me and arranged for presentations of my work at adoption-related events in Stockholm, including a stimulating and productive seminar in 2006 at Stockholm University, as a guest of professor of ethnology Lena Gerholm. Eva Hedén and Elisabet Sandberg also helped me obtain permissions for illustrations in the book. And I appreciate Ewa Westman's highly professional and sensitive transcription of my Swedish interviews.

Although the base of my research was in Sweden, I also spent many weeks in India and South America, accompanying staff of AC on trips to children's homes and visits to aid projects funded by the Swedish International Development Agency. I am grateful to individuals and organizations in Bangalore, Chennai, Delhi, Kolkata, and Mumbai, and particularly to Nomita Chandy, secretary of the Ashraya Children's Home in Bangalore;

to Swaran Chaudhry, secretary of the Society for Indian Children's Welfare in Kolkata; to Andal Damodaran, who was secretary general of the Indian Council for Child Welfare in Tamil Nadu at the time of my research and subsequently the director of CARA, India's Central Adoption Research Agency; to the late Aruna Kumar, secretary of the Delhi Council for Child Welfare, whose unexpected death in 2006 was a great loss to her professional colleagues and to the children for whom she worked with such dedication; to Girija Kumarababu, a child welfare organizer in Tamil Nadu when I visited there in the 1990s; to Aloma Lobo, who was director of CARA during the last part of my research; and to Nina Nayak, a social worker who is active in advocacy for foster care and domestic adoption in India. In addition, I want to thank the directors and staff of children's homes in Cali and Bogotá, Colombia, especially Chiquitines, FANA, and Los Pisingos, which I visited in the course of my research.

This project began with travel to Asia and South America in the company of AC staff, but in the last few years of the research, I spent more of my time interviewing adopted adults who had grown up mostly in Sweden, as well as some of their parents. I will not mention all of them by name, since some prefer to remain anonymous and the experiences of others were the focus of an earlier publication (Yngvesson 2005). But special thanks go to Sara Nordin Grönroos, ChuChu Schindele, Amanda Fredriksson, Mikael Jarnlo, Daniel Rosenlind, and the Association for Adopted Ethiopians and Eritreans in Stockholm; also to Jaclyn Aronson, Barbara Rall, and Maria Brunn. Hanna Wallensteen, who generously agreed to attend an adoption conference I organized in Amherst, Massachusetts, with Kay Johnson in 2003, performed (in English) her wonderful monologue about transnational adoption and identity, *Know Your Place*, at that conference. I have also benefited greatly from the published work of Anna von Melen and Astrid Trotzig. Their work is unfortunately available only in Swedish, but it is among the first publications by transnationally adopted adults that focus on issues of identity and belonging.

Numerous colleagues have contributed to this project through their friendship, intellectual energy, and moral support. They include Maureen Mahoney, with whom I have taught and written collaboratively for years. Maureen's insights and theoretical acumen have shaped my work in countless ways, and she generously read through and commented on the entire manuscript. Susan Coutin has been a close friend and intellectual collaborator over the past several years, during which many of the ideas developed in this book came to fruition. Together with Bill Maurer and Tom Boellstorff, we spent several weeks at the International Institute for the Sociology of Law in Oñati, Spain, where Susan, Bill, and I produced a draft for a paper

we later published discussing the connections between immigration, adoption, and offshore finance. Subsequently, Susan and I collaborated on two other papers that brought our research on adoption and immigration into conversation. I am also indebted to the writers' group of which I have been a member for many years—Michelle Bigenho, Julie Hemment, Beth Notar, and Joshua Roth—for careful reading of many chapter drafts, culinary adventures prior to our meetings, and the support they provided as we saw each of our most recent books through to publication.

Nina Payne read through an early draft of my manuscript for this book. For years, I counted on her sensitivity to language and phrasing to guide me through one or another dense passage in an article or chapter and to suggest what in retrospect seemed the perfect words to capture what I was trying to say. She is sorely missed. Christine Harrington has talked through with me many of the ideas in this research and has been a wonderful and supportive friend. Jan Hoffman French read and commented helpfully on an early draft of chapter 1. I have also valued the intellectual support and friendship of David and Jaruwan Engel, Carol Greenhouse, Dirk Hartog, Lynn Mather, and Toby Volkman. Marlene Fried, with whom I have taught a course at Hampshire College titled "Creating Families" for many years, has been crucial in broadening my perspective on the issues I have been studying; Kay Johnson's expertise on China and her experience with adoption more generally have also been invaluable. Thanks also to Lourdes Mattei for discussions about psychological literature on adoption; to Peter Selman for his amazingly detailed knowledge of the demographics of transnational adoption and his willingness to send me the most up-to-date information on very short notice; and to Falguni Sheth for thought-provoking conversations on topics related to adoption, immigration, and race. In addition, I would like to acknowledge the invaluable support of Emily Gallivan, Chyrell George, Paula Harmon, and Rae-Ann Wentworth, all administrative staff at Hampshire College.

To the anonymous readers of my book manuscript (and to Lynn Mather, who provided detailed comments on the semifinal draft) I extend my appreciation for your careful reading and the insight you provided regarding blind spots and possible improvements that strengthened the final draft. John Conley's interest in the manuscript (as Law and Society Series editor, together with Lynn Mather) is also very much appreciated. To John Tryneski, my editor at the University of Chicago Press, I am indebted for his enthusiasm, his flexibility, his guidance through various stages of the publication process, and his good sense regarding questions both substantive and aesthetic; and I thank Rodney F. Powell, his assistant, who has so ably responded to my questions and concerns.

Finally, I have no adequate way of expressing my gratitude to my husband Sigfrid, my sons Dag and Finn, and my parents, William and Julia Belton, on whose porch I wrote many early drafts of this book. While my mother did not live to see it published, her influence pervades it. My father continues to send me articles on adoption and has been consistently supportive of my work. Thanks also to my brother and sister-in-law, Hugh and Jennifer Belton, for reading one of the last drafts of chapter 1. But most especially, my love and thanks go to Dag for his detailed reading of the entire manuscript and long discussions about it; to Finn for reading drafts, designing artwork, and being the source of my inspiration to undertake the research; and to my husband Sigfrid, who read various parts of the book multiple times and whose unstinting belief in me helped to bring it to completion.

The section titled "A Form of Consent" in the prologue is adapted from Yngvesson 1997, 34–38. My research was supported by the National Science Foundation, award numbers SES-9113894 and SBR-9511937, as well as by faculty research grants from Hampshire College.

A Letter

This is a shortened and translated version of a letter written by a birth mother in Colombia to the adoptive parents of her infant son. Identifying information (including names and the date) has been changed. The letter was produced at a time when institutional children's homes in Colombia and elsewhere were increasingly receiving inquiries from adoptees about their preadoptive history. Adoptees were asking specifically, "Why was I abandoned?" In response, some homes were encouraging the relinquishing mother to write a letter to the child or the adoptive parents that could be included in the adoption file, in case the child or the parents had questions about the circumstances of the mother's decision to relinquish the child.

July 1999

To the parents of Antonio Andrés·

Before all else, I send you a respectful greeting and please excuse me if I inconvenience you by writing these sad words. My name is María Antonia, mother of Andrés, of whom you have become the legitimate parents and even though it is hard for me to accept this I respect it and am resigned that I must learn to accept it, since because of my love of my child his wellbeing is more important than anything else. Perhaps you think that I am giving you my child because I don't love him but it isn't that way, my son is everything to me, but because of that I don't want him to lack what he needs or to suffer, no. I don't want that for him and that is why I cede my place as his mother to you because I am sure that you can offer him a better quality of life different from the one I could offer him.

I am sure you understand that this is very painful for me and I know that you have suffered because you cannot have a child and although we know about pain in different ways, we share the sorrow and anguish.

Now life is giving you the opportunity to be happy and enjoy the joy that a child can offer his parents and although my heart is breaking to have to give him away I know that with you he will be much better off because my unstable situation makes it impossible for me to keep him, in addition to the lack of support of my family and of his father.

You cannot imagine the suffering or the pain that I feel in separating from my child but I have to do it because I don't want him to lack for anything. For this reason, with my heart in my hand, I pray that you will take good care of my child, since he is legally your child. Care for him as much as you can, offer him all the love you can, guide him along a good path, love him as though he were your own. . . .

Cordially,
María Antonia Guzmán

I include this letter not because it is representative of others (nor because it speaks for other birth mothers who do not leave written messages for the future parents of their children), but to provide some sense of a relinquishment narrative, the circumstances that can lead to the "abandonment" of a child, and a particular historical moment when awareness of the child's interest in his or her "identity" led officials in sending nations to support the production of such documents. For a very different representation of the "abandoning" mother, see "Space-Blankets," pages 86–87.

Prologue

A Form of Consent

I first met my son Finn in the office of our lawyer, David Kaplan, in Northampton, Massachusetts. We had arranged for his parents to fly in from California the night before; the lawyer we had hired for them had met them at the airport in the morning and brought them to the law offices of our lawyer. There we all came together to sign the papers that would "irrevocably terminate" Finn's birth mother's parental rights. Finn was then four months old. I remember that he was tired and crying; that his mother, Diana, nursed him there in the lawyer's office, to soothe him, and that as we signed what seemed to be endless paperwork, our older son Dag carried Finn around the office, bouncing him gently, thrilled to be entrusted with the brother he had so longed for. Diana had brought with her all of Finn's baby toys, the cards and presents he had received when he was born, his favorite blanket, a plastic bluebird we could hang from the ceiling in his room, and a Japanese kite of blue and white fabric, shaped like a giant fish. These belongings, familiar from his first few months of life, came in a well-worn blue canvas duffel bag, its red handle secured with a diaper pin covered in yellow plastic. We still use this bag today, and the yellow safety pin is still there.

The documents we signed that morning included papers authorizing me and my husband Sigfrid to become Finn's legal guardians and a "form of consent" signed by his mother in which she "finally and irrevocably" surrendered her legal rights to her child. Because Finn was born out of wedlock, only Diana signed the form, which reads as follows: "I, as the mother of Finn, age 4 months, of the male sex, born in San Rafael, California on June 25, 1981 do hereby voluntarily and unconditionally surrender Finn to the care and custody of Barbara and Sigfrid Yngvesson for the purpose of adoption or other such disposition as may be made by a court of competent jurisdiction. I waive notice of any legal proceedings affecting the custody, guardianship, adoption or other disposition of Finn." At the end of the signings, everyone in the law office joined us to drink champagne and toast this moment of transfer and of Finn's new life with us. His birth parents flew back to California that afternoon.

When we had first imagined the transfer of parental rights, two weeks before, our lawyer had arranged that the physical handing over of this baby would not involve an actual meeting of the two sets of parents. Massachusetts law at the time forbade such a meeting. Thus the plan had been that we would bring Finn's mother to Northampton, where she would hand her baby over to her lawyer, her lawyer would hand him to our lawyer, and our lawyer would give the baby to us. We would be in separate rooms. When his parents heard about this arrangement, they asked (through my brother, who had made the initial contact for the adoption) to speak with me, and so I called Diana, with great trepidation. My social worker friends had warned me that this was a woman who was not ready to part with her child and that any contact we had would bode ill for the future. Our phone call was not the difficult event I feared, however. She simply said that she was entrusting us with her baby and that she wanted to hand him to me, not to a lawyer. She told me about her difficulties in weaning him, since he seemed to be allergic to cow's milk and had developed a bad rash, of her efforts to accustom him to goat's milk, and her worry that he would not look beautiful when we first saw him. She told me, too, about the insensitivity of people in her small town, most of whom "can't forgive me for giving him away." A few people thought she was courageous to do so.

By the end of our conversation, it was clear to me not only that I should receive Finn into my arms from Diana's, but that Finn's father should accompany them to Northampton for the exchange and that we should all—my husband Sigfrid, our son Dag, and I—be there to participate in this ceremony of severance and of joining. The legal moment that was to separate Finn "irrevocably" from his mother and join him temporarily to us (the adoption was not to become final for several months) became inseparable from an "illegal moment," an outlaw time in which we violated Massachusetts adoption law. We agreed that this was not only a transaction between a birth mother and the state, and between potential adoptive parents and the state, but that it was also, in Finn's birth father's words, a "parent-to-parent matter." He wrote in a letter he gave to us that morning in Northampton:

> We do feel responsible that he join a family that wants him, and cannot blindly turn him over to the surrogate parenthood of the state. So the one thing we ask of you, is to make an arrangement with us, so that if for any rea-

son his adoption to you does *not* occur, that we regain custody—rather than have him go to a foster home chosen by a social agency. There are several other families that want to adopt him, so there is no point whatsoever in his becoming a ward of the state of Massachusetts. I realize the laws are formal here in regard to "property" claim, but this is a parent-to-parent matter, not a question of a child supported at public expense. We feel that we express Finn's "best interest" by turning him over to you, and that if that doesn't work out, you would express his "best interest" by turning him back over to us rather than to a professional agency. Until the adoption is completed, I think both Diana and I will continue to feel somewhat responsible and ambivalent. I hope you would understand this.

Finn's father went on to describe his son's birth—"without anesthetics, surrounded by friends, immediately breast-fed, and always cared for conscientiously"—and habits: "He doesn't like his diapers to be changed. When he's tired, he makes a kind of coughing cry. He likes to be rocked in a rocking chair and sung to when he's tired. . . . He doesn't crawl yet but likes to be held so that he can walk." And he concluded with a brief P.S.: "Please don't interpret this note as a bid for personal relationship, or an embarrassment of any kind to you. I only mean to put this child properly into your safekeeping, and convey my regards, and assure you of our availability *if* for some reason the adoption process can't be completed at that end."

Seven months later, our adoption of Finn was finalized in a brief legal ceremony at the Franklin County probate court in Greenfield, Massachusetts. Shortly thereafter, we received his new birth certificate in the mail. The certificate named me and my husband Sigfrid as Finn's parents. There was no mention of his adoption. In effect, if the new birth certificate was to be believed, Barbara Yngvesson, born in the Dominican Republic, age thirty-nine, had given birth to Finn Fort Yngvesson at the Marin County General Hospital in Greenbrae, California, on June 25, 1981. The only available record of his birth to Diana Morrison-McGuire was an outlaw record, kept in the slowly expanding folders of letters and pictures that Diana and I collected and that documented our relationship and our connection to each other through the son to whom she gave birth and whom Sigfrid and I were raising.

I recount this brief story of how Finn came to us in part because it illuminates the contradictions embedded in American adoptive kinship. It also speaks to the multiple ways in which birth parents, adoptive parents, and others construct and rework adoptive kinship through and in the power of these silences and disjunctions. But I also imagine this story and the adoption that it is about as a way of reflecting on a central theme in the construction of American social order and disorder, a theme that historian Michael Grossberg has termed "the persistent attraction of illegitimacy" in American history (1985, 228). This "persistent attraction" can be seen both in the refusal of the illegitimate family to disappear, in spite of repeated efforts to eradicate it, and in the seeming compulsion of the established order to make illegitimacy a focus of its attention. Illegitimacy is, to use Judith Butler's phrase, the "constitutive 'outside'" of American social order, and the splitting of legitimate from illegitimate families is an "enabling cultural condition" for the emergence and reaffirmation of patriarchy (Butler 1993, 8).[1]

Patriarchy materializes over time in the repeated, disruptive return over the past three centuries in the United States of the unmarried mother as a "social problem"; and it takes shape in countless reiterations of the difference between the dyadic unit of mother and child and "the place where a society enters a child, and a child learns the laws of a society" (Steedman 1986, 79). These reiterations naturalize the mother-child dyad as an intimate, emotionally charged connection that "can never be severed, *whatever its legal position*. . . . An ex-husband or ex-wife is possible, and so is an ex-mother-in-law. But an ex-mother is not" (Schneider 1968, 24, emphasis added). Likewise, the reiterations denaturalize law, making it a separate order from the order of nature, "imposed by man and consist[ing] of rules and regulations" (24). In this way a boundary materializes between two orders—one of natural substance patterned according to "the way things are in nature," the other a code for conduct, a "rule of order, the government of action by morality and the self-restraint of human reason" (26).

This cultural interpretation of motherhood as fundamentally outside the law, grounded in a biologically based intimacy (and, conversely, of fatherhood as fundamentally within the law, grounded in property rights over his child), is at the root of prohibitions that represent the unwed mother as chaotic, disruptive, asocial—a "mother in name only" (Kunzel 1993, 130). The *kind* of chaos she represents differs according to her race, her class, and her age; and the solutions proposed are shaped by social, cultural, and economic concerns that are specific to the particular historical moment. In my research on open adoption in the United States, my informants were white, lower- to middle-class, unmarried mothers and the white, broadly middle-class, adoptive families in which they placed their infant children in the decade 1981–1991. In these adoptions, it was the birth mother's choice of adoptive parents for her child that created an adoptive family, whole and "complete" in itself, to use the words of a

young birth mother who placed her child for adoption in 1994. The matching of a baby to a family (that is, the "completion" of identity for the parents and for the child) constructed a racialized hierarchy of families and
of unwed (unfit) mothers, who together fulfilled the "postwar family imperative" (Solinger 1992, 154) in the United States, while reinscribing the
racial borders through which the interpretation of family wholeness was
measured.

The "Abandoned" Child

My present project continues the exploration of such issues in a global
arena. Beginning with the journeys of white, relatively affluent Swedish
women to India and Africa in the 1960s to adopt or arrange for the adoption of children from orphanages in Delhi, Kolkata, or Addis Ababa, I examine the power of the "abandoned" child (the "different" child) to compel
prospective adoptive parents, as the most desired domestic adoptee—a
healthy white infant—became increasingly scarce in Euro-American
adopting nations. The appeal of the orphanage child was precisely its lack
(of a mother) and the corollary of that lack, the need for maternal love.
This "need," and the assumed capacity of the adoptive mother to provide
it, obviated increasingly complex questions raised by psychologists, social workers, birth mothers, and adopted adults in domestic adoptions
about the importance for the child of engaging with its preadoptive history, however fragmentary the narratives of this history might be. Abandonment—what one prominent U.S. social worker, herself the parent of
a child adopted from China, referred to as "the 'A' word" (Brown 2000,
32)—was at the same time constructed as the central experience of the
transnationally adopted child, the source of "early disturbances" that
might follow her or him through life, and considered unspeakable, "the
worst thing that could happen to any child" (Henningson 1999).

As increasing numbers of adopted adults returned in the final decade of
the twentieth century and the first years of the twenty-first to their countries of birth in search of some trace of the elusive figure of the "biological
mother," the stories that took shape, whether in her absence or in the presence of the woman who could have been their mother, have complicated
our understanding of the meanings both of motherhood and of "return."
Building on the insight of Swedish social worker Ingrid Stjerna that "there
is no such thing as a motherless child[;] even if she is dead she is important,"[2] I consider the central place of the abandoning mother in the legal
family, as well as the pull exerted by this figure on adoptees and, in no less

powerful ways, on their adoptive parents, to return to the imagined "before" of abandonment, where "real" belongings can be found. The tensions between legal (adoptive) relations and blood ties that were the focus of my research on open adoption in the United States (Yngvesson 1997) become the tension between legal belongings and the pull toward a mother(land), culture, or native soil in a global context. In both cases, I argue, the "as if" relations established by adoption law catalyze the pull back to an allegedly prior (more natural) state of completion, even as such journeys complicate belongings, entangling us in relations that can never be complete.

In the chapters that follow, I develop this analysis of the power of law to make and unmake "natural" belongings, while drawing on narratives of the lived experience of adoption to suggest unexpected ways in which adoptive kinship may transform understandings of identity and the belongings in which it is implicated. Chapter 1 provides an overview of key themes, focusing on the place of adoptive kinship in realizing, rather than displacing, a genealogical "real" that is evoked by the "as if" quality of families and nations that are constituted by adoption. I examine the tension between humanitarian ideals that are expressed in the figure of a generalized child who can be "loved by anyone" but must be freed of his or her preadoptive history to become adoptable, on the one hand, and the racialized hierarchies and inequalities that materialize around a specific child, whose difference is inscribed in and on her or his body in ways that both call forth and unsettle expectations about where "real" belongings are to be found, on the other hand. These hierarchies predate the child's adoption and are a dimension of systems of stratified reproduction that constitute some families and nations as givers or senders of children in adoption and others as receivers. They are expressed in the longings of adoptive parents for a "different" child and in the transformations of a child's "value" that accompany the child's becoming adoptable and being placed in the adoptive family and nation.

Drawing on fieldwork in Sweden and India, two nations that played a key role in the development and regulation of transnational adoption, chapters 2 and 3 move between Sweden's principal adoption organization, Adoption Centre (AC), located in a suburb of Stockholm, and orphanages and child welfare organizations in Bangalore, Kolkata, Mumbai, and Delhi. Through interviews with the pioneer generation of transnational adopters in Sweden and persons in India who were involved in the process, I trace the emergence of informal networks dedicated to finding families for abandoned children and the work of such networks in making the "value" of the abandoned child visible. A central theme is the connection of the emerging value of the abandoned child to its commoditization and the ambiguous role of legal instruments that seek to regulate transnational adoption. I examine, for example, the roles of the 1985 Indian Supreme Court judgment in *Lakshmi Kant Pandey v. Union of India* and the 1993 Hague Convention on Intercountry Adoption in transforming an adoptable child who is not "one of us" into a national resource that has the potential to become "one of ours." Chapter 3 concludes with a discussion of the efforts of child welfare activists in India to secure resources for poor children and their mothers and the entanglement of these efforts in processes such as transnational adoption that transform children into resources for the nation.

The fourth and fifth chapters move from the sending to the receiving nation, building on participant observation, interviews, and archival research in Sweden, a nation that has one of the world's highest adoption ratios (number of adoptees per one thousand live births) and has played a prominent role in developing guidelines for transnational adoption policy. The chapters explore the tension between Swedish ideals that even the most "different" child can become fully Swedish as long as he or she is placed in a proper Swedish family and the lived experience of the adopted that they do not fully belong in their adoptive nation. I focus on the ambiguous position of the adoptee as both inside the family and nation and outside it—as culturally and racially different—during the period of Sweden's transition to becoming an immigrant nation. I also critically examine the conventional assumption that "difference" in the adoptee is an effect of "early disturbances" that occurred before the child's arrival in the adopting nation, rather than an effect of postadoptive relations of an adoptee to his or her social surround, such as parents, school teachers, friends, and strangers.

My final two chapters draw on extensive interviews I conducted with adopted adults of African or Asian descent who were raised in Sweden and the United States, some of whom have made multiple trips back to their countries of birth and have visited with birth families, at orphanages, or at the hospitals where they were born. I explore the connections between adoption practices that cancel the adopted child's history so that it can be completely incorporated into the adoptive family and nation and the pull back to a place or person with its promise of providing a ground of identity. I suggest that the pull back is fundamental to the logic of (biogenetic) identity but that going back may complicate the experience of identity, constituting it as dynamic, discontinuous, and always in need of one more return.

The Safehouse of Identity

Adopt 1. To take into one's family through legal means and raise as one's own child. 2. To select and bring into a new relationship, as a friend, heir, or citizen. 3. To take and follow (a course of action, for example) by choice or assent. 4. To take up and use as one's own, as an idea, word, or the like. 5. To take on or assume. . . . [Latin *adoptare*, to choose for oneself : *ad-*, to + *optare*, to choose, desire.]

—*American Heritage Dictionary of the English Language*, New College Edition

Genealogical Fictions

In July of 1999, my son Finn and I visited my parents in West Virginia. My mother, age eighty-five, frail and just released from the hospital, was sitting with us in her favorite spot on a balcony that overlooks their meadow and the steep wooded hill beyond. In the past weeks, we had all wondered whether she would sit on this balcony again, and so the moment was especially poignant. Finn, who had turned eighteen in June, had been working with my father—repairing a leaking pond, sawing fallen trees, hauling cut wood to the barn. As we relaxed in the cool of the evening, my mother turned to Finn and said, "You know, Finn, I feel that you are *really* one of us. You know what I mean—*really* part of our family." Finn looked back at her, the hint of a smile in his eyes. My mother spoke out of the deepest affection for Finn, and saying he was "really one of us" was her highest compliment.

My father, who has devoted months of research over the past several years to family genealogy, was similarly affirming his grandson's place in the family when he offered to use his Family Tree Maker software to develop a genealogical chart for Finn if I would just provide the names of parents and grandparents for him to start with. When I asked why genealogical research was so compelling, my father replied, "I like puzzles." But he agreed that his interest was captured no less by the assumption that he was putting together "his own" puzzle, and he hoped that the information would be of interest to his children and grandchildren "one of these days." At the same time, the idea that Finn, whom we had adopted almost eighteen years previously, needed a separate genealogy if he was to locate himself properly in relation to us and to his "own" family, reflected my mother's need to reassure him that he was *really* one of us, *really* part of our family." In both cases, the implicit ground of family—of what it means to be "one of us"—in the genealogical connection of parent to child is reaffirmed, even as real families take shape in ways that radically and irreversibly transform both the lived experience of belonging and the narratives that shape it for those one considers "one's own."

Adoption writer and consultant Betty Jean Lifton captures the emotional resonance of the biogenetic narrative in her account (1994, 36) of "the story," as told by a friend to his seven-year-old daughter:

> It made his daughter very happy and secure to hear the story that began not with her but with her parents who created her. Sometimes her grandparents and other relatives showed up in the details of the story of before she was born. The child knew without having to be told that her narrative was connected to the narrative of her parents, grandparents, and great-grandparents down through the generations, and so she was connected. Her narrative revealed her identity. It told her who she was. If there had been essential people missing from the narrative—her Mommy, Daddy, grandparents, and other members of her clan—it would have been difficult for her to feel connected as she did.
>
> For most children, like my friend's daughter, their narrative is as much a part of them as their shadow; it develops with them over the years and cannot be torn away. Unless, of course, they are adopted.

The idea of a biogenetic narrative as the shadow other of a child that must be "torn away" to place a child in adoption underscores the erasures that constitute adoptive kinship. But it is also revealing of blind spots that accompany efforts to think and practice a narrative of family—or even of connection—outside the genealogical frame (Povinelli 2002).[1] The image of tearing away the genealogical shadow of a child recalls a passage in the memoir of Swedish adoptee Astrid Trotzig (1996), who explains that the baby picture in the passport that allowed her to enter the Kingdom of Sweden from Korea in 1970 was "torn away" from a larger photograph that included her Korean foster mother holding her (at the time she had the name Park Suh-Yeo, given by Korean child placement authorities) (23).[2] The foster mother was Trotzig's only link to a complicated past that included reproductive policies of the Republic of Korea and its marginalization of women whose out-of-wedlock children could not be accommodated in Korea's strongly patrilineal society.

Here, a national narrative that privileges connection to paternal parents and grandparents "down through the generations" excluded Park Suh-Yeo from belonging in her native land. Indeed, to create an adoptable child from the foundling taken by police to child placement authorities, officials in Seoul first provided Trotzig with a fictive genealogy, in which Park Suh-Yeo was established as the family head and her family's only member (Trotzig 1996, 34–35), then positioned as if she had no (foster) mother. Thus she qualified for adoption in Sweden, where her fictive genealogy was canceled so she could become a completely Swedish child.

The story of Trotzig's adoption, a variation on a familiar narrative in which children must be abandoned so that "family" can be preserved, illuminates a central thread in the emergence, consolidation, and (in the post-1950s period) globalization of the liberal legal form of adoptive kinship. Neither the birth mother nor the adoptive parents constitute a "real" (two-parent, biogenetic) family, but both are constant reminders, as in the case of our son Finn's adoption, of the power of a genealogical imaginary in defining what a real family consists in. The constant slippage (as in the conversations with my parents, above) between real and fictive belongings positions the adoptee and the adoptive family and, in very different ways, the birth mother in a virtual space where they are simultaneously real and not real. The adoptive family is the only de facto family of the child; yet it never becomes an unmarked (nonadoptive) family. The birth mother ceases to be the adopted child's mother; but the promise of "papers" documenting her existence or even her death may pull the adopted child (and the adoptive family) "back" to seek some trace of her (or may pull the birth mother "forward" to seek information about the adopted child) (Yngvesson 1997; Yngvesson and Coutin 2006).

Finn's adoption also involved the legal erasure of his preadoptive history and the legal construction of our family "as if" it were genealogical (Modell 1994, 2). But the circumstances surrounding his placement with us made it possible for us to forge connections with his birth family and remain in contact with them. This contact, focused initially on my relationship with Finn's birth mother, Diana, substantiated my own connection to Finn, my sense that he was my child because he was her child. Connections such as these, developed in juxtaposition to and always in tension with the closures and cut-offs that establish the adoptive family as if it were the only family of the child, both challenge the autonomy of that family and help to constitute it as real. The labor of kinship in adoption begins with this emotional work, whether it involves the birth family, as in our case, or records found in a children's home, hospital, or court archive, as may be the case in transnational adoptions.

For our family, the emotional work began when my brother relocated to Bolinas, California, on the day of Finn's birth, moved into a house with Finn's birth mother's best friend, and gradually became an intermediary between Finn's birth family and ours. What started as a series of chance events, culminating with Finn's formal adoption almost a year later, became in retrospect (and from my perspective) the frame for an adoption story that seemed to move almost in spite of itself toward Finn's becoming our child. My brother's involvement was crucial to my experience of these events "as if" they were taking place within our family, while their fortuitousness imbued the narrative of Finn's adoption with a sense that it was meant to be, a quality remarked on by other adoptive parents with stories that differ significantly from ours.

The emotional experience of adoption as "meant to be" both mythologizes and realizes adoptive kinship. A relationship that is "only legal" is in some sense (in a Euro-American socio-legal universe) "only" a paper relationship (only a chosen relationship) and lacks the emotional and cultural force of a "natural" connection, a connection that compels us in spite of ourselves and is believed to precede and to endure beyond the more planned beginnings and endings of legal parentage, legal marriage, or legal citizenship.[3] A birth mother I interviewed some years ago as part of my research on open adoption conveyed the importance of this sense of kinship as natural connection when she described the adoptive parents with whom she placed her child as "not just anybody, it's not just somebody [my lawyer] knows, it's somebody that Jim [her boyfriend] knows, it's somebody that *I* know" (Yngvesson 1997, 55).

As anthropologist Marilyn Strathern (1995, 351) points out in a paper on kinship and technology: "What gave Euro-American culture its modernist cast . . . was that the core of the family was constituted in the procreative act of the conjugal pair in such a way that *the child's biogenetic closeness to its parents endorsed the nurturing closeness of the conjugal couple. Though the parents were not born kin to each other, the child was born kin to both of them. The child they produced created a closeness*" (emphasis added).[4] The labor of jointly producing a child retroactively *creates* the (genealogical) kinship of the parents in a Euro-American cultural universe, and in this sense the child completes the family by making the parents "naturally" kin to one another in a way that law alone cannot.[5] In an analogous way, the birth mother I interviewed completed the adoptive family by placing her child with known parents, people she considered "like" her in fundamental ways

and with whom she hoped to maintain an ongoing relationship. Her identification with the adoptive parents as the ideal family she could not provide for her child elided the distinction between genealogical and adoptive
kinship by "creating a closeness" between adoptive parents and child that
derived from her own connection to both.[6]

In the chapters that follow, the tension inherent in adoptive kinship—
that it simultaneously constitutes and disrupts a genealogical imaginary
for what a "real" family consists in—is a central theme. The work of the
birth mother interviewee, like my own work in creating a narrative that
made (natural) sense of Finn's adoption, are part of this process of simultaneous production and disruption of genealogical kinship. A similar process goes on discursively, where the implicit difference between an *adoptive*
(that is, a legal) relationship of parent to child and the procreative (more
"natural," more "real") relationship of giving birth naturalizes the latter.[7]
Without the assumption that *before* the adoption there is a natural real,
there would be no need for adoption law to cancel the prior relation of
birth parent to child, for adoptees to search for a birth parent, or for the
adopted child and the adoptive family to remain forever "as if."

The Work of Adoption

> Most troubling is always to meet questions about myself and my origin.
> As though it is not natural that I am here.
>
> —Astrid Trotzig, *Blood Is Thicker than Water*

The efforts of my father to trace Finn's real history, my mother's affirmation of his real connection to our family, and our own sense that he was
fated to become our child are all dimensions of the emotional, cultural,
and legal work that is required to transform adopted families into real
ones, families that are "one of us," families that can be imagined as part of
a larger Euro-American narrative of the "meant-to-be." At the same time,
as Astrid Trotzig's observation in the epigraph suggests, the lived experience of adoption is in tension with what and who this "real" (this "us") and
this "meant-to-be" consist of.

The work of adoption takes place in multiple ways and in multiple settings: in the first encounters of adoptive parents with their children in
the orphanages of Delhi, Addis Ababa, Cali, or Guangzhou; in the private
struggles of adoptees to fit into their adoptive families, birth families,
schools, and workplaces; in organizations of adult adoptees, such as AEF

(the Association of Adopted Eritreans and Ethiopians) in Sweden or AKA ("Also Known As," the adopted Koreans' association) in the United States; on Internet chat groups and adoption research Web sites; in moments such as those on the balcony with my parents and Finn; and in public, collective gatherings in the United States, Korea, Sweden, and elsewhere.

One of the smallest but most visible of such public gatherings took place in Seoul in October 1998, when 29 Korean adoptees from eight Western nations gathered at the Blue House for a ceremony in which President Kim Dae Jung described his nation as "filled with shame" over practices that had sent so many of Korea's children abroad during the previous forty years (Kim 1999). A year later, in Washington, DC, more than 400 Korean-born adoptees from thirty-six U.S states and several western European countries met for the first Gathering of the First Generation of Korean Adoptees, an event that has since been repeated in Oslo and Seoul and has led to a reimagining of what a "Korean" diaspora might (or might not) consist in (Hübinette 2004; E. Kim 2005, 2007). And in May 1999, 2,700 adoptees and their families, agency and government representatives, and staff from children's homes and welfare organizations on four continents gathered at a *"jubileum* celebration" to mark the thirtieth anniversary of Adoption Centre, Sweden's premier organization for transnational adoption.

Each of these gatherings testified to the ways in which adoption opens up conventional understandings of individual identity, national belonging, and family form. In the sheer emotional energy they generated, the gatherings contributed to this opening up. At the same time, the conversations that were begun there and continued in other arenas spoke to the contradictions of a practice that has been shaped by the felt needs of adoptive parents to complete (rather than open up) their families and by the concerns of adopting states to control (rather than bridge) their national boundaries. These needs and concerns work to reproduce rather than unsettle inequalities that are realized in the relationship between sending and receiving nations and birth and adoptive mothers and especially in the figure of the adoptee.

I was present at the largest of these gatherings, which took place at Sollentunamässan, a vast exhibition hall in the center of Stockholm, on a chilly spring day in 1999. Adoption Centre (AC), Sweden's principal adoption organization and one of the largest such organizations in Europe, was hosting a weeklong series of events. AC, known for its pioneering work in the field of transnational adoption, is responsible for Sweden's place as the nation with the highest per capita population of transnational adoptees in the world—approximately 1.5 percent of cohorts born in the 1970s and 80s

(Cederblad et al. 1999). Beginning with a conference at Stockholm University's School of Social Work that focused on problems of residential care and the importance of providing a family for every child who needs one, the events continued as a series of workshops, organized by region (Latin America, South and Southeast Asia, eastern Europe, Africa, and so forth). Child welfare professionals from Sweden's main sending nations, as well as from other adopting nations, were present at the celebration.

Funded by grants from the National Science Foundation to support research on open adoption in the United States and transnational adoption in Sweden, I attended the Stockholm meetings as both participant and observer in a project that had begun four years earlier and involved fieldwork in India, Bolivia, Colombia, Ecuador, Chile, and Hong Kong, as well as in Sweden.[8] Many of those present were familiar to me from visits together with AC representatives to children's homes and aid projects and from previous conferences and workshops in Asia, Latin America, and Europe, and I had been invited to present the results of my research to the assembled participants. On the last day of the weeklong series of events, the focus shifted from research and policy to a celebration of the work of adoption, as the visitors gathered with adoptive families and AC staff at Sollentunamässan for a collective meal.

The exhibition hall, normally used by transnational companies for the display and marketing of new products, was packed. Parents with toddlers, teenagers, and older children gathered at long tables that were grouped by nation and by children's home. Parents, children, and the directors of children's homes ate together, aided when necessary by an interpreter from AC. There were emotional reunions of children with caretakers whom they had not seen for years. Carmen Borrero de Hleap, the founder of Chiquitines, a children's home in Cali, Colombia, stood in a receiving line for four hours as parents and children waited to embrace her and recall the circumstances, in some cases almost twenty years in the past, that had brought them from a first meeting in Colombia to this celebratory moment in Stockholm. Carmen was responsible for the adoption of some two thousand Colombian children to Sweden, and the Chiquitines families filled five long tables. In another section of the hall, Nomita Chandy of Ashraya Children's Home in Bangalore, India, and Nina Nayak, also from Bangalore, visited with children they had placed in Sweden over nearly two decades. At a Chile table, Marta Garcia and Marta Hermosilla from Santiago reminisced with families who had traveled to Chile a year previously on a "roots trip" that took them to hospitals, foster families, and children's homes where their children had spent weeks or months 15, 18, or 20 years previously.

At Sollentunamässan on May 9, 1999, the "crazy dream" of "making a family with an orphanage" that AC's Gunilla Andersson, a founder of the organization, had realized when she traveled to India to adopt her daughter in 1964, took unexpected forms as orphanages became the link between families, the ground for memories, an experience joining past with present. But this potential for the orphanage to "make" a family, and in this way to become (once again) a part of Swedish society, was dependent on a radical intervention in the discourse of blood belonging and national sovereignty, an intervention that repeatedly bumps up against assumptions about what real belongings consist in and where they are to be found.[9]

The moment on the balcony with my parents and Finn and the celebration in Stockholm that joined families with staff of children's homes speak to the powerful feelings adoption provokes. Adoption both challenges and instantiates conventional notions of belonging, as children whose ties to a specific, historically grounded, social surround—whether domestic, as in our case, or in Asia, Africa, Latin America, or eastern Europe, as in the Sollentunamässan gathering—are legally nullified so that they can become completely the adoptive family's and the adopting nation's "own." But the experiences of adoptive families and adopting nations suggest that however much the ideal of completeness inspires the legal project of adoption, the origins of a child *do* matter, whether coded as a difference of kinship, of culture, or of national identity. The different origins of the child, as reflected in the fantasies, longings, and fears of adoptive parents, make themselves felt from the very beginning: from the moment prospective parents choose a country or are asked to select the skin color of their child, perhaps imagining what a Chilean, Korean, Ethiopian, or Indian child might be (like) or considering how they, as parents, might relate to these children. But in what ways does difference count, and how does it contribute to (or disrupt) the project of completing the identity of the child, the family, or the nation that adoption of a child is supposed to bring about?

The Right to an Identity

My research on transnational adoption began in 1995, two years after the signing of the 1993 Hague Convention on Protection of Children and Cooperation in Respect of Intercountry Adoption, an outcome of the Hague

Conference on Private International Law.[10] I examined the tension between
a system of exclusive belongings (national, familial, individual) secured
by the closures imposed by adoption law, on the one hand, and the experiences of not belonging anywhere that have shaped the lives of so many
transnationally adopted children and adults in the last decades of the
twentieth century, on the other. The Convention marked the official recognition of a significant shift in practice over the forty years since the first
adoptions of children from Korea, India, and other Third World nations by
Euro-American parents in the 1950s and 1960s. The experiences of these
children (like those adopted domestically in the first half of the twentieth
century) raised questions about the conventional wisdom that it was in
the "best interest" of the child to make a "clean break" (Duncan 1993, 51)
from the past, pointing rather to the complex meanings of this "past" for
the identity of the child as he or she matured. Thus, while the Convention affirmed the principle endorsed by laws in Euro-American adopting
nations that adoptions should be "strong"—that is, that the child's legal
connection to preadoptive kin should be terminated so the child could be
fully incorporated into the adoptive family—the Convention also recognized the importance of preserving information about the adopted child's
origin, and specifically about the identity of its parents.[11] This recognition
was in keeping with the 1989 UN Convention on the Rights of the Child
(UNCRC), which endorses "the right of the child to preserve his or her
identity, including nationality, name and family relations as recognized
by law" (United Nations 1989, article 8).[12]

The Hague Convention was the outcome of complex negotiations
among the delegates over differences in perspective that tended to divide
the conference into two rough camps: nonmember sending nations who
were invited to the conference made up one group, and receiving nations
who were members of the conference made up the other (Carlson 1994,
257). Key sending nations during the decade leading up to the conference
were the Republic of Korea, India, Colombia, Brazil, and Sri Lanka, all nonmembers of the conference. Principal receiving nations between 1980 and
1989 were the United States (the world's leading transnational adopter in
terms of the actual numbers of children involved), France, Sweden, the
Netherlands, and Italy.

One of the most sensitive issues dividing participants at the conference was whether the Convention should endorse transnational adoption
and facilitate the adoption process, or whether the aim of the Convention
should be restrictive: "to eliminate abuses such as baby-selling; to protect

a child's right to grow up in the land of its birth, or a nation's right to prevent the loss of its natural resources—children—to other nations; and with the possible effect of reducing intercountry adoption" (Carlson 1994, 256). As Richard Carlson notes, "differences in perspective were especially troublesome because they touched emotional issues of child welfare and national interests" and because they tended to divide the participants into senders and receivers (257). In this context, and considering the stratification between members and nonmembers of the conference, a key achievement from the point of view of the U.S. delegation was that the conference became "a forum for mutual education about the situation of children without families and the virtues of adoption" (264; see Yngvesson 2004, 215–216).

An earlier convention (the UN General Assembly's 1986 Declaration on Social and Legal Principles Relating to the Protection and Welfare of Children) favored foster care or even appropriate institutional placement in the birth country of the child over transnational adoption, and there was a move among delegates from sending nations at The Hague as well to prioritize in-country foster care over adoption in another nation (Carlson 1994, 260–262). Ultimately, a compromise was worked out, framed in the rhetoric of the child's need for "a family environment" (Hague Convention, Preamble; see Carlson 1994, 264). This allowed for language in the Convention stating a preference for in-country adoption but not requiring it—only "due consideration" of possibilities for local placement was mandated—and privileging transnational adoption over foster or institutional care in the child's birth country.

As this discussion suggests, understandings about the child's need for a family emerged in tension with the child's right to identity, understood as fundamental to the child's well-being and inseparable from its birth parents; its ethnic, cultural, and religious background; and its national origins. Both positions were framed in terms of a shared concern with the best interest of the child, but each derived from *national* interests and debates over which of those interests was tethered to the child's best interests and needs. For sending nations, the child's right to identity was inseparable from the nation's right to its "natural resources—children" (Carlson 1994, 256). For receiving nations, the child's need for a family was inseparable from the needs of childless couples for children and adopting countries' needs to bolster declining fertility rates. In both cases, the dislocation of the child triggered and was occasioned by concerns about the nation and its potential loss of identity.

Difference and Identity

The origins of transnational adoption conventionally are traced to the mid-1950s, when missionaries, medical personnel, returning U.S. and UN soldiers, and other foreign nationals publicized the plight of Korean "war orphans" in the aftermath of the Korean War. Similar in some ways to rescue efforts directed at finding substitute families for German, Polish, and Finnish children during World War I and World War II, the adoption of children from Korea in the 1950s (or from India, another popular source of adoptions from the mid-1960s to the mid-1980s) marked a turning point, because the children were obviously "different" from the adopting parents and because their placements were understood as permanent. In Sweden, the difference was marked by the designation of adoptees in the post-1950s period as "non-Nordic." Celebrated by adopting parents in subsequent years as a "cultural" difference, but experienced by many adopted children and adults as invoking a more radical (and racialized) form of "otherness," the difference of the transnational adoptee became "a dense locus of desire and value" for adopting parents in the ensuing decades (Anagnost 2000, 403; see Volkman 2005b; Dorow 2006). It also emerged as a central theme in the memoirs, films, and scholarly publications of transnational adoptees from the 1990s onward (Trotzig 1996; von Melen 1998; Borshay Liem 2000; Wallensteen 2000; Trenka, Oparah, and Shin 2006).

The difference of the adopted child has long been an issue that has troubled Euro-American adoptive kinship. The child's difference took shape in conjunction with the emergence of adoption laws in the nineteenth and early twentieth centuries, as child welfare advocates sought to regulate the conditions (and mitigate the threat) of thousands of homeless, neglected, and delinquent children whose number far exceeded the capacity of public institutions set up to provide for them (Presser 1971–72; Grossberg 1985, 271). Officially identified as "vagrants," "orphans," or "abandoned," many of these children had mothers whose marital status and poverty made it impossible for them to care for a child, as rapid industrialization and accompanying migration to urban centers left women isolated and with no family support system. Similar patterns can be found in most industrializing nations at the time, but I focus here on the United States and Sweden, which illuminate key issues.

In Sweden, where early adoption legislation was influenced by American law and practice, the Swedish Adoption Act, passed in 1917, was part of a new body of law relating to the welfare of illegitimate children. The

Adoption Act marked the end of a period, dating to the "Adultery Ordinance" of 1778, in which baby-farming flourished, child mortality was high, and older children were placed in foster homes where they worked as farmhands or domestic servants (Bohman n.d.; Agell and Saldeen 1991). Like adoption laws passed in the United States between 1851 and 1929, the Swedish Adoption Act of 1917 was a turning point, both from the perspective of child welfare and in the increasing involvement of the state in regulating the relations of parent and child.

In the United States, the transformation of adoption into a legal procedure dates to the landmark Massachusetts Adoption Act of 1851. This statute charged the courts with evaluating the suitability of the parents, and in what became a central tenet of legal adoption in most Anglo-European nations over the course of the next century, dissolved the "natural family ties" of the child and replaced them with legally created ties to the child's new parents (Grossberg 1985, 272). Historian Michael Grossberg notes that "adoption spread at a phenomenal rate" in the United States, displacing other forms of custody transfer (272).[13] But even as adoption was seen as a positive intervention in that it provided children with what was legally deemed a more suitable family, the idea of using law to create "artificial families" (275) posed problems for common-law understandings of property rights and set in question the extent to which adoptive relations could fully replace "natural" ones. As the Ohio Supreme Court noted in 1898, in deciding a contested inheritance claim that turned on the meaning of the word *issue*, "Adoption does not make the adopted child of the blood of its adopter, nor of the blood of his ancestors" (277, quoting *Phillips v. McConica*, 59 Ohio St. 1, 8 [1898]; see Modell 1994, 25). The question whether an adopted child is fully equal to "blood issue" in contested inheritance claims persisted in the United States to the end of the twentieth century, even as this country developed some of the most stringent policies for making the child's biological family disappear.[14]

As adoption laws were revised over the course of the twentieth century, western Europe (with France a notable exception) followed the American example of progressively strengthening the legal status of the adoptive family, moving away from "weak" or "simple" adoptions, in which the biological family retained connections to the adopted child, to "strong" or "plenary" ones that canceled these connections. In Sweden, where strong adoptions became mandatory in 1971, adoptions were also declared irrevocable, suggesting that adoptive ties are stronger than "biological" ones, since the latter *can* be legally canceled.[15]

This seeming paradox highlights continuing tensions in adoptive kinship and points to the unexpected ways in which implicit assumptions

about the power of a natural connection between biological parent and child can make themselves felt, even (and perhaps most insistently) in those nations where efforts to eradicate such a connection have been most thorough. In the United States, for example, an adoptive parent-child relationship is legally constructed as "exactly like a natural relationship: the child *as-if-begotten*, the parent *as-if-genealogical*" (Modell 1994, 2). This construction is secured by policies (in most states) to seal records that pertain to birth and adoptive parents, as well as to adoptees, even after adoptees have reached majority; altered birth certificates in which the adoptive mother is listed as the child's birth mother; and, in U.S. domestic adoptions, practices of matching adoptive parent and child with each other in terms of ethnicity, race, religion, physical likeness, personality "traits," and so forth (Bartholet 1993, 95–117; Modell 1994, 43–45; Wegar 1997; Yngvesson 1997; Carp 1998).[16] In this sense, American adoption law replicates the very entanglement in blood relations that adoption would seem to undo, an entanglement that is also suggested in the ambiguities that linger surrounding the entitlements of adoptive kin in contested inheritance claims.

In Sweden, where *blodsband* (blood ties) are deemed central to the relationship of parent and child (Boholm 1983, 118), unease with the permanent cancellation of these ties has led to a controversial policy, implemented in 1980 and continuing into the present, of placing Swedish children who have been removed from the care of their birth parents in long-term foster care, rather than releasing them for domestic adoption.[17] Known as "the Swedish model for family care" (*Vård i familjehem* 1995, 77–78), the policy is based on assumptions about the key place of the biological parents in the life of the child, as well as on "the great importance of the child for the biological parents and for its whole family of origin" (33). The role of the foster parents is to maintain the child's ties to the birth parent, a responsibility that is regarded by opponents of this practice as undermining the potential for a meaningful relationship to develop between foster parent and child, particularly in cases where children remain in foster care throughout their childhood (Andersson 1990; Barth 1992). Swedish child welfare policy dictates foster care over adoption, even if the birth parents are unwilling to care for their children and even if they prefer that the child be adopted (Barth 1992, 41). This policy has been maintained for almost three decades, in the face of mounting clinical evidence that it is highly detrimental to the child's well-being (Barth 1998; Hjern, Vinnerljung, and Lindblad 2004; Vinnerljung, Hjern, and Lindblad 2006).

In this context, Sweden's passionate defense of the exclusiveness of adoptive family ties in a widely publicized case in which the maternal grandparents of a child born in Colombia sought visitation rights (Yngvesson 2000) bespeaks both the tensions that underpin a policy of strong adoptions and a kind of doublethink. The relationship of a child to its birth parent or birth family is prioritized in the Swedish domestic context (in that foster care is regarded as preferable to adoption), whereas adoption and its required cut-off from the birth family is privileged over foster care in a transnational context.[18] This set of views was apparent in the concerns of Sweden and other adopting nations that the 1993 Hague Convention might rank domestic foster care in the nations providing children for adoption over transnational adoption for children in need of substitute parents. The same perspective could be seen in the efforts of these nations to restrict the definition of an appropriate "family environment" to a "permanent" (that is, an adoptive) family.

The importance of descent (*härstammning*) to individual identity in Sweden is made explicit in the strong Swedish support of the rights of the adopted child (or of a child conceived by reproductive technologies such as donor insemination) to obtain records of her or his birth (Rädda Barnen 1992, 282). These rights are widely supported in other Anglo-European nations, with the exception of the United States and, to some extent, France, where a long tradition of supporting the birth mother's right to anonymity conflicts with a 1993 law supporting children's right to know their identity (O'Donovan 2002, 362).[19]

More recently, the tension between a family of "blood" and a family of "choice" flared up in France in the context of a proposed French immigration strategy "to verify the bloodlines of would-be immigrants who want to join family members already living in France" (Sciolino 2007, A3). Opposition to the new policy was articulated in terms of a long French tradition in which "parental choice, rather than birth" has been determinative in the filiation of children whose biological origins are in question (O'Donovan 2002, 361). French president Nicolas Sarkozy, himself the son of a Hungarian immigrant, supports DNA testing for immigrants; he noted that such testing would be used only "where there were no clear records 'to prove that children are really your own,'" (Sciolino 2007, A3). French controversy over this issue hints at the ways a discourse of (biogenetic) identity may surface not simply in the context of what makes a family (and what makes it one's own), but perhaps more significantly in defining the boundaries of the nation against those whose difference is seen as threatening national identity.

As this discussion suggests, the difference of the adopted child takes shape against a backdrop of assumption that "blood," "genes," or "descent" constitute "natural" identity in an Anglo-European cultural and legal universe.[20] As anthropologist Judith Modell (1994, 28) argues in a discussion of the tensions implicit in U.S. adoption law that is applicable to adoption laws in western Europe as well, "emphasis in adoption law on terms of consent, on grounds for termination, and on the permanence of contract reveals a suspicion that the legal transfer does not erode the claims of nature." Modell adds that in alienating a child from the biological parent, "whatever the basis for removal or relinquishment, the course of 'nature' has been disrupted. . . . This seems so extreme an act precisely because in American culture the 'physical realities of conception and birth' establish an enduring 'emotional attachment' to the child" (28, quoting Blustein 1982, 142).

The silences that surrounded domestic "same race" adoptions in both Sweden and the United States in the middle decades of the twentieth century and the efforts to produce adoptive families that reproduced the ideal of what a biological family was imagined to be—permanent, loving, and attentive to the needs of the child—have played out in complex ways in the lives of adopted children in both nations. This pattern is illuminated in a dissertation published by Susanna Matwejeff in 2004 that draws on interviews with adults adopted domestically in Sweden. Matwejeff notes that "the adoption and their origin [were] delicate topics during their childhood in the adoptive family, with elements of irritation and silence" (2004, 137), and she suggests that the silence associated with the birth family of the adopted child "actualizes a state of tension" for the adoptee as she or he matures (139).

This state of tension is a product (as Modell's observations in the preceding paragraph suggest) of the seeming irreconcilability of a template for constructing parent-child relations that is based on choice (whether by the parent, by agents of the state, or in the case of older children, by the child) and sealed by contract with a template for belonging that is experienced as taking shape in an "enduring emotional attachment" made possible by the "physical realities of conception and birth" and the assumed continuity of these realities with a natural order of things. Although I agree with Modell's insight, I suggest that the state of tension experienced by the adopted child, and to a greater or lesser degree by the adoptive parents, is equally a product of other physical realities: the social and economic circumstances that compel some women to relinquish their children, while others can "choose" to adopt them or be paid to foster them (as in the "Swedish model of family care"); the constraints of such circumstances on the capacity of a woman who conceives and gives birth to a child to develop an enduring emotional attachment to the child; and more generally, the effects of a "highly stratified system of reproduction" in which "hierarchies of class, race, ethnicity, gender, place in a global economy and migration status" position women differentially for the accomplishment of reproductive tasks (Colen 1995, 78).[21]

Legal fictions that underpin adoptive kinship, such as the voluntary consent of the birth mother to the child's relinquishment (the child as "gift"), the legal orphan status of the child (the child's "abandonment"), and in some nations the reinvention of the child as the biogenetic descendant of the adopting parents, work to maintain this stratified system of reproduction, while affirming the centrality of blood (and of the "natural" connection of mother and child) as the foundation of familial and national belonging. In this way, the contingency of the mother-child relationship on circumstances that may affect the belonging of *both* mother and child is left unexamined by interventions that displace the child while affirming the value of its "natural" connection to its original mother. Adoption operates as a kind of legal "laundering" of a child whose capacity for belonging in its nation of birth is jeopardized by such factors as the marital status of its mother; its gender, ethnic identity, skin color, and health status; and more generally its "origins" in a population whose poverty bespeaks its abandonment by the nation state, so that it can be transformed into "one of ours" in its new family and nation and potentially (should it return to its native land as an adult) into "one of ours" in that nation, as well.[22]

Family Disturbances

Tensions infusing the invisible domestic adoptive family intensified in the 1970s and 1980s (Modell 1994, 143–145, 169–199) and were accompanied by a steady decline of domestic adoptions in western Europe and the United States. The declines were due in large part to the increased availability of contraception, the legalization of abortion, and an ensuing decrease in unwanted pregnancies. Declines were influenced as well by the emergence of welfare states in Scandinavia and elsewhere in western Europe that guaranteed benefits to women with children, regardless of their marital status. In Sweden, for example, domestic adoptions fell from 3,600 in 1947 to 1,000 in 1965. By the early 1990s, only 15–20 Swedish children were placed in domestic adoption per year (Andersson 1986; Selman 1989, 154–155).[23] (The emergence of the welfare state in Sweden is discussed in greater detail in chapter 2). In the United States, domestic adoptions by nonrelatives peaked in 1970 at 89,200 and declined rapidly in subsequent years.[24] As the most desirable adoptive children—healthy white infants—became increasingly scarce and (in the United States) increasingly expensive, and as rates of involuntary childlessness rose, would-be adoptive parents turned to alternatives, including "open" adoption, which encourages various forms of contact between birth and adoptive families, and to domestic transracial adoption and transnational adoption.

Open adoption, which began in the United States in the 1970s and remains largely confined to this country, provides a potential variant on the exclusiveness of adoptive kinship.[25] In an open adoption, birth and adoptive parents may meet before the birth of the child; the birth parent may choose the adoptive parents; and there may be varying degrees of ongoing contact after the child's birth, ranging from exchanges of pictures and letters, to occasional visits, to more regular engagement over time (see, e.g., Yngvesson 1997; Mundy 2007; Winerip 2008). Openness in adoption was developed in part as a way of encouraging single women to relinquish their children at a time when the availability of healthy white infants was declining (Baran, Pannor, and Sorosky 1976). Openness does not change the legal cancellation of a child's ties to his or her birth parents. But including the birth mother (however briefly) in the space reserved for the "as-if" adoptive family reveals the complex transactions in motherhood that are necessary to make that family "complete" (Yngvesson 1997).

Like open adoption, transracial adoption (whether domestic or transnational) makes visible the exclusions on which complete families (and complete nations) are premised. But unlike open adoption, where the birth mother is unlikely to be visible outside the adoptive family context (and may have a negligible role within it), the disturbance created by transracial adoption is publicly apparent and has raised complex questions about the politics of racial identity that were long contained by the construction of likeness in adoptive families.[26]

Domestic transracial adoptions in the United States were made possible when state laws prohibiting them were held unconstitutional or overturned by state legislatures in the aftermath of *Loving v. Virginia*, the 1967 Supreme Court case that struck down laws prohibiting interracial marriage (Simon, Altstein, and Melli 1994, 23). Between 1968 and 1975, some twelve thousand African American children were placed domestically with white families (3). On a more limited basis, African American children were also sent in adoption to western Europe, a practice that continues into the present.[27]

Domestic transracial adoptions of African American and Native American children, like the transnational transracial placements that began in the 1950s, were celebrated by advocates as a key move in the realization of humanitarian ideals and specifically the capacity to see beyond race to the needs of the child, regardless of that child's "genetic heritage" (Andersson 1991, 2; Simon, Altstein, and Melli 1994; Bates 1993; Bartholet 1993). Children without parents would be given a "loving home," and transracial adoptive homes would provide a model for a color-blind society. But the implementation of these ideals through an adoption program that erased the child's connection to preadoptive kin in order to facilitate its complete incorporation into a white adoptive family made domestic transracial adoption—like transnational adoptions in the 1980s and 1990s—the site for intense battles over the rights of communities (African American, Native American) to their children and the rights of children from such communities to their identity.[28]

Domestic adoptive placements of African American children were brought to a halt when the National Association of Black Social Workers (NABSW 1972) publicly opposed them on grounds that they amounted to a form of racial genocide.[29] Similar opposition to the placement of Native American children in adoption with white families led to passage of the Indian Child Welfare Act in 1978.[30] The debate over U.S. domestic transracial adoption in the 1960s and 1970s and subsequent controversy over transnational adoption in the 1980s, 1990s, and early years of the twenty-first century illuminate the ways that adoption works simultaneously to normalize and to racialize the national body.[31] In transracial adoption, whether domestic or transnational, a project that embodies humanitarian ideals pursued in the interests of a "generalized child" (Stephens 1995b) whose need for "a family" transcends divisions of class, race, or gender leads to the elaboration and proliferation of the very differences that adoption ostensibly seeks to overcome.[32] The tension between a generalized child whose canceled past makes her or him adoptable and the racialized child that re-emerges in the adoptive family and nation recalls Carolyn Steedman's analysis (1995, 5) of the figure of the child as "a true thing" that took shape in European law, literature, and science from the late eighteenth through the early twentieth century.

The figure of the child and the idea of childhood, Steedman argues, represent the "depths of historicity within individuals, the historicity that was 'linked to them, essentially'" (1995, 12, citing Foucault 1970, 368–369).[33] This child figure emerged in conjunction with modern conventions of historical practice and the accompanying assumption that life is lived as a story of the self: "The child *was* the story waiting to be told" (Steedman

1995, 11), a story that would unfold in a familiar developmental trajectory. By displacing a specific child who is the product of a complex (colonial) past with an imagined, interior, child—the dream child, the "child of any color"—that resides in everyone, it seems possible to incorporate the "different" child into the adoptive family and transform him or her into a child like any other.[34]

The power of this fable of transformation has captured not only adoptive parents but adopted children, placing both child and parents in a struggle with experiences that are in tension with the standard narrative, as I discuss in chapters 4 and 5. Likewise, I suggest, the figure of the transnational transracial adoptee, the displaced child, has come to represent the "depths of historicity" within the (postcolonial) nation, a "true thing" that is imagined as "linked to [that nation], essentially" and whose return can make that nation (like the adoptee herself or himself) whole.

In a world where the immigrant, the undocumented, and other forms of "alien" are increasingly targeted as disruptions to national identity and belonging, transnational adoption has been a particularly intense site for this imagining. Constructed as a "legal orphan" whose need for "a family" allows it to circulate between nations, the adoptee becomes "Chinese" or "Korean" in his or her adoptive country and ultimately "Swedish," "Italian," or "American," should the child return as an adult to the native land. Exploring this dynamic requires moving between the narratives of real people, living in particular times and places, and the power of cultural forms (the child, the adoptee, the family, the nation) that figure their lives.

Mobile Children

The shifting patterns of sending and receiving nations highlight the complex forces shaping the movement of children in transnational adoption (see tables 1 and 2, in the appendix). The specifics differ from case to case, but always there is a combination of conditions that are simultaneously local and global and have the effect of placing certain categories of children at risk of becoming a liability in one location, even as they become objects of desire in another. These conditions include the Korean War in the 1950s, the war in Vietnam in the 1960s and 1970s, the "civil" war in El Salvador in the 1980s, the fall of Communism in the 1990s, and wars in Africa in the 1990s and the early years of the twenty-first century, as well as the dramatic rise in children orphaned by HIV/AIDS in South Africa, Ethiopia, and elsewhere from the 1990s on. In addition, population policies such as the one-child policy in China, pronatalist policies in Ceausescu's Romania, and the marginalization of illegitimate and "mixed-race" children in Korea have contributed to the movement of children in transnational adoption, as have such demographic variables as dropping birthrates, rising rates of involuntary childlessness, and decreasing availability of domestic children for adoption in Western liberal democracies.[35]

South Korea became the world's major country in terms of "sending" children for adoption in the period from 1955 to the late 1980s. This pattern began during the Korean War, when some 4,000 children were placed overseas, principally in the United States. The number of foreign adoptions from Korea grew steadily during the 1960s and 1970s, when 60,000 were processed; by the mid-1980s, Korean transnational adoptions peaked, with almost 9,000 placements each year, mostly to the United States and European nations such as France, Sweden, Denmark, and the Netherlands. Korean overseas adoptions dropped significantly in the 1990s, following adverse publicity about the practice at the Seoul Olympics in 1988, but it was not until 2006 that annual placements fell below 2,000, for the first time in four decades. By the end of 2007, South Korea had sent almost 161,000 children to Euro-American nations in adoption.[36]

While the exodus of children in adoption from Korea was triggered by the Korean War, "war orphans" at that time included not only children whose parents died in the war, but others whose mixed heritage placed them outside belonging in Korea. Aided by media campaigns in what became "receiving" or adopting nations in North America, western Europe, and Australasia and by the complicity of a Korean military government intent on rapid economic and social development, South Korea passed the Orphan Adoption Special Law in 1961 and shortly thereafter the Korean Child Welfare Act. These were followed by the negotiation of agreements in the 1960s with the United States, Sweden, Denmark, and other Euro-American nations that facilitated the emergence of transnational adoption as an alternative to institutional care for thousands of children who were deemed unacceptable in Korean society. Over the ensuing half century, the terms for authorizing the removal of these children varied, from their "mixed-race" status as children of Korean women and U.S. or UN soldiers, to full-blooded Korean "orphans" who were relinquished owing to the poverty or marital status of their mothers and a lack of social service options in a patrilineal society that gave primacy to consanguineal relations (Hübinette 2006; E. Kim 2005).

South Korea provides a striking example of the use of foreign adoption as a strategy for eliminating children who do not qualify as the "truth" of the nation, because of the record numbers of children adopted, the range of circumstances that qualified them for removal, the time span involved, and the methodical way that this redistribution of Korean-born children to other nations by the South Korean government was organized. In 1989 South Korea sent 5.4 children in adoption overseas for every 1,000 live births; in 2005, the adoption ratio was 4.8 (Selman 2002, 218; Selman 2008, table 14). The latter figure is striking in the context of South Korea's high per capita gross national income and low fertility rate in the last years of the twentieth century and first years of the twenty-first.[37] South Korea remained one of the top five sending nations in the first six years of the 2000s, dropping in 2007 to a lower rank. Other key sending nations between 2003 and 2007 were China, Russia, and Guatemala, with Vietnam and Ethiopia steadily moving into more dominant positions (table 1, appendix).

Likewise, the adoption of children from China, which began with the end of the Cold War in the early 1990s, was brought about by a biopolitical dynamic that included decreases in transnational placements from Korea, India, and some parts of Latin America in response to negative publicity about the pressures placed on women in these nations to abandon, sell, or "place" their children in adoption, together with the "excess" of abandoned girl children in China that resulted from China's one-child policy and the historical preference for males in that nation.[38] In adopting nations, Chinese girl children became what the fashion magazine *Vanity Fair* described in the summer of 1998 as "the season's hot accessory in the Hamptons" (Fein 1998, 30), at least in part because of the attention devoted by the world media to the plight of abandoned (and potentially adoptable) children languishing in Chinese orphanages.[39] China quickly became and remained the leading country of origin for transnationally adopted children in the United States and other adopting nations such as Sweden, Spain, Netherlands, and Norway through 2007, although changes in Chinese government regulations for transnational adoption (specifically in defining the qualifications of adoptive parents) resulted in a significant drop in adoptions from China, beginning in 2006. Between 1998 and 2006, China sent 66,447 children in adoption to the top twenty-two receiving nations (Selman 2008, table 12).[40]

The surge in adoptions from Ethiopia at the beginning of the twenty-first century is the most recent example of the social, political, and economic forces shaping the movement of children in transnational adoption. Between 2002 and 2005, Ethiopian adoptions to twenty-two receiving nations increased by 150 percent, an effect of famine, war, and the mounting toll of HIV/AIDS in Ethiopia, as well as a spate of what has been called "celebrity adoptions" from Africa that brought widespread media attention to orphans on that continent. Adoptions from Ethiopia continued to rise steeply between 2005 and 2007, years in which tightening eligibility requirements in China, new requirements for registration of agencies in Russia, and falling numbers of adoptions from Korea affected the flow of children from these nations (tables 3 and 4, appendix).

Described in a front-page article in the *New York Times* in 2007 as "a hot spot for international adoption" even before "the actress Angelina Jolie put adoption in Ethiopia on the cover of People magazine in 2004," the increase in adoptions from Ethiopia to the United States (from 82 in 1997 to 732 in 2006) "is the steepest adoption officials have ever seen. Ethiopia now ranks 5th among countries for adoption by Americans, up from 16th in 2000," and the number of American agencies licensed to operate there grew from one to twenty-two between 2000 and 2007 (Gross and Connors 2007, A1). Adoptions to the United States from Ethiopia increased by 320 percent between 2002 and 2005 alone (table 3, appendix). Likewise, in 2005 Ethiopia was second only to China in number of children placed with agencies that belong to the European association Euradopt (Selman 2006, table 10).

A nation "more often associated by Americans with drought, famine and conflict" than with adoption, Ethiopia was recently described as having "model centers for orphans" (Gross and Connors 2007, A1), but there is concern about its ability to handle the steep increase in demand. With a population of 76 million and an estimated 5 million orphans, Ethiopia, unlike many other African nations, "has welcomed American and European families who are willing to provide homes for children who have lost both parents to AIDS, malaria, tuberculosis or starvation, or who come from families too destitute to feed and clothe them" (A16). The *New York Times* article adds, in parentheses, that the adoption process "includes routine screening for HIV infection."

The flurry of publicity about Ethiopia on the Internet and in the popular press—what one author (Kyazze 2006) termed "this Hollywood clamor to adopt 'darkies'"—is emblematic of the complex issues that surround Euro-American adoptions of children from the developing world and the narrative of rescue that seems almost inevitably to surround these adoptions.[41] Like the "war orphan" from Korea or the rescue of children from "dying rooms" in Chinese orphanages, Ethiopian orphans are associated in the popular imagination with what a National Public Radio program described as "one of the least developed nations on earth" (Report on archaeological discovery 2007). They are also associated with the HIV/AIDS epidemic in Africa, but *those* orphans are "screened out" in the "clamor to adopt 'darkies.'"[42]

The rescue narrative is implicit in questions raised by researcher and adoptive parent Anna Rastas in a talk given at the first global research conference on transnational adoption in Copenhagen in 2005. Rastas, who lives in Finland and is herself the parent of two adopted children born in Ethiopia, cautions that the "white wannabe" parent adopting a "non-white" child is always positioned differently in racialized social relations and that "any decisions that the 'wannabe parents' make, or reasoning underlying their decisions, can be understood as racist acts" (2005, 2). Although Rastas is primarily referring to adoptive parent competence in understanding the ways racism affects the lives of their children, her observation about positioning of "'the non-white' body" in a society structured by unequal racial hierarchies (5) is related to the concerns expressed by Kyazze and others about the "rush to Africa" by the rich and famous and the ways this rush can be seen as a way of "projecting" oneself through the (black, orphan, HIV/AIDS-infected) body of the child.[43] As Rastas argues, "transnational adoptions offer a kind of an arena where many different kinds of questions related to racism arise" (1).

The Crossroads of Ambiguity

The greatest fanatic is the greatest doubter. Without knowing it.
He is a pact between two
where the one is a hundred percent visible
and the other invisible.
How I hate that expression "a hundred percent."

—Tomas Tranströmer, "Golden Wasp"

Hanna Wallensteen, who was born in Ethiopia in 1971 and adopted by Swedish parents a few months later, hints at the contradictions surrounding full belonging in her portrayal of Lotta, the protagonist in Wallensteen's monologue *Veta sin plats* (Know your place) (2000), which she has performed to critical acclaim in Sweden and at a conference on transnational adoption in the United States in 2002. Lotta (whose name is remarkable in Sweden only for its ordinariness) was born in Africa and adopted by a Swedish family when she was nine months old. She grew up with Swedish parents, "danced around the midsummer pole, the whole business." Her parents taught her to speak perfect Swedish, and thus, Lotta insists, she "blends in," she is "at home in this culture," unlike immigrants who "stumble in" and have no idea what they must do to adapt. Lotta's alter ego is Kunta Kinte, an immigrant child she encountered while riding the bus.[44] Kunta Kinte can't sit still and has a "fat nigger mamma" with too many children, who "stare and scream like wild animals." Lotta suggests that Sweden marks itself as a civilized land in its openness to people such as Kunta Kinte, a trope for the *hottentotsk* (the "Hottentotish"), the category most remote from the "Swedish."

Knowing how to blend in, to adapt (by acting perfectly Swedish, perfectly civilized), is a key theme in Wallensteen's monologue. But blending in, as Lotta makes clear, is impossible, however much the adoptee tries to conform. To be "completely normal" in Sweden means having "straight hair that blows in the wind and beautiful, blue eyes. To be able to blush if one receives a compliment and blanch if one sees a horror film." "Imagine," Lotta says, "having pink nipples under a skin-colored bra. . . . Then no one would notice you." Provoked by Kunta Kinte's behavior, Lotta is accused by others of striking him and is arrested for assault and disorderly behavior. The monologue takes place from the jail cell where she is being held, and it moves between her own experience of herself as completely Swedish and her representation of the perception of others that she is exotic ("Africa? I hear they have a mighty fine culture there!") and emotionally unstable (she struck the child on the bus for no reason) (Wallensteen 2000).

Wallensteen's characterization of Lotta points to the complex hierarchies of identity and belonging that materialize around the adoptee. Taught to be "at home in this culture" by parents whose Swedishness manifests itself in their capacity to "treat everyone as though they have equal value," she is nonetheless mistaken for "immigrants," whose difference is realized (like her own) in their inability to conform to civilized behavior (Wallensteen 2000). The contradiction between her self-image as Swedish and her identification by others as an immigrant is the central theme of the monologue, in which the reader (but not the protagonist, who persists in seeing herself as Swedish) can see Lotta's impossible dilemma.

Sara Nordin, another Swedish adoptee born in Ethiopia, refers to this dilemma in an article written for the magazine *SvartVitt* [Black-white] in 1996:

BLACK!
The meaning of this word has grown with each passing year, until I have finally understood that I am black. It is something big, personal, and hard. It is a fact for me.

The people who only see my color don't see all of me. The people who suggest they can see beyond my color don't see all of me. When I try to gather together all the bits of myself, I easily lose myself. In colors and stories. In theories and dreams. When I go by the mirror I see something exotic that I barely recognize from TV, newspapers, and books. Sometimes it makes me happy, sometimes sad, and sometimes amazed. But most often the reflection in the mirror evokes questions that have no easy answers.

I have tried to absorb the "black" but then I have difficulty holding onto the Swedish. I have tried to absorb the "Swedish" but then I haven't understood what I see in the mirror. (1996, 4–5, freely translated)

These portrayals of the paradoxes of belonging that constitute the lived experience of transnational adoption in Sweden are captured in the narratives of adoptive parents and adopted adults elsewhere. Friends of mine living in Italy who adopted a child from Haiti expressed their dismay when the little girl, then five years old, began approaching North African immigrants who could be found on benches in a park near their home. She wanted to touch them and was resistant to her parents' and grandparents' explanation that these were strangers who had no part in her life. Although the instinct of this child hinted at a more complex truth than that conveyed by her parents' words, she also spoke to her mother of her longing to look like her parents and (white) sister. In spite of her engaging smile, sparkling brown eyes, and outgoing personality, she did not feel that she was beautiful. At the time of my visit, she was playing with a very blond, very light-skinned Barbie doll.

Jaclyn Aronson, who was born in South Korea and adopted by American parents in the mid-1980s, describes similar longings in her senior thesis, "Not My Homeland" (1997). She recalls her experience as a participant in a high school panel discussion for adoptive parents when she was a teenager. At that time she told of her desire as she was growing up to resemble the Barbie dolls she played with. The parents in the audience laughed, and one mother noted that "We all wanted to look like Barbie." But Aronson notes:

For me, and for some Korean adoptees (as perhaps for international adoptees from other countries and transracial adoptees), this desire is very real. It is not only reflective of desiring the "perfect woman" that Barbie represents in American society. It goes beyond the perfect breasts, the unattainable waistline and long, sexy legs. What is represented as American, white, blond hair, big, blue eyes and prominent nose, is what I was after. And outside the context of the popularized image of the "all American," my desires came from what I felt I mirrored. Everyone around me, with the exception of my brother Josh, who is biracially of Caucasian and black birth parents, and my black friends, was white. My mom, dad, two brothers, grandmother, teachers, soccer coaches, friends were white. My immediate surroundings were white and inside, I mirrored them. But on the outside, often unbeknownst to me, I was not. (1997, 26)[45]

The idea of full belonging as embodied in a physical type that the adoptee can/must/should mimic but can never master because of what she or he sees in the mirror is the unarticulated (racial) dynamic that grounds whiteness. It is the unquestioned logic of identity that helps us, as Stuart Hall suggests, "to sleep well at night" (1997, 43). It is lived as the tension of "blood" difference by white adoptees, for whom race-matching policies work to render invisible the difference that blood makes. In transracial adoption, blood manifests itself on the skin in ways that are compelling for the public and painful to live.[46] The transracial adoptee placed in a white, middle-class family in Stockholm, Milan, or New York becomes the embodiment of difference, inhabiting the space of a tug-of-war between the "me" and the "not me" through which the givens of a coherent, grounded, and singular identity are constituted.

As the locus of ambiguity, of a likeness (she acts "Swedish") that is simultaneously a not-likeness (she "is" black), the adoptee evokes discomfort, curiosity, and a pull to self-definition in selves—both adoptive and native-born—that are always in process and never complete. Just as my mother felt that Finn's obvious belonging in our family called for affirmation that this belonging was "real" and my father was moved to include Finn in a genealogical project that situated him (genealogically) vis-à-vis our family, so too the presence of adopted women such as Hanna Wallensteen and Sara Nordin in Sweden and Jaclyn Aronson in the United States evokes a "real" that materializes in an ambiguous moment of likeness and not-likeness in which a "past" that was foreclosed so that a child could be reared as "one's own" makes itself felt in the present.[47]

On a warm summer morning in 2003, my husband Sigfrid was browsing with Anna ChuChu Petersson, a twenty-seven-year-old Swedish woman who was born in Ethiopia, at the farmer's market on the Amherst (Massachusetts) town common. Approached by a stranger who was provoked by the contrast of a tall blond man in his mid-sixties standing with a slender young black woman who had intricate braids and what would be considered (in Amherst) "exotic" dress, ChuChu was asked where she was from. "Sweden," she responded. She confessed to me later her pleasure in the obvious confusion of her questioner and her own sense of déjà-vu when strangers assume they are entitled to ask such questions.

A question like this is of course not adoption-specific but a dimension of gendered and racialized discourses in which "adoptees," "immigrants," "refugees," and other subject categories whose belonging might be considered questionable take shape. But transnational adoption works today as a particularly fraught site through which these discourses operate. Adoption, in its mimicry of "natural" families and the genealogical grids for which they stand, inscribes the borders of the genealogical "real."[48] Likewise, as anthropologist Susan Coutin (2003) has argued, as a trope for the incorporation of "naturalized" immigrants who have "adopted" a new nation, adoption becomes a template for the simultaneous incorporation and exclusion of subjects or citizens and thus acts to inscribe the borders not simply of families but also of nations that depend on "adoptees" of various kinds to sustain themselves, both materially and symbolically (see Coutin, Maurer, and Yngvesson 2002). Adoption unsettles "the safehouse of identity" by introducing those who do not belong; but in this very process it "realizes" the families, nations, and persons that (naturally) lie just beyond the reach of adopted ones.[49]

The realization of "natural" families by adoptive ones, of "birth" nations by those that receive their children in adoption, and of "real" identities by those that are legally made through adoption is a central theme in the chapters that follow. This realization of the natural through the adoptive means that adoption is both a site for the reenactment of identity thinking and a "crossroads of ambiguity" (to quote Anna Deavere Smith's evocative phrase [2003]) at which identity seems to break apart. The concept of adoption as "*trans*national," with an emphasis on "*trans*," captures this sense of simultaneously making and unmaking not only the child who is adopted but the nations and families that are involved in this process as well; this concept can avoid the tendency to essentialize identity (the "Indian" or "Ethiopian" child; the "completely Swedish" person). Transnationality suggests "both moving through space or across lines, as well as changing the nature of something" (Ong 1999, 4).[50]

The shift in nature begins with the ways the child is imagined by the first generation of transnational adopters. It continues as the migration of children in adoption is interpreted as "traffic" and the child as "a commodity" and as the early narratives of rescue are transformed into a "business in babies." Throughout the final decades of the twentieth century, the movement in children from global South to global North has constituted adopted children as more (or less) precious resources of the nations where they were born and those in which they find new homes. They become "Ethiopian" or "Korean," "Colombian" or "Indian" in this process, identifying the nations from which they come (and to which they may feel compelled to return) as grounds of their identity. My book contributes to a growing body of literature that examines such changes in "nature" by focusing on the complex implications of transnational adoption for those who live (with) it and the potential of this practice for transforming (and not simply reproducing) the system of relations that brought it into being.

2 The Only Thing
We Can Give Away Is Children

When I came to India in 1970 and took my son, someone asked me,
"Are you taking one of *those?*" Now there are lots of Indians who
come forward to adopt. So I feel the value of the children has gone up.

   —Ann-Charlotte Gudmundsson, vice president of AC, 1995.

The policy to seek adoptive families, either domestically or abroad,
as a solution to poverty distracts us from the thousands of families and
populations who exist in a state of abandonment. We must privilege
a politics that gives resources to the poor before developing policies to
seek substitute families for poor children.

   —Guillermo Dávalos, Bolivian lawyer and activist, 1995

In this chapter and the next, I explore the emergence of the "abandoned child" as an object of desire for adopting parents in Euro-American nations and consider the key role of parental desire in the child's commoditization as a "good" worth saving for nations that give and receive children in adoption. I argue that transnational adoption transformed children who were marginal in their countries of birth into a precious national resource, a transformation that both undermined and enhanced the "best interest" of the child.

I begin with the journey of Gunilla Andersson, one of the earliest Swedish transnational adopters, to fetch her daughter-to-be from an orphanage in India, a nation that became a key supplier of children for families in the United States, Sweden, and other Euro-American nations in the 1970s and 1980s.[1] Andersson, who in 1972 became a founding member of Adoption Centre, Sweden's premier adoption organization, was in charge of Indian adoptions during the 1970s and 1980s, a period in which Sweden's annual transnational adoption rate was the world's highest.[2] She was also my point of entry to the organization in the mid-1990s, when she served as the director of research for the organization until her retirement in the first years of the twenty-first century.

A Purple Silk Dress with Fringes

Gunilla and I are sitting in her cramped office at Adoption Centre on a May afternoon in 1997. It is the end of an intense week in which I have gathered as much information as possible about the organization and its history, interviewing staff who were responsible for specific countries or projects, reading and copying archival material, and duplicating copies of newsletters published over some thirty years. As our conversation draws to a close, I ask Gunilla if she can tell me about the adoption of her daughter from India in 1964. It was one of the earliest foreign adoptions from India to Sweden and marked the emergence of both nations as central players in what became a global practice involving some forty-five thousand children a year by the early twenty-first century.

It is late in the day and we are both tired. Her personal experience more than thirty years ago—if I correctly interpret her inquiring look and initial silence—would appear to have little relevance to the challenges confront-ing transnational adoption in the late twentieth century. These challenges included efforts to promote domestic adoption in sending nations, even as childless men and women in Euro-American countries pressed for ever-younger children to complete their families; rising adoption costs and the relation of high costs to the thin line separating child placement from child trafficking; and perhaps most significantly, a growing international network of adults who had been adopted as children and were pressing for more regulation of transnational adoption and in some cases working to shut down such adoptions completely. These issues were hard to imagine at the time Gunilla, pregnant with what was to be her second child, trav-eled to India to fetch her daughter from an orphanage in Delhi in 1964.

Her determination to do so, at a time when adoption between nations was virtually unknown in India and was considered "crazy" by her family and friends had to do, Gunilla explains, "with my mother going to Sunday school":

> And now we are somewhere between 1910 and 20—and they had magazines already at that time with those kind of stories where you learnt morals. She collected those and had them made into books, heavy books, which I read as I grew up. And I started to read quite early, so I sat in a corner and read those stories, and two things remain within me from those two thick books. One is to do with gambling . . . because there were many stories about fathers who drank and gambled and left their children starving. . . . And the other thing was a picture, and that picture was a picture of an angel holding the

hand of a small child going over a small bridge over a cliff, and *this picture of*

*children needing someone helping them not to fall down on the cliffs—this I kept
in my mind.* When I grew up and read in the newspapers and when television came and showed pictures of children sitting in the orphanages in the world, I said to my husband-to-be that "When we marry, I'd like to adopt." So he said *"Ja, ja"*—he's used to my crazy ideas. So he said, *"Ja,* why not, if you want that, it's ok with me." We *knew* when we were married that this is what we were going to try.[3]

Finding a baby in an orphanage at that time proved challenging. Gunilla continued: "I wrote to Geneva, and I wrote to Hong Kong, and I wrote to Jordan, and I don't know what places I wrote to—just to ask if it was possible—'Could I adopt a child in your country?' Very naive. At the start, I was the only person I knew doing this, probably around '60–'61. And if they answered, they said 'Forget this crazy idea.' So we weren't exactly encouraged." Not until 1964, when she had become pregnant, assuming it might take years to adopt, did Gunilla receive a letter from an orphanage in Delhi saying, "There's a baby. Will you come?" So they went, without telling anyone she was pregnant, because "in 1964 to tell my mother that I was going pregnant to India, I mean it was almost like saying you were going to the moon."

During a second conversation on an August evening two years later at an Indian restaurant in Stockholm with me and her daughter, Maria Brunn, then thirty-five, Gunilla recalled that trip and her first experience of an orphanage, with Maria occasionally adding a wry comment or correction. Gunilla described the length and complexity of the trip, the "appalling conditions" at the orphanage, and the emotional intensity of the moment when the doctor led her, with her husband, to the crib where the baby called Renu by orphanage staff was lying.

It was our first time in such an orphanage, with small children coming running to you, taking your skirt and saying "Hello, hello" and small babies in cradles, and the doctor took us to the cradle where Maria was and said, *"This is your daughter."* So then—she was 10 months—we, we just looked at her. The doctor said, "There are lots of children." But we said, *"No, we're not looking at anybody else, we're not looking at any child. We're looking at—this is our baby—I don't want to see the other child!"* So—and that was quite pathetic, the whole of it. You [addressing Maria] had almost nothing on. You had some, some kind of little cloth, a little loincloth or something, and there was a rubber sheet on the mattress and that was all. And you—oh, I don't know if I can tell this [crying]—so we [Gunilla and her husband] looked at each other and then said, "So what do we do now?" I, I was allowed to hold you for a little while. So we said, "What do we do now?" And we started the paperwork.

Gunilla described what seemed like an endless process of writing, over and over again, an explanation of why they wanted to adopt a child, and her fears that every time they left the orphanage, Renu wouldn't be there when they got back. Officials kept asking them:

> "Why on earth are you doing anything like this?" We tried to explain we wanted a baby, and I tried to look not too pregnant. Finally, the official signed the paper, and then they sent us to the reserve bank because if she had any means, I mean it might be we take her for her riches and goods and everything. So we went to the reserve bank and they said, "Why do you want to do this?" And we told them, and they said, "Write it down." So we sat down and made in handwriting a long story. I know we wrote that story at least four times. . . . And this went on for some days. It was only five days, but it was a long time.

When the day came for them to leave the orphanage for the last time and return to Sweden, Gunilla explained, turning to Maria: "We went to take a photograph and they dressed you up, I'll never forget that, in a purple silk dress with fringes. And you were so tiny, and you had no fat anywhere, you were so skinny, and that purple dress with all those fringes. Ah, it was horrible. It was probably the most beautiful dress they had in the entire orphanage, but you just disappeared in it."

Renu's disappearance into the "horrible" dress on her departure from the orphanage speaks to the power of the adopting parent to transform the "pathetic child" into a precious resource, not only for the nation that adopts her, but for the country (and the orphanage) that gives her away. The transformative power of the parent is suggested both in the moment of claiming the baby as the parent's own—"We're looking at—this is our baby"—and in Gunilla's horrified rejection of the doctor's suggestion that she might look at other children: "I don't want to see the other child!"[4] The rejection of the other child is implied as well in her ironic comment about the requirement that they go to the reserve bank in Delhi so bank officials could confirm that Renu "had no means," since "it might be we take her for her riches and goods and everything." The proximity of the commoditized child to "our baby" makes itself felt in each of these moments, hinting at the inseparability of "the other child" (Renu, the child who was left behind, the child who might have been me) from the one who became Maria (the "sublime object," the "true thing" at the heart of the parent's desire).[5] It points as well to the centrality of a child's "orphan status"—the legal clean break that is required to make him or her available for adoption—to its capacity for completing the "fully Swedish" (or American, French, or Italian) family and nation.

The official erasure of the child who was left behind is signaled ten years later, when Gunilla and Maria return to the orphanage seeking possible records of Renu's preadoptive history and are presented with files containing Gunilla's letters. The moment was devastating for Gunilla: "It was a big disappointment when we went to India together. We went round to find papers and everywhere we went, there were copies of *my* letters before and after the adoption, but *no* papers. That was so terrible. They sent us to the town hall and we had lots of hope, and— "These are *my letters*." It was painful. It was terribly painful."

The painfulness of this experience speaks to the paradox that underpins the value of the "pathetic child" for the adoptive parent who claims her: that the value of the child for the parent is defined by the very quality that must be left behind if she is to become "my child" (the Swedish child, Maria).[6] The desire to recover some trace of this child may drive both adoptive parent and adoptee back to the orphanage, as in this case (and see chapter 7), but as Maria explained, "That hope was completely extinguished after three weeks in that country. It was a result of that trip that I realized there is just no trace. It was just to accept it, it's just to accept that fact of your life."[7]

This narrative of parental longing for a child and of the journey in which she finds her points to key issues surrounding the project of transnational (or what is referred to in Europe as "intercountry") adoption that engaged Euro-American nations with the developing world from the mid-1950s forward. It speaks to the passion with which the first adopters approached a project that was considered "crazy" by others (including officials in many of the birth countries of the children); and it testifies to their belief in the transformative power of family (and especially the adoptive mother) to convert such craziness—such deprivation—into what an Indian Supreme Court justice, writing almost three decades later, described as a "a supremely important national asset" on which "the future well-being of the nation is dependent" (*Lakshmi Kant Pandey v. Union of India* 1985, 4). At the core of this process of transformation is the simultaneous affirmation and disavowal of the child's difference—her radical otherness—in the eyes of the adopting parent. The difference of the child is part of her fascination for the parent, even as the parent's immediate conviction that "this is my baby" works to deny difference, anticipating its transformation into the same: the *child*—*my* child—that threatened to disappear each time she left the orphanage.

In the remainder of this chapter, by examining Sweden's familialist project (Balibar 1991, 102) and the ways it was transformed through transnational adoption, I point to the ways that placement of children across national, cultural, and what are understood to be ethnic or racial boundaries contributes to the reinscription of racialized communities and nationalities that transnational adoption might seem to unsettle.[8] At the same time I suggest how this movement of children may work in unexpected ways to disturb the family form and the racialized communities and identities to which this form is tied.

Non-Nordic Children

Official records of transnational adoption in Sweden show a slow trickle of children in the sixteen-year period between 1950 and 1966, when a total of 240 children immigrated with a view to their subsequent adoption. Included were children from Greece and South Korea as well as smaller numbers from India, Iran, Pakistan, and Thailand (*Adoption av utländska barn* 1967, 22–23). Before the 1950s, there had been foster and adoptive placements in Sweden of children dislocated as a result of World War I and especially World War II, when some seventy thousand children from Finland were placed in Swedish homes. But the adoptions that began in the 1950s and 1960s were experienced as significantly different by those undertaking them and regarded with suspicion by others. As Gunilla Andersson explained, "For most people here, it *sounded* crazy. You sit in a little corner here up in Sweden and say, 'I'd like to make a family with an orphanage in India.' They'd never *heard* of the idea. So someone had to prove to them it could work." Those people who "proved it could work" were what Andersson describes as "the pioneers, the naivists" (1991, 3) of intercountry adoption:

> We had then in Sweden a society where equality was THE word, the ideology par excellence. This political view was supported by the scientific trend of the "nature and nurture" debate where the stress was heavily on nurture. Moreover, Swedes are a homogeneous population with no colonial past, which means very little perceived racism or experience with majority/minority clashes. All this made Sweden a well prepared soil for the idea of intercountry adoption to grow. The Swedish adopters felt that it didn't matter that the child came from another country or that he had another genetic

heritage, once he was adopted into his family and new society he would become fully "Andersson" and fully Swedish, integrated with the family as well
as a citizen. (2)

The key sentence in that passage is the last one, voicing the belief that
even radical difference ("another genetic heritage") could be transformed
into sameness (the "fully Swedish") in the context of a nurturing family.
This family-centered ideology has been a cornerstone of Sweden's social
welfare state and took shape as part of a broader vision in which "the Swedish" as *folkhem* (home of the people) has been imagined by utopian thinkers
since the first decades of the twentieth century (Hirdman 1989; Lewis and
Åström 1992; Freiburg 1993). The idea of Sweden as *folkhem* is expressed
in the desires of individual parents such as Gunilla Andersson to "make a
family with an orphanage"; of Ann-Charlotte Gudmundsson, who adopted
from India in 1971, to make "one of those" a part of her family; and of Margareta Blomqvist, another of the early Swedish adopters, who describes the
power of an image in the book *Family of Man* (Steichen 2003)—"a picture of
a little Chinese girl with small braids which stick straight out and who is
trying to catch a soap bubble"—to cement her decision to adopt children
rather than "having" more of them.

The commitment of the pioneer generation of transnational adopters
was in marked tension with the concerns of child welfare officials, whose
perspective was voiced in the first official report on transnational adoption
in Sweden, published in 1967 in the prestigious SOU (Statens Offentliga
Utredningar [Sweden's Official Reports]) series. The report, titled *Adoption
av utländska barn* (Adoption of foreign children), appeared in the context
of the 240 adoptions that took place during the 1950s and 1960s and immediately before the steep rise of foreign adoptions in Sweden that began
in 1969 and continued until 1981 (table 6, appendix).[9] Arguably, a key event
influencing the decision to commission such a report was the December
1966 signing of an agreement negotiated by the Swedish National Board of
Health and Welfare with the Korean Child Placement Service, facilitating
the adoption of Korean-born children in Sweden.[10] Before this agreement,
ninety-four Korean-born children had arrived in Sweden for the purpose
of adoption, as a result of media publicity and the efforts of Sweden's
koreaambulansen (the "Korea ambulance," a medical team sent to Korea in
the 1950s) to raise public consciousness about the plight of so-called war
orphans. Between January and September 1967, following the agreement
with South Korea, an additional ninety Korean-born children immigrated
to Sweden for the purpose of later adoption. The sudden influx of Korean

children hinted at the potential impact foreign adoptees might have in Sweden, if agreements similar to that negotiated with South Korea were to be worked out with other sending nations.[11]

The 1967 report provides an overview of ongoing debates in Sweden at the time regarding the pros and cons of adopting "non-Nordic children" (*utomnordiska barn*).[12] For example, it summarizes a discussion that took place on the board of Rädda Barnen (the Swedish branch of the Save the Children Foundation) in the early 1960s; board members considered whether it was preferable to provide foreign aid to homeless children who were citizens of Third World nations or to provide a new family for them in Sweden. An advantage of the latter, it was argued, was that Swedish citizens would acquire "greater knowledge about and understanding for the problems of foreign nations; [and] potentially, over time, less repudiation of people whose appearance differs sharply from that of Scandinavians" (*Adoption av utländska barn* 1967, 16). At the same time, participants in the Rädda Barnen debate pointed out that a child whose appearance differed in this way was at risk of remaining an outsider, especially if he was a "*neger*" (16).[13]

Drawing on material provided by social workers who had been in contact with the adoptive and foster parents of some one hundred children who originated in Korea, Greece, India, Pakistan, Ethiopia, and a handful of other nations and had immigrated before 1966 with a view to their subsequent adoption, the report noted that all but five of these children were doing well. Of the five that were not, four were described as "mulatto" or of mixed racial heritage and one was adopted from Kenya. Child welfare officials and adoptive parents in these cases expressed grave reservations about the placement in Sweden of children "who, with regard to appearance, differ too much" from their Swedish parents. One official argued that "it can lead to suffering for the child of a kind that . . . should be avoided if the child is to have a happy future" (*Adoption av utländska barn* 1967, 27).

The report also provided information on interviews that had been conducted with officials in the nations of origin of adopted children, and in the majority of cases—with the notable exception of South Korea, where officials were described as "very positively disposed to the adoption of parentless children by foreigners" (*Adoption av utländska barn* 1967, 38)—concerns were raised by local authorities regarding cultural, religious, national, demographic, psychological, and/or legal implications of transnational adoption. For example, the Ethiopian Women's Welfare Association was concerned that the skin color of Ethiopian children would lead to social difficulties for them in Sweden; moreover, the association noted that Ethi-

opia "was not overpopulated" and needed its children, and that parents
who were temporarily unable to care for them because of illness, famine,
or civil conflict, would expect to have their children returned (49). There
was no concept of a plenary adoption in Ethiopia at this time.[14] In India,
where only Hindus were allowed to adopt, attitudes toward the adoption
by foreigners of children born in India were no less negative (54–58).

The 1967 report is instructive in the (prophetic?) insight it provides regarding potentially serious problems accompanying any national project
for incorporating adopted children into Sweden from what were termed
at the time "undeveloped nations" (*uländer*) and the report's cautious en-
dorsement (in spite of this insight) of individuals who were willing to attempt such adoptions. In this connection, the report underscored "that
there can be no question of Sweden applying racially motivated restrictions to
such adoptions" (*Adoption av utländska barn* 1967, 7, emphasis added). From
the outset, then, the issue of race was a matter of official concern in non-
Nordic adoptions by families in Sweden, if only as a disavowal of any "racially motivated restriction" by the Swedish state in developing adoption
policy. Nonetheless, in light of reservations among prospective sending
nations, the report concluded that it was *not* appropriate for the Swedish
government to facilitate more widespread adoption of foreign children in
Sweden.[15]

Despite this conclusion, other pressures were at work that ultimately
made it imperative to do so. In Sweden, as in other Scandinavian countries,
the number of children available for domestic adoption decreased steadily;
the decline had begun in the late 1940s. A policy of pronatalism in the 1930s
successfully turned Sweden's declining birthrate around in the first half of
the twentieth century, while abortion, access to more effective contraception, and legislation strengthening and expanding child subsidy payments
in the second half of the century meant that fewer unwanted children were
born and that it was increasingly easy for parents, single or married, to
care for their children.[16] The number of out-of-wedlock childbirths increased dramatically between 1966 and 1989, but the number of Swedish
children placed for adoption in this period fell just as dramatically, from
1,000 in 1965 to a maximum of 20–30 per year in the early 1990s.[17] At the
same time, the incidence of involuntary childlessness among couples of
childbearing age in Sweden was reported to be 10–15 percent (Andersson
1986, 24). In Stockholm alone, the office of child welfare reported a waiting list of 500 applicants for adoptive children at the end of 1964 and an
anticipated waiting period of four to five years to receive a child (*Adoption
av utländska barn* 1967, 18).

These social and demographic patterns are one dimension of Sweden's growth as an adopting nation in the 1970s and 1980s (table 6, appendix) and of Adoption Centre's emergence as the most influential European organization for transnational adoption and one of the key such organizations worldwide. The expansion of the organization began as the earliest adopters began to make contact with one another around their shared interest in finding families for children in Third World orphanages. Two fledgling associations took shape out of these early interactions, the Indiska-Svensk Föreningen (Indo-Swedish Society), which promoted adoptions from India, and Adoption Centre, which was more widely based. By the early 1970s, the work of their members in making calls, giving talks, writing letters, and publishing newspaper articles paid off, and they were overwhelmed with requests for children from abroad. This response led to the consolidation of the two associations into one organization, Adoption Centre, in 1972. "We weren't so structured," Gunilla Andersson noted of the Indo-Swedish Society, "while they [AC] had the best organizers and bureaucrats. . . . You can't survive only as enthusiasts, you have to have structure and organization." Once the two groups joined, they formed a board of directors, hired three people, got an office—"a small office, a couple of people in a former milk shop"—and "the whole thing came to be administered from there."

The organizational structure and policy for transnational adoption in Sweden forged by AC became a model for other nations.[18] Key features were AC's nonprofit status (the term in Swedish is *ideel*, which suggests an organization motivated by idealistic rather than self-interested goals), support that came from parent fees, procedural transparency based on published guidelines, and oversight by a special government committee, the National Board for Intercountry Adoptions (NIA), which existed to ensure that adoption organizations abided by established legal principles regulating transnational child placements. The features of this model, established in Sweden in the 1970s, resemble the requirements of the 1993 Hague Convention on Intercountry Adoption and standards complied with by all European organizations by the first years of the 2000s (but not endorsed by the United States until it became one of the last nations to ratify the Hague Convention in December 2007).[19] AC was to a large extent responsible for Sweden's position as the country with the world's highest adoption rate in the late 1970s and early 1980s.[20]

During this same period, AC was actively engaged in sponsoring and participating in workshops and conferences focused on regulating what was increasingly perceived as a traffic in children from global South to global North (Yngvesson 2000). In the United States alone, the number of "orphans" who immigrated for the purpose of adoption increased from 2,080 in 1969 to 8,102 in 1989. In Sweden, adoptions rose throughout the 1960s and 1970s, reaching a high of 1,864 in 1977 (table 6, appendix). In other European countries, such as the Netherlands, Norway, Denmark, France, and Italy, adoptions also increased steadily in the 1970s, and by the end of the 1980s, 16,268 children from Asia (predominantly South Korea and India), Latin America (predominantly Colombia), and Africa had been adopted by Euro-American parents (Selman 1989; 2002, 210).

A Right to "a Family"

Concerns about traffic, and especially about the sale of children—for multiple purposes, including adoption—were one dimension of a much larger international movement for human rights, including women's and children's rights, in the 1970s and 1980s, which led ultimately to the UN Convention on the Rights of the Child (UNCRC) in 1989.[21] In this movement, transnational adoption has had a complicated place. Efforts to regulate it, and especially to prevent the sale of children, have focused on procedural guidelines securing the voluntary consent of a parent to the child's relinquishment, or documenting that the physical abandonment of the child was not induced by monetary compensation.[22] In effect, the abandonment of the child (its status as freestanding, so that it can move to a new family and nation) is *required* by international convention (Yngvesson 2002). In a similar way, the idea of children's rights could not fully take shape until the child could be thought as an entity *separable* from the family. This separation was contingent on an even more radical move: "the refusal to take [the family] as a given collectivity, as 'the foundation of society'" (Therborn 1996, 35).

For AC and other advocates of transnational adoption who worked to regulate the practice in the 1970s and 1980s, the (heteronormative) family remained at the center of a practice that insisted on children's rights (to a family) and on their separability from preadoptive kin so they could acquire one. This right was subsequently authorized by the Hague Convention and remains at the center of transnational adoption practice (Yngvesson 2004).[23] As anthropologist Sharon Stephens argues (1995b, 40–41), individualist discourse both challenges the articulated coherences of modernity and entails risks for children. This means, Stephens suggests, that tools such as the UNCRC need to be used strategically, in ways that enable "an expanded vision of the risks—and social possibilities" of a modernist emphasis on children's individual rights. The same argument can be made with regard to the Hague Convention on Intercountry Adoption, which Stephens does not discuss but which arguably has the potential not only for strategic use in "protecting and reconstructing spaces of childhood and adulthood in a time of far-reaching local and global change and un-certainty," but also for strategic use in ways that place certain groups of children—*the most adaptable, and thus most adoptable*—at particular risk for exploitation.

The tension between the universal fact of children's dependence and need for care, on the one hand, and the translation of this fact into their need for or right to "a family," on the other, is an unresolved contradiction that underpins the policies of transnational adoption. Transnational adop-tion both advocates for children's rights as individuals, allowing them to be separated from nations and families in which—in the view of adoption professionals—they cannot thrive; and it insists that the *only* context in which a child can thrive is a familial (and by implication, a national) one. The simultaneous discovery of children's separability, their adoptability, and their right to *a* [family] name, *a* nationality, and *a* cultural identity (as specified in the UNCRC) reveals the entanglement of children's rights in the very family and nationalist politics from which "rights" were to liber-ate children.[24]

This family and nationalist politics hints at the implicit connection be-tween the idealistic goals of the pioneers who founded AC in the 1960s (for example, to "make a family with an orphanage") and the seemingly more self-interested longings of what one AC memo in the 1980s described as the "large mass of applicants" (*det stora massa sökande*) who adopted "from childlessness" in the ensuing decades. In both cases, the figure of the adoptee is at the center of a process in which family building and nation building are proceeding simultaneously (if not always intentionally). For the pioneer generation, transnational adoption involved a commitment to providing homeless children (children abandoned in orphanages, hos-pitals, or on the streets) in Asia, Africa, and Latin America with "a fam-ily" in Sweden, a commitment that was realized as Sweden became one of the world's principal adopting nations in the second half of the twentieth century. For those who followed, the desire for children so that they could become "a family" is arguably the flip side of the same familialist logic, in which (to quote AC's motto): "Children Need Parents Need Children." Indeed, the stories of longing, fulfillment, hope, and fear found in narra-tives such as Gunilla Andersson's at the beginning of this chapter, in books such as Kerstin Weigl's *Children of Longing: Adoptive Parents Tell Their Stories* (1997), or in several decades of AC's adoptive parent journal tell us more about the continuity between parental desire and the "traffic" in children's bodies, or between a child's "best interest" and its transformation into "a valuable commodity worth stealing" (Goodman 2006, A1), than about a sea change in the forces underpinning intercountry adoption in the mid-twentieth century and transnational adoption today.

In both periods, the transnational adoptee (like the domestically adopted child in previous decades) is envisioned as requiring a specific *kind* of family (heterosexual, two-parent, and married) in order to thrive. This stereotypical (adoptive) family, iconic as the natural family form in much of the Euro-American world throughout the twentieth century, is a conundrum in Sweden, a nation that is known for its generous policies in support of women and children, regardless of the marital status of a child's mother, and for its liberal policy with regard to same-sex marriage. In this sense, the *adoptive* family, the family that must absorb radical difference— the Asian or African child, the nonbiogenetic child—is charged with a particular kind of civic function by the state, one that is tied to the perceived needs of the "different" child and the associated needs of the nation form if it is to absorb radical difference.[25] This is a topic to which I return in chapters 4 and 5.

The politics of the adoptive family in Sweden and its connection to the construction of national identity, at a time when involuntarily childless couples were having increasing difficulty finding adoptive children and non-Nordic immigrants were a growing presence in Swedish society, provide a way for thinking more generally about the relationship of transnational adoption to the construction of ethnicity and identity at a national level.[26] As suggested above, a striking characteristic of the discourse of family surrounding the practice of adoption in Euro-American nations is its normativity. Requirements relating to the marital status, age, health, sexual orientation, and income of adoptive parents contrast with the absence of restrictions on most nonadoptive parents. As divorce rates soared in the second half of the twentieth century, single motherhood increased (with fewer children voluntarily placed for adoption in countries such as the United States, Sweden, and other welfare states in western Europe), gay marriage achieved increasing recognition, and assistive reproductive technologies catering to the infertile led to ever-more-complex arrangements for producing a child, only the adoptive family remained virtually intact as a model of what a "real" (as-if biogenetic) family should be. The one nonnormative feature of this family was its incorporation of the racially "different" child. In Sweden, a nation otherwise seemingly open to nonnormative families, the *racial* difference of the child became the rationale for an adoption policy *requiring* a conventional family form, pointing to the ways that racialization, familialization (as heteronormativity), and projects to construct a national identity are intertwined formations.

The questions raised by Sweden's project in transnational adoption, like those that followed the first wave of non-Nordic immigration to Sweden in the post–World War II period and those that arose in the 1980s, when Swedish eugenics policies came to light (Broberg and Tydén 1991), involve just how (and through whom) a national "home for the people" can be fashioned. How different can the child who is "different" be and still belong in Sweden? Perhaps more worrisome: how might the different child (and the adult she or he becomes) transform not only the adoptive family, but Swedish society and the terms for belonging in it, as well? This issue has been of particular concern in a nation renowned for its whiteness and homogeneity, illuminating the paradoxes of an adoption policy that simultaneously recruits and cuts off the difference of the child. These paradoxes are suggestive of the ways that transnational adoption contributes to the production of what Etienne Balibar (1991, 102) terms "fictive ethnicity" or the articulation of a "community of race" in sending and receiving nations alike. The adoptive family (as imagined ideal and as more chaotic practice) both realizes and unsettles this community of race, at a time when the nation form is under increasing pressure from the "implosion of difference" (Kramer 2005, 41) that began in western Europe after World War II and continued with increasing intensity as colonial empires came apart in the following decades.

A Home-Grown, Backyard Thing

The growth of transnational adoption from a child-saving venture of middle- and upper-middle-class women—an endeavor described (von Melen 1998, 185) as a "genuine Swedish folk movement, a grass roots project generated by spirits of fire" (*eldsjälar*)—into a global process that has transformed both families and nations during the past half century is illustrated in the close friendships that developed between the pioneer generation of Swedish adopters and child welfare advocates in India, women whom Gunilla Andersson describes as "wealthy upper class women who were making volunteer work and had discovered the orphanages." Their relationship involved "cooperation built very much on personal trust and a shared belief that children fared better in families than in institutions" (1991, 7). Thirty years later, as I researched the history of transnational adoption in Sweden, I was referred to three-ring binders containing hun-

dreds of letters received from these advocates for children's welfare during
the 1960s, 1970s, and 1980s.

53

*The Only
Thing We
Can Give
Away Is
Children*

One of AC's earliest contacts was Rama Ananth. Ananth visited Sweden
in 1965, when she served as group leader for an exchange program, what
she describes as "kind of . . . ambassadors-at-people-level kind of thing."
The family she stayed with included

> a gentlemen from FAO—Food and Agriculture Organization. He was also
> with SIDA [the Swedish International Development Agency] and he'd been in
> India. His wife was a writer. A little intellectual family and, you know, music
> in the house and all that kind of stuff. They were very much like our family
> in India, and we kept writing to each other after I got back. . . . Then this
> gentleman wrote to me in 1969, I think, to say that a friend of his, a couple
> who lived very close to his house, wanted to adopt a baby from India. And
> they needed a local guarantor for the whole procedure. . . . And that's just
> about the time that I started—in fact, I didn't even know that there were . . .
> that it was possible for an adoption to take place. It was the first I'd ever
> heard of intercountry adoption.[27]

After facilitating this first adoption, Ananth received a letter from
Adoption Centre, her paraphrase of which, together with her response,
follows:

> "Dear Madam,
>   I believe that you've done one adoption in Sweden. We have all these fami-
> lies. And do you care to help us, we have so many families on our waiting
> list?" . . . That was Ann-Charlotte, she said "We have the Adoption Centre,
> we just started the Adoption Centre." So I wrote back and said I'd be only
> too happy to help them. . . . And then we had all these [children's] homes
> I had contacted. And we started doing quite a number of cases. Then Den-
> mark contacted me, Norway contacted me, they all wanted me to help, they
> wanted a power of attorney, and so I would be as power of attorney, I'd be the
> guarantor too. . . . So that's how it started, my long association with Adop-
> tion Centre.

Nomita Chandy, an early co-worker for Adoption Centre in Bangalore,
describes the first years of India-Sweden adoptions as a "home-grown,
backyard thing" in which the shared goal of finding families for children
was at the center of the enterprise. Procedures were informal, and in Rama
Ananth's words, "all very haphazard . . . we just gave them the name of the
child and maybe the approximate date of birth. A little bit maybe about the
medical . . . and I remember that at the homes, we always selected the best
looking and healthy babies for foreign adoption. Because there were no

Indian adoptions in any case. . . . Whereas, you know, the whole attitude has changed now."

Recalling her participation in the first World Conference on Adoption and Foster Care, held in Milan, Italy, in 1971, Ananth noted, "We had a lot of people approaching, you know, because we were the giving country, and all kinds of people came and left their cards and said, "Will you work there?" *And it felt very good at a number of conferences to be a person that, you know, we are an underdeveloped country, the only thing we can give away is children, you know?*" (emphasis added).

The Milan conference is considered by many professionals in the field today as a turning point, marking the emergence of transnational adoption as a dimension of international child welfare policy and consequently as in need of professional regulation. Francisco Pilotti, affiliated for a number of years with the Inter-American Children's Institute in Montevideo, Uruguay, states that the conference was "instrumental in prodding the United Nations to initiate work on international standards for intercountry adoption" (1993, 167), an effort that eventually produced the UN Declaration on Social and Legal Principles Relating to the Protection and Welfare of Children, with Special Reference to Foster Placement and Adoption, Nationally and Internationally (United Nations 1986).[28] For participants such as Rama Ananth, however, the significance of the Milan conference lay primarily in the recognition it offered that India had something to provide to the developed world: the "gift" of children.

The tension between Ananth's sense that "it felt very good" to be the giving country, when children were all that India had to give, and the emerging concerns voiced by Pilotti and others at the Milan conference that this "giving" was in need of guidelines and regulation illuminates issues that dominated the field of transnational adoption until the signing of the Hague Convention in 1993 and that continue to provoke heated debate in the twenty-first century. These concerns were voiced by Nina Nyak, who worked with Adoption Centre in the early 1980s at what was then the Swedish Society for Indian Child Welfare (SICW) in Kolkata but is now known as the Society for Indian Children's Welfare. What later became SICW began in 1980 as an informal arrangement that AC established with a Swedish woman whose husband worked for Lutheran World Service, a Pentecostal organization, in the 1970s. Oriented exclusively toward finding homes for babies in Sweden, the informal operation was initially managed from the missionaries' home but was relocated to an apartment as the number of children increased.[29] Nayak, in an interview in 1995, described the new location as a three-room flat and . . . they just had the management of one person who was the secretary, who'd just come a few hours and since they didn't have any guidelines, they just had this pile of home studies waiting, a hundred per year, and these families, [assigned] to the first baby that came and there was no waiting period. There was nothing. . . . And there were so many babies. And when I asked them—"Where are all these children going?"—I would say 99.9% were going in Swedish adoption. And the organization was not doing anything else but adoption. . . . They weren't an orphanage. They were not getting them from another orphanage, they were getting children directly, from the families, from the hospitals, from the nursing homes, wherever the child was abandoned. . . . The moment they came in, if the health was good, immediately within one week, two weeks, they were afoot for a Swedish adoption. So the child was there within two months, two and a half, three months.

Nayak's words point to the shift in orientation between the 1970s and the 1980s, as Euro-American adoption agencies expanded their activities in India. The "homegrown, backyard" network that Adoption Centre established through contacts with people such as Rama Ananth and others in the 1960s and 1970s—Shanthi Chacko and Nomita Chandy in Bangalore, Andal Damodaran in Chennai (then Madras), contacts in Orissa and Maharashtra—produced a steadily growing number of Indian adoptions in Sweden. From the first official adoptions through the Indo-Swedish Society in 1969, when 37 children were placed in Swedish homes, the number of such placements peaked at 460 in 1981. That same year, adoptions from India to the United States, which were also increasing steadily and outpaced those to Sweden later in the 1980s, reached 314.[30]

The "Indian Child"

The rapid growth of transnational adoptions from India led to concerns such as those alluded to in Nina Nayak's statement above, about procedures and the implied need for guidelines: how, where, and by whom were the babies found, how were adoptive families identified, and how was the decision made to place a particular baby in a particular family? Nayak's observation that the babies handled by the precursor to SICW were coming not from an orphanage but "directly from the families, from the hospitals," pointed to issues of relinquishment and consent that moved to the forefront in India and internationally in the following two decades, provoking calls for a halt to transnational adoption on grounds that it was contributing to an unregulated traffic in children. Nayak became a strong opponent of such adoptions in subsequent years and was active in efforts to promote foster care and adoption in India.

Others, such as Andal Damodaran, who became the director of CARA (India's Central Adoption Resource Agency) in the late 1990s and served as general secretary of the Tamil Nadu Council for Child Welfare in Chennai during the 1980s and 1990s, condemned the unregulated flow of children from India but pointed to the ways that transnational adoption contributed to a change in attitude toward destitute and abandoned children in that nation, a change that Damodaran characterizes as a shift from a "welfare approach" in the 1950s and 1960s to an approach focused on "issues of children's rights, human rights" in the following decades. Damodaran, who worked with Gunilla Andersson (then the staff person at AC in charge of Indian adoptions) on twenty-three adoptions from India to Sweden in the late 1970s and early 1980s, attributed this shift in approach by Indian child welfare advocates at least in part to their work with people such as Andersson. She recounted for me an "almost" adoption, which she had helped to facilitate for Sweden and which fell through at the last minute because the father of the children intervened to prevent it. Damodaran was not convinced the children involved would be better off with the birth parents, and official papers approving the adoption had been signed (with the mother's consent) before the father objected. Nevertheless, and although an adoptive family had been arranged for and was expecting the children in Sweden, Andersson was clear about the need to return them to their father.

Damodaran pointed out that complex questions about what it meant to consider the rights (and "best interest") of the child were raised in such situations. She became part of a loose international working group that met regularly at national and international conferences in the 1970s and 1980s, triggered by concerns that adoption was increasingly oriented toward finding children for would-be adoptive parents and that pressures to do so, accompanied by monetary incentives to children's homes and other involved parties, deflected attention from the needs of poor women and their children in sending nations. This working group formulated what are known as the Bombay Guidelines, at a regional meeting of the International Council for Social Welfare in Mumbai in 1981. These guidelines, in turn, were incorporated into a decision by the Indian Supreme Court (*Lakshmi Kant Pandey v. Union of India*) in 1985 that transformed the landscape of Indian transnational adoption and provided a blueprint for international conventions in the following decade.

A key provision of the court's judgment, which I discuss in more detail in chapter 3, was to limit transnational adoptions from India, while instructing children's homes and child welfare societies to develop domestic adoption programs for needy children. In doing so, it defined the welfare of the "destitute" child as an issue of national concern and the body of the child as a national body, recalling similar measures undertaken in Europe to cope with child abandonment in the nineteenth century, specifically the emergence of abandoned children as *enfants de la patrie* in nineteenth-century France (Donzelot 1979, 31). These new definitions had implications not only for what was deemed to be in the best interest of the destitute child but, perhaps more significantly, for what was in the best interest of nations that might give and receive such children in adoption, as well.[31] *Lakshmi Kant Pandey v. Union of India* marks the transformation of transnational adoption from a set of informal practices that were understood in the 1950s, 1960s, and even into the 1970s as a matter of charitable impulse—the domain of missionaries, of "crazy" idealists, and ultimately of infertile couples who would travel "to the ends of the earth" (Serrill 1991, 41) to complete their families—into a global biopolitical practice. The practice is characterized by systematic state policies that target specific populations of children as in need of or benefiting from transnational adoption and ultimately as *entitled* to such an intervention in order to secure their right to life.[32]

The normalization of transnational adoption as a dimension of state child welfare policy, though aimed at constraining the use of children to complete families in Euro-American nations, had complex implications for the lives of poor children and their mothers in the global South. By defining as adoptable in other nations those children who were least desirable "at home"—children whose abandonment was a function of the marital status of their mothers (an induced delivery late in pregnancy and accompanying low birth weight), their gender, their (dark) skin color, their age, or their health status, "a novel form of recognition" was bestowed on populations who could become, through adoption in other nations, "one of ours" *without* becoming "one of us" (Sunder Rajan 2003, 55).[33] This ambiguous status as *both* excluded *and* "ours" was crucial, I suggest, to the emergence of the destitute child as a subject of rights in its own nation (including the right to adoption, or to protection from adoption), as well.

The shift from child as object of welfare to child as a subject of rights, articulated in forums such as the United Nations, The Hague, and regional and international conferences on child welfare in the 1980s and 1990s tracks the increasing vulnerability of particular groups of children as " '*at risk' of intercountry adoption*" (Pilotti 1993, 171, emphasis added) —that is, at risk for becoming "one of ours." For children and parents whose life is defined by their abandonment by the nation-state (as noted by Guillermo Dávalos, the Bolivian activist and lawyer who is quoted in the epigraph to this chapter), transnational adoption holds out a promise of "inclusion," but one that is premised on a fundamental rupture—the death of the child with a specific (tainted) history that leads to its exclusion or abandonment, or both, and the birth of "our" child in its place. That this new national subject can exist only "outside" the nation, as a signifier or testimony to the value of what lies "inside"—of a fictive "truth" at the heart of the nation (Steedman 1995, 5) that is unadulterated by the upheavals that produce both nations (Anderson 1983, 204–205) and their adoptable children—is the contradiction that confounds efforts by activists to create more permanent bans on transnational adoption on grounds that it is in the best interest of "the child" (but of *which* child?) to remain in its native land.[34]

This reading of best interest—not unlike the issue of "returns," which is taken up in chapter 7—assumes that the belonging of the adoptee in his or her birth country *precedes* adoption in another nation. By contrast, my argument is that *the capacity for belonging (among children deemed adoptable and other marginalized populations) is created by the very potential for alienage and the necessary exclusions and abandonments that precede it.* There is no "Indian" (or "Colombian," or "Korean") child prior to its adoption in other nations, only a specific child whose inclusion in a population that defines the limits of "us" constitutes him or (most likely) her as available for exchange, a condition that transforms the abandoned child into a "good" both for the country where it was born and for the adopting nation.

In this sense, the market in children does not so much devalue the adoptable child (by commoditizing it), as establish a central condition in constituting its value (its entitlement to political or physical life, or both); and the regulation of this market through national laws and international conventions is part of a technology of rule in which this newly valued life is deployed: as a means to complete families, as a form of exchange for resources from abroad, and as a long-term investment that may bear unexpected returns in the future. The nuances of this technology of rule are explored in the chapter 3. Its complex implications for adoptees, their birth parents, and their adoptive parents are considered in the second half of this book.

If India is to play her role as mother, she must protect
her children wherever they are.

> —Dhundev Banhadoor, head of the Global
> Organization of People of Indian Origin

How can we give a personal color to a human problem?
We aren't an industry. How to manage our resources?

> —Swaran Chaudhry, Society for Indian Children's Welfare

Speaking Law with a Social Worker's Tongue

In 1981, the death of a child en route to the United States for adoption from
India precipitated an outcry in the Indian press and demands for a mora-
torium on transnational adoptions. These demands were formalized in a
"writ petition" filed with the Indian Supreme Court by a Mr. Lakshmi Kant
Pandey, complaining of malpractice by "social organizations and voluntary agencies engaged in the work of offering *Indian children in adoption to
foreign parents*" and accusing the organizations and agencies of exposing
such children to "want of proper care" and to the dangers of becoming
beggars or prostitutes in their adoptive nations (*Lakshmi Kant Pandey v.
Union of India* 1985, 1, emphasis in original). The ruling in this case, issued
by the chief justice of the Indian Supreme Court, P. N. Bhagwati, in 1985,
is widely regarded both in India and in adopting nations as a landmark. It
directed child welfare organizations to develop domestic adoption programs in India, placed a quota on foreign adoptions (only 50% of adoptions
could be by foreigners), and expanded the mandate of child placement organizations to include a range of services for children. The ultimate goal
of these organizations should be to prevent abandonment, not to promote
adoption, a goal, Justice Bhagwati argued, that could be achieved only if

adoption was treated as "part of a child welfare programme," rather than as "an independent activity by itself."

In making this case, Justice Bhagwati argued that "children are a 'supremely important national asset'" on which "the future well-being of the nation" is dependent. Quoting Milton, he noted,

> "Child shows the man as morning shows the day" and the Study Team on Social Welfare said much to the same effect when it observed that "the physical and mental health of the nation is determined largely by the manner in which it is shaped in the early stages." The child is a soul with a being, a nature and capacities of its own, who must be helped to find them, to grow into their maturity, into a fullness of physical and vital energy and the utmost breadth, depth and height of its emotional, intellectual and spiritual being: otherwise there cannot be a healthy growth of the nation. . . . That is why there is a growing realisation in every part of the globe that children must be brought up in an atmosphere of love and affection and under the tender care and attention of parents so that they may be able to attain full emotional, intellectual and spiritual stability and maturity and acquire self-confidence and self-respect and a balanced view of life with full appreciation and realisation of the role which they have to play in the nation building process (*Lakshmi Kant Pandey v. Union of India* 1985, 4–5).

The celebration of *Lakshmi Kant Pandey v. Union of India* by adoption professionals in the mid-1980s and its standing today as a model ruling aimed at protecting potentially adoptable children in sending nations are a function of Justice Bhagwati's skill in formulating a decision that was politically acceptable to both sending and receiving nations, while presenting a complex representation of the adoptable child as a national resource. Framed in Miltonian rhetoric that evokes a child figure simultaneously Christian and romantic, the ruling skillfully lays out the link between the best interest of the child and the interest of the nation in two key moves.

First, it reconfigures the abandoned child vis-à-vis the welfare of the nations that give it away. By defining such children as "supremely important national assets" that contribute to "the physical and mental health of the nation," the judgment underscores the potential detriment to the nation of alienating its children by placing them in adoption overseas and simultaneously positions them as assets that can be used both at home and abroad. A decade later, this position was given international support at the Hague Conference, where delegates from sending countries insisted on "a nation's right to prevent the loss of its natural resources—children—to other nations" (Carlson 1994, 256).

Second, the Supreme Court judgment redefines transnational adoption as part of a broad program of child welfare. In this sense, according to Adoption Centre's Gunilla Andersson, who was in charge of adoptions from India to Sweden in the 1970s and 1980s, Bhagwati's ruling is an example of "law speaking with a social worker's tongue,"[1] in that it focused on the best interest of the child. Specifically, the judgment stipulated that transnational adoption should not be "an independent activity in itself," because of the likelihood that it would "tend to degenerate into trading" and thus *promote* abandonment, an implicit reference to the growth of adoptions from India to the overdeveloped world in the preceding fifteen years and the monetary incentives involved in this growth (*Lakshmi Kant Pandey v. Union of India* 1985, 19).

These two moves are not necessarily incompatible. Instructing child welfare organizations to provide a range of services for children and to make family reunification a priority makes sense in the context of a vision of the child as a resource of the nation. But the figure of the child as resource is also potentially in tension with an agenda that favors family reunification over adoption. Programs to reunite families and to prevent abandonment *expend* resources and may only slowly produce them. Children who are adopted transnationally, however, *generate* immediate resources in the form of "donations" to the orphanages and nations that "give" them away, while relieving their nation of origin of the responsibility to care for the children. Moreover, such children have the potential to generate a range of possible returns in the future. Thus there are reasons for the staffs of children's homes to privilege foreign over domestic adoptions and to accept a child who appears to have been abandoned, or whose mother wants to relinquish him or her, rather than attempting (under what may seem highly unlikely circumstances) to reunite the child with birth kin.[2] Likewise, agencies in receiving countries may support the ideal of preventing abandonment or encouraging the development of domestic adoption programs in sending nations, or both, but the everyday pressures of aspiring parents who want children and of children who need homes get in the way of such ideals, particularly since the paying clients (by contrast to those whom many agencies depict as their "real" clients, children in need of homes) are men and women from wealthy nations who are in search of the youngest, healthiest children for adoption. This tension between the goals of preventing abandonment and developing domestic adoption programs in sending countries, on the one hand, and the economic realities of parents in search of children and children in need of care, on the other, is central to the business of transnational adoption today and is particularly significant in the work that goes into defining transnational adoption as *not* a business in babies.

Seeing Children Differently

The emergence of the abandoned, adoptable child as a good of and for the nation was realized both in the details of Justice Bhagwati's 1985 ruling and in the practices of child welfare professionals in India in the decades that followed. *Lakshmi Kant Pandey v. Union of India* resulted in an aggressive program for the promotion of domestic Indian adoptions, a policy that proved successful but was challenging to implement because, as Bhagwati noted, "By and large, Indian parents are not enthusiastic about taking a stranger child in adoption."[3] (Recall as well the suspicion in Sweden when the earliest transnational adopters arrived with "one of those" from India, a point that is taken up in chapter 2). As a result of such concerns, adoption advocates in India undertook a nationwide campaign to promote both foster care and domestic adoption in the post-1985 period, a campaign that was still evident at the time of my research in 1995. Large billboards along the highway in cities such as Chennai encouraged Indian couples to adopt, booklets were circulated that promoted the joys of adoption, and child welfare councils sponsored presentations by parents who had adopted. The illustrations in this section (copies of fliers and posters that I collected on visits to south India in 1995, 1996, and 1997) provide some sense of the rhetoric used in marketing adoption and foster care in that area: adoption was presented as a familiar form of family-building, and the foster child was depicted as no different from the adopted child (see figs. 1 and 2). In this way, adoptive and foster families were portrayed as family forms like any other.

Even as this campaign achieved remarkable success, Justice Bhagwati was prescient in predicting its limits. His observation about the lack of enthusiasm for a "stranger child" among Indian parents was followed by the comment that "even if [Indian parents] decide to take such a [stranger] child in adoption they prefer to adopt a boy rather than a girl and they are wholly averse to adopting a handicapped child, with the result that the majority of abandoned, destitute or orphan girls and handicapped children have very little possibility of finding adoptive parents within the country and their future lies only in adoption by foreign parents" (*Lakshmi Kant Pandey v. Union of India* 1985, 15).

To ensure that children were given the maximum possibility for adop-

I can draw nicely.
And I can read and write a little.

Will you take me home with you?

Be a foster parent
Give a child a home

Would you like to know more about adoption/foster care? Contact us at:

FIGURE 1. A flier used to promote adoption and foster care in India.

tion within India in the years following the Supreme Court judgment, children's homes were required to "exhaust" all possibilities for domestic adoption before requesting approval (in the form of what came to be known as a "no objection certificate," or NOC) for foreign adoption. Elaborating on this requirement, Justice Bhagwati specified:

> Whenever any Indian family approaches a recognized social or child welfare agency for taking a child in adoption, all facilities must be provided by such social or child welfare agency to the Indian family to have a look at the children available with it for adoption and if the Indian family wants to see the child study report in respect of any particular child, such child study report must also be made available to the Indian family in order to enable the Indian family to decide whether they would take the child in adoption. It is only if no Indian family comes forward to take a child in adoption within a

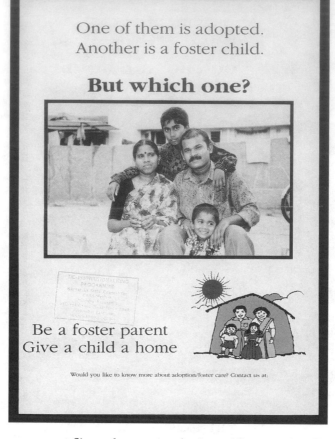

One of them is adopted.
Another is a foster child.

But which one?

Be a foster parent
Give a child a home

Would you like to know more about adoption/foster care? Contact us at:

FIGURE 2. A flier used to promote adoption and foster care in India.

maximum period of two months that the child may be regarded as available for inter-country adoption, subject only to one exception, namely, that if the child is handicapped or is in a bad state of health needing urgent medical attention, which is not possible for the social or child welfare agency looking after the child to provide, the recognized social or child welfare agency need not wait for a period of two months and it can and must take immediate steps for the purpose of giving such child in inter-country adoption (*Lakshmi Kant Pandey v. Union of India* 1985, 21).

In practice, this requirement was interpreted to mean that each "suitable" child had to be offered to at least three Indian couples before it was made available for adoption abroad.

In the late 1990s, directors of Indian child welfare societies reported waiting lists of Indian adoptive parents and a gradual shift in the bias against adopting girl children. As the director of CARA (India's Central Adoption Resource Agency), Aloma Lobo, explained to me in 2005, "Indian domestic adoption has increased remarkably over the last twenty years. . . . There is a greater awareness that adoption is 'acceptable,' that these children are 'normal' and come from backgrounds that may be underprivileged but are definitely not 'suspect.' . . . Education and the media have gone a long way in promoting awareness that it is possible to adopt a child and to complete one's family."[4]

Even as the understanding that adoption is an acceptable way of completing a family in India increased, however, the *kind* of stranger child that Indian parents were willing to adopt remained limited, with a few exceptions. During my visits to several children's homes in south India in the late 1990s, all directed by dedicated, energetic women strongly committed to fostering domestic Indian adoptions, the common theme among parents adopting domestically was their desire for a healthy, light-skinned infant (whether male or female). These preferences are comparable to those of transnational adoptive parents but take on inflections that are nation- or region-specific. For example, during a visit to SICW (the Society for Indian Children's Welfare) in Kolkata in 1997, I was in the office of the director, Swaran Chaudhry, when a couple who were in the process of adopting a newborn baby boy arrived, together with the husband's mother. They became involved in a heated exchange with Chaudhry about whether the infant should be given an electrocardiogram. Chaudhry insisted that "the child has no heart problem," and advised the parents: "You are getting too tense about the whole situation. We'll get the tests that need to be done. Let the child be six weeks, we'll do all the tests." As they left, Chaudhry commented to me that the attitude of these parents was typical. They wanted guarantees that the child they adopted would have no defects. Furthermore, she noted, the preference of most parents for light-skinned children is in tension with their reluctance to acknowledge the adopted status of their child outside of their immediate family. Even parents who themselves have very dark skin prefer to adopt a light-skinned child.[5]

Justice Bhagwati's ruling also required that the directors of children's homes work with representatives of overseas agencies to broaden the range of children they were willing to accept for adoption, in this way expanding notions of what constitutes a "normal" child and a "normal" family and increasing the possibility of finding a home for every child who needs one. I was introduced to these efforts on a visit to Ashraya, a children's home in Bangalore, in 1997. The director of the home, Nomita Chandy, is strongly committed to the goals of the 1985 ruling and works both domestically and with overseas agencies to accomplish them. She mentioned numerous organizations in the United States and western Europe that had shaped her own approach to placing special-needs children and explained that while she used to think "you can't place an eight year old or a seven year old," because "they're too old, they can't settle down, now we're placing thirteen year olds. We were proved totally wrong."

Ashraya, which was established with support from Sweden in the early 1980s, had by the 1990s "weaned ourselves off Swedish help totally, with a push from Sweden also, which was necessary, which was good." In subsequent years, as adoptions to Sweden from India declined, Sweden paid adoption costs for children placed with Swedish families and the salary of one of Ashraya's staff members. Chandy laments Sweden's reluctance to take special-needs (specifically, older) children and the consequent drop in the number of placements they can make to Swedish homes.

> They don't work hard enough with their special-needs program. There are all these studies that say it's the Swedish language and they can't cope. But English is as alien a language to these children, you know? So . . . I don't buy that argument anymore, you know, frankly. I'm told Sweden's a small country and they can't absorb these children, and you see countries like Switzerland and Italy absorbing them. And unfortunately, it's coming to a point where we're able to place less and less children in Sweden. . . . If I offer Sweden a five-year old child, it's a problem. If I offer that same child to America or Italy, I would get a reply within a week and place that child.[6]

Sweden was (and remains) reluctant to take children with most disabilities. The AC staff member with whom I was traveling in 1997 was offered a one-and-a-half-month-old little girl, a sweet-looking, alert baby who was missing a right forearm. We were told by Ashraya staff that she had been born to an eighteen-year-old mother and her twenty-six-year-old husband, who were planning to kill the child: "They couldn't return to the village with her because she looked like a payment for past sins." A nurse at the hospital persuaded the mother to let her call Ashraya, and after meeting with a social worker, the parents agreed to relinquish her to the shelter. When she was offered to the AC staff person during our visit, she explained that while the child's age was ideal, her defect was too serious for Swedish parents, who would accept only "small handicaps."

By contrast, on a visit to the Guild of Service Children's Home in Hyderabad, I was introduced to a five-year-old boy, Samir, who was missing both forearms and both legs below the knee. Samir had been abandoned at birth and Dechu Banerjee, the social worker in charge of his case, had recently succeeded in finding a placement for him overseas. An obvious favorite with the staff, Samir moved easily and freely around the children's home, in spite of his physical disability. Sitting in a chair in Banerjee's office, I would suddenly find him beside me, offering to show me pictures of his family-to-be, which he carried with him in small plastic frames attached to a chain that circled his arm. He was amazingly skillful with his limbs; he could do jigsaw puzzles, could write his name by grasping a pen between his two arms, and had learned a few words of English.

When I returned to the United States in November 1997, I encountered Samir once more, on the Internet. His new mother, herself a grandmother and the wife of a pediatrician who specialized in prosthetic limbs for children, was writing in response to an exchange on ICHILD (an Internet list server for adoptive parents with children from India) as to how prospective adoptive parents choose a child. She responded that she and her husband had seen Samir on an Internet posting of "waiting children." They felt immediately that this was a child they should adopt. "We didn't choose him," his mother wrote, referring to how compelled they were by the child's picture. "He chose us."[7]

Indian child welfare professionals have made limited inroads in changing the perceptions of potential adoptive parents in India regarding special-needs children. Aloma Lobo, the director of CARA, noted that in Bangalore a small number of parents—typically older, educated parents with grown children—have adopted children with conditions that range in severity from visual impairment to such severe disabilities as spina bifida, autism, and lamellar ichthyosis.[8] She emphasized that "these families are few and far between and so far have been limited to Bangalore, where perhaps the inclination has been to make an effort to at least attempt to place these children before clearing them for intercountry adoption." This "inclination to make an effort," Lobo explained, is related to the capacity for "seeing these children differently": for staff of children's homes and for parents to move beyond superstition and for parents to overcome "the fear that society will see their family as being 'imperfect' and therefore a liability for marriage etc."[9]

Making Value Visible

These examples of the challenges encountered by child welfare advocates in India as they have sought to move adoption away from the "trade" into which it had "degenerated" in the years leading up to the 1985 Supreme Court judgment illuminate the complex ways that trade is entangled with the value of the (potentially adoptable) child. For adoption to become acceptable as an aspect of child welfare in India, the value of a "stranger child" had to be promoted among prospective adoptive parents. This required the directors of children's homes steadily to push the boundaries of what the perfect (Indian) family might be, while at the same time working to expand standards of adoptability among professionals and parents in receiving nations, encouraging them to accept ever older, more seriously challenged, and previously unadoptable children.

In this sense, an unintended consequence of the Indian Supreme Court decision was that while it sought to prevent an (illegal) trade in children to foreign parents, it *expanded* the legal market in adoptable children, both in India and abroad. By this I mean that it transformed more children who were, in effect, "priceless" in the sense that they had no apparent value in India—girl children, dark children, other kinds of special-needs children—into resources of the nation to which they belonged. As anthropologist Igor Kopytoff noted in his insightful commentary on commoditization as a process in which "things" acquire value, "to be a non-commodity is to be 'priceless' in the full possible sense of the term, ranging from the uniquely valuable to the uniquely worthless" (1986, 75).[10]

Commoditization works, in effect, as a process of "making value visible" (Strathern 1992, 172). The pressures brought by parents and adoption agencies in receiving nations on child welfare advocates, social workers, and children's homes in sending countries to find adoptable children for them worked to make previously invisible children visible, in this sense. They were transformed, through the desire of those who sought to adopt them, from the "uniquely worthless" to "supremely important national assets," a transformation that made such children priceless "in the full possible sense of the term." This simultaneous embodiment of worthlessness (recall the statement of the Indian associate for AC, quoted in chapter 2, that "as an underdeveloped nation, the only thing we can give away is children, you know") and supreme value is a central dimension of adoptive identities, a point to which I return in chapters 6 and 7.

Commoditization is an effect of such practices as promoting adoption on billboards along the highways in south India, offering different "kinds" of children to representatives of overseas adoption agencies and to prospective adoptive parents in sending countries such as India, and listing "waiting" (hard-to-place) children on the Internet, as a way of securing homes for the widest range of children. Through such processes of displaying and offering, children become qualified in different ways for adoption and a "hierarchy of comparable goods" is created (Callon, Méadel, and

Raberharisoa 2002, 199).[11] Such promotion and the hierarchies it creates are implicitly (if not always explicitly) authorized by legal rulings such as the 1985 Indian Supreme Court judgment and by international conventions such as the one signed at The Hague in 1993, which insist that all "appropriate measures" be taken to keep a child in its nation of origin before it can be considered for transnational placement.[12]

Qualities that are taken on by potential adoptees in the process of qualification as adoptable include cultural or national identity, color or racial identity, and status as hard to place. These qualities are assumed to be intrinsic to the child (the child "is" Indian, she or he "is" black, or older, or physically challenged), but they emerge as different "kinds" of children (or reports and images of such children) circulate among the staff of children's homes, representatives of foreign agencies, and domestic or foreign adoptive parents.[13] The child *becomes* "Indian," "Colombian," "Korean," or "Chinese" "moreno/mulatto," "black," or "any color"—in this process, taking on qualities or properties that are both intrinsic to the child and closely bound to extrinsic characteristics generated by "evaluations and judgements which vary from one agent to the next" (Callon, Méadel, and Raberharisoa 2002, 199). The relationship of "intrinsic" to "extrinsic" characteristics is apparent in a range of transactions that accompany placement of the child.

The following example of transactions surrounding the color of a child demonstrates the relationship of intrinsic to extrinsic characteristics. It was described to me by a Colombian social worker who worked closely with AC during the late 1970s and early 1980s, when the organization was building what became a long-term relationship with Colombia as a source of adoptable children. This relationship eventually came to include ties with children's homes in Bogotá and Medellín, as well as in Cali, a city in the south of Colombia with a significant Afro-Colombian population. From AC's perspective, Cali was both a desirable and a challenging area for developing its work. Babies from the region, according to Colombian co-workers of AC, were predominantly dark-skinned, many of "indigenous" origin or "negritos."[14] According to staff in a range of Colombian orphanages in Cali and in Bogotá, dark-skinned children were not sent to the United States in the 1980s and 1990s because of the perceived racism in this country.[15] This perception provided a potential opening for AC, which noted in a 1980s memo that Colombia had become a "big [sending] country, but not only for us" (a thinly veiled reference to the aggressive pursuit of adoptions in Colombia by U.S. agencies, and especially by lawyers with agency connections). The United States, which has received approximately half of all children placed in adoption transnationally during the past five decades and is perceived by European organizations as driven by a "baby hunt" mentality, is seen as a major obstacle to developing transnational adoption practices that are not simply driven by market forces of supply and demand.

The interest of Colombian officials and social workers in developing adoptive placements for dark-skinned children and the interest among AC staff in developing a less pressured economic and social environment for adoption (one they judged to be less likely to foster an unethical traffic in infants) shaped the emergence of an innovative approach to placement of children from the Cali area in Sweden. This approach may have been influenced as well by commitment of AC staff to a policy of encouraging parental openness to darker-skinned children, a move that was viewed by the staff as controversial and as potentially alienating prospective adoptive parents. Memos circulated in the 1980s gave voice to this concern, asking what one senior staff member described as "the least comfortable question, and the fundamental one. . . . *For which children do we have parents?*" Noting that "when children of African origin, older, or handicapped children are at issue, our possibilities today are extremely limited" and that "hopefully families who apply will become more open in their desires," AC was clear that in order to retain the "'large mass' [of parents] as applicants," the organization would have to adapt its practice to their interests, while working toward change in parental preferences over time.[16]

The efforts of AC to change parental preferences were facilitated by the close relationship of staff with social workers in Cali who could influence the ways prospective adoptive children from specific orphanages were classified, and thus their adoptability in different receiving countries. On the one hand (according to a Colombian social worker), a range of babies available for adoption came to be classified as "black" in the 1980s with a view to influencing their potential placement in Sweden. On the other, an innovative system for "color coding" Colombian children was developed, so that the greatest range of skin shades was made acceptable to a highly cautious adoptive parent pool. The categories still available (in the early twenty-first century) to prospective adoptive parents of Colombian children are the following: "*un niño de cualquier color*" (a child of any color): opting for this category implies that the parents have no particular preference as to a child's color but is always interpreted as openness to placement of a black child; "*no negro*" (not black): implies that the parents are open only to a "light-skinned" child; "*moreno/mulatto*" (brown/mixed race): implies parental openness to a darker-skinned, but not black, child.

Ambiguity surrounding skin color and its relationship to the transnationally adopted child's desirability is also suggested in literature provided by children's homes. For example, SICW, a children's home in Kolkata with which AC has had a long relationship, prepares a small album
for each child it places for adoption overseas. Known as a "Life Book," the
album opens with a full-size cartoon of a smiling baby (fig. 3), ambigu-
ously shaded the palest of pale tans (on first appearance, the child appears
to have been left uncolored), with a vivid orange and yellow cloud over
her head (her rhinestone-studded diapers are bright pink) containing the
words "I remember. . . ." The album also has photographs of the institution, including the "S.C.I.W. office entrance," the "Foundling Home" (for
infants), and Ashirwad (The blessed haven) (where toddlers and older children live), and of the staff. There are a hand-drawn map of India, a page
depicting various Hindu and Christian festivals (Holi, Kali Puja, Diwali,
Easter, Christmas, and others), and depictions of familiar sites in Kolkata—Howrah Bridge, Birla Planetarium, Victoria Memorial, the Metro
Railway. See figures 3–11.

The "Life Book" presents a vision of an adopted child who is simultaneously "Indian" and not-Indian: a pale-skinned baby indistinguishable
from a Caucasian child who might be born into a Swedish or American
home, but with a past situated in an orphanage in Kolkata. In representations such as these, identity—imagined as an intrinsic property of the
child that derives from a specific family and national history—is also constituted in global terms, where the lightest, youngest, and healthiest children are the most adoptable, both in their native countries and abroad.

This analysis of commoditization as a process in which children circulate and, in circulating, take on value as "goods" of various kinds has two
important consequences for child welfare policy, particularly where transnational adoption is concerned. First, the child is not independent of the
bodies (national, familial, organizational) that are involved in promoting
its best interests. The interests and needs of the child (indeed, the concept
of a particular entity as "a child" with distinct interests that the nation-
state must protect) take shape in the context of transactions between parties (orphanages and agencies, giving and receiving nations, birth and
adoptive parents) whose relationship is a function of their mutual engagement in defining these interests and needs. Second, the "diverse internal
qualities" that give any particular child value do not preexist the transactions, negotiations, and exchanges that surround an activity such as transnational adoption. Rather, these "internal qualities" are elicited or made
visible "in dealings with others," and this happens in the context of a "set

I REMEMBER....

My birth parents gave me a very special gift—

They gave me the gift of LIFE

And a birthday to celebrate every year.

My birthday is on _____

FIGURES 3 AND 4. Created and designed exclusively for the children of the Society for Indian Children's Welfare, Kolkata, India.

SOCIETY FOR INDIAN CHILDRENS WELFARE

This is the S.I.C.W. office entrance.

The nurseries are on the first floor.

They are known as the "FOUNDLING HOME"

The Nurseries at the FOUNDLING HOME

FIGURES 5 AND 6.
Created and designed
exclusively for the
children of the Society
for Indian Children's
Welfare, Kolkata, India.

FIGURE 7. Created and designed exclusively for the children of the Society for Indian Children's Welfare, Kolkata, India.

FIGURE 8. Staff of the Society for Indian Children's Welfare, with some of the children. Created and designed exclusively for the children of the Society for Indian Children's Welfare, Kolkata, India.

The backyard at Ashirwad : a place for playing — and drying clothes!

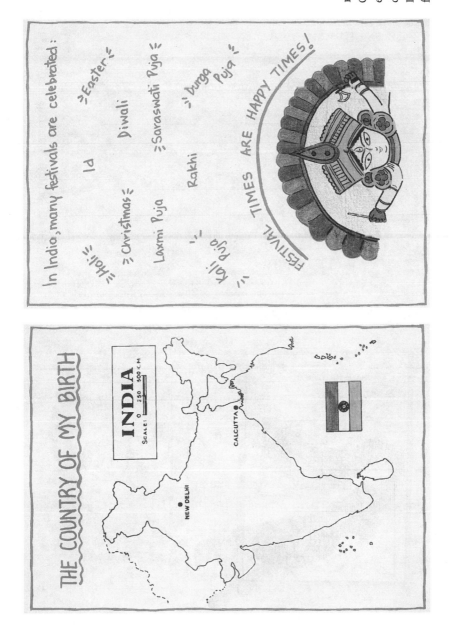

THE COUNTRY OF MY BIRTH

INDIA
SCALE: 0 250 500 K.M

NEW DELHI
CALCUTTA

In India, many festivals are celebrated:

Holi Id Easter

Christmas Diwali

Laxmi Puja Saraswati Puja

Rakhi Durga Puja

Kali Puja

FESTIVAL TIMES ARE HAPPY TIMES!

FIGURES 9 AND 10. Created and designed exclusively for the children of the Society for Indian Children's Welfare, Kolkata, India.

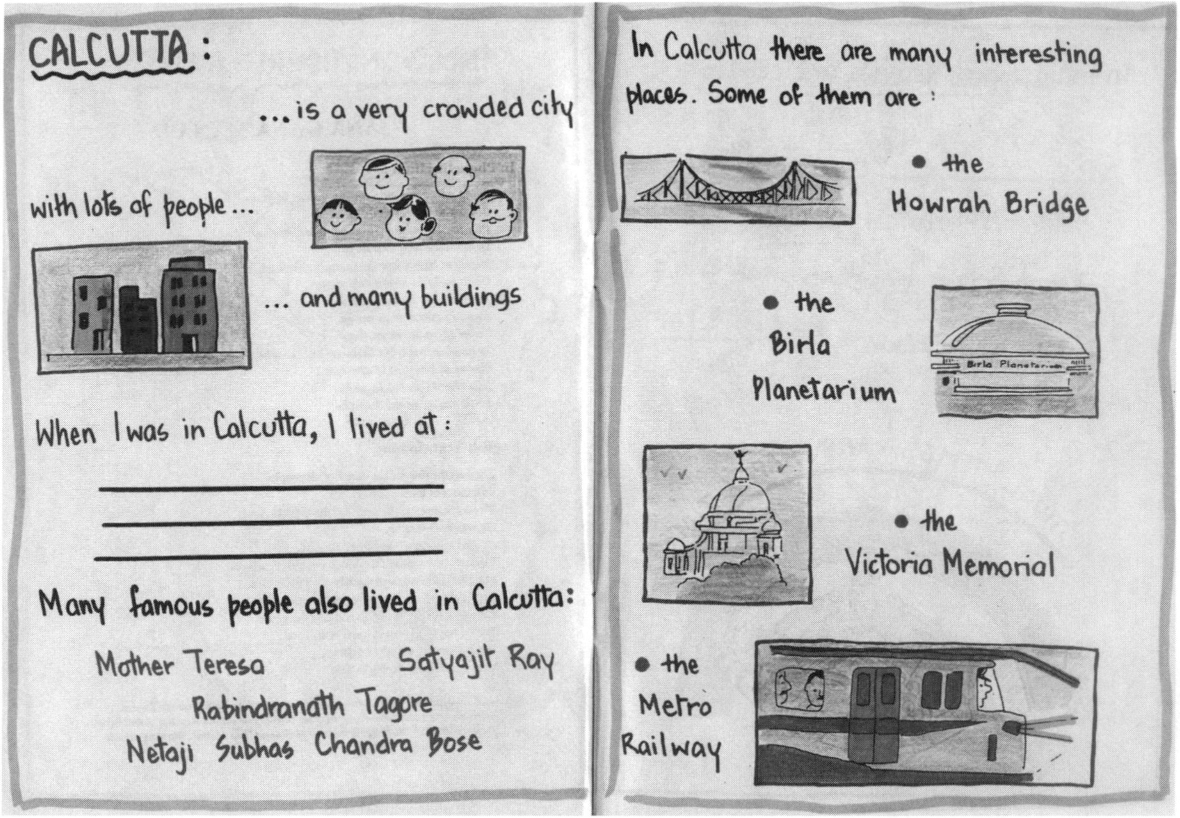

FIGURE 11. Created and designed exclusively for the children of the Society for Indian Children's Welfare, Kolkata, India.

of dependencies" that may influence which qualities become objectified as the child's "value" in a particular transaction.[17] For Sweden, these dependencies include religious and economic ties with Ethiopia that began in the nineteenth century and continued throughout much of the twentieth, as Sweden provided economic counsel and aid to that nation (see chapter 4); a relationship with India that was consolidated around shared interests of affluent women in child welfare and children's rights and the mutual "need" of Swedish parents for children and of Indian children for parents (see chapter 2); and a relationship with Colombia in which Sweden's perceived openness to Afro-Colombian infants was advantageous to both nations.

Relations such as these between giving and receiving nations established the underpinning for a legal market in children through which an ever-increasing range of children, defined as "abandoned" according to various criteria in their nations of origin, could be given homes either in the developing or the overdeveloped world. *Only* by entering such a market could the value of the (potentially) adoptable child be established. But only by demonstrating that this was *not* an ordinary market could the child's pricelessness—his or her fundamental quality as a child—be secured.[18]

The Rules of the Game

In 2001, the state of Andra Pradesh became the focus of a baby-selling scandal in which two orphanages were accused of "procuring children since 1996 for the purpose of giving [them] . . . in intercountry adoption for huge monetary considerations." The scandal was precipitated by a group of activists opposing transnational adoption, led by Gita Ramaswamy. Activists claimed that biological parents, driven by poverty, were selling their (girl) children for as little as twenty dollars. Baby girls are regarded as a particular burden since, unlike boys, who remain with their families after marriage and contribute to the family income, a girl must be provided with a dowry at marriage, "leaving her parents with nothing or even a debt" (Bonner 2003a, A3). The activists, who successfully shut down transnational adoptions from Andra Pradesh for a time and claimed victory for their lawsuit when the director of one of the children's homes was sent to prison, argue that foreign adoptions drive baby-selling because they are so lucrative. Thus there is little incentive for orphanages to place children domestically, although there are Indian parents willing to adopt them (2003a, A3; 2003b, A3).

Stories such as this are notable chiefly because they are so common and because they continue to be front-page news in 2008, after more than forty years in which advocates of transnational adoption have sought to draw a bright line between adoption and a business in babies. Legal judgments and conventions such as *Lakshmi Kant Pandey v. Union of India* in 1985, the UN Declaration on Social and Legal Principles Relating to the Protection and Welfare of Children in 1986, and the Hague Convention in 1993 all prohibit traffic in children.[19] Central authorities such as CARA (the Central Adoption Resource Agency) in New Delhi, CCAA (the China Center of Adoption Affairs) in Beijing, SENAME (the Servicio Nacional del Menor) in Santiago, Chile, ICBF (the Instituto Colombiano de Bienestar Familiar) in Bogota, MIA (the Swedish Intercountry Adoption Authority) in Stockholm, and countless other forms of oversight have been established to regulate transnational adoption. Nonetheless, the movement of children across national borders (or within those borders) for placement in adoptive homes remains a suspect operation, the subject of media attention and the object of grassroots movements to stop the sale of children. Legally approved agencies and children's homes are regularly accused of intentional or unwitting involvement in this illicit activity.

Sweden's strong position in support of the Hague Convention on Intercountry Adoption and other guidelines for principled transnational placements has not shielded that country from such accusations.[20] A report published by the Swedish government in 2003, *Adoption—till vilket pris?* (Adoption—at what price?), notes (2003, 149) that one of the criticisms leveled by sending countries at Swedish adoption practices is that Swedish parents are "*spädbarnsfixerade*" (fixated on newborns), a veiled allusion to what Nomita Chandy of Ashraya Children's Home describes as a "baby hunt" and the implicit trail of money that accompanies a search for the youngest and healthiest children. The Swedish report passes over this concern with little comment, but it pinpoints the rising costs of Swedish transnational adoption (for Swedish parents and for the Swedish state) as a sign that more control is needed in a process where paying for services (social, psychological, medical, or legal) or for programs that benefit women and children is often hard to distinguish from payment for a child.

Focusing on the issue of cost and its assumed connection to a business in babies, the report recommends restricting the costs that adoptive parents (and, by extension, the state, which provides adoption subsidies) must absorb. The report voices particular concern that state agencies such as SIDA (the Swedish International Development Agency) may be "'paying' so that adults in Sweden might have the possibility of completing a family" (148). As a consequence, it recommends that subsidy of programs by SIDA devoted to the welfare of women and children in sending nations and aimed at preventing abandonment be counted as "excessive costs." This restriction would eliminate the fifty-one foreign aid projects that AC has supported, with a budget of 5 million Swedish kronor provided by SIDA, since 1988. Twenty-four of these projects were funded in India, a particular focus of criticism in the Swedish report because *"children's homes themselves choose which organizations they collaborate with, and choose . . . organizations . . . which are prepared to support all of their [child welfare] projects"* (*Adoption—till vilket pris?* 2003, 139, emphasis added; also see 149).

The report concludes by pointing to the ethical dilemma posed by its recommendations: "Development activity that in the eyes of the sending country guarantees the integrity of the Swedish organizations, diminishes integrity for those who seek cleanness [*renhet*] in the practice of adoption" (*Adoption—till vilket pris?* 2003, 149). For an adoption to be clean, development aid, like the gift of a child, must be unconditional (*villkorslös*), given in such a way that there is no direct connection between projects that are aimed at preventing abandonment and improving the welfare of women and children, on the one hand, and the receipt of adoptable children, on the other. Only by keeping the two processes separate can the cleanness of children adopted to Sweden (and the cleanness of Sweden as an adopting nation) be maintained.

The authors of the report pay lip service to the idea that transnational adoption "must be placed in a larger context than is typical today, when [it] is primarily seen as an alternative way of creating a family" (*Adoption— till vilket pris?* 2003, 146). But the idea of cleanness requires narrowing, rather than broadening, the context of transnational adoption, in this way undermining a key feature that marked the Indian Supreme Court judgment of 1985 as a landmark: that transnational adoption should be carried out *only* as part of a more general program of child welfare and should never be engaged in as "an independent activity in itself." This more general program would be aimed at preventing abandonment and should promote adoption (whether domestic or transnational) only when family reunification is impossible. To this end, foreign adoption organizations *must* be actively engaged with children's homes in India in programs to prevent abandonment and to encourage domestic adoption. Transnational adoption should be a last resort, to be considered when it is impossible to place children in homes in India. These same principles are endorsed by the 1993 Hague

Convention and are at least supported (if not always acted upon) by major adoption organizations worldwide.

The focus on cleanness is in tension with the goal of broadening the context in which transnational adoption is viewed, but it is critical to a smoothly functioning process of finding children for parents. "Cleanness" is not simply about cost but refers to the production of an alienable (a free-standing) child, one who has no messy strings attached (to the women and nations that produce such children). Cleanness is intimately related to the principle of the legal clean break in domestic and transnational adoptions. It requires that the parent or parents of a child either physically abandon the child or voluntarily consent to the child's relinquishment, so that it can be declared a "legal orphan" and transferred to the care of an approved facility, which subsequently makes it available for domestic or transnational adoption. By requiring that (potentially adoptable) children be "free" (as legal orphans) from the broad range of conditions that make them vulnerable to abandonment, cleanness may actually contribute to, rather than mitigate, children's vulnerability to exploitation, specifically the risk that they will be targeted as desirable for adoption abroad. By contrast, greater transparency about the fact that many if not most adopted children are not orphans, in that they have a living parent or parents, could open up other options for their care, including social and monetary assistance to their mothers so that they would not have to relinquish or abandon their children.[21]

A key distinction in keeping adoptions clean is the legal fiction that money is never paid for the child but only for services performed in connection with the adoption. As legal scholar Margaret Radin argues, relinquishment of a child is feared (in a market economy) only if it is "accompanied by—understood in terms of, structured by—market rhetoric." Baby-giving can be interpreted as "admirable altruism"; in contrast, baby-selling (in the context of Euro-American understandings of persons as radically different from "things") threatens our very understanding of what it means to be (a person) and in this sense destabilizes not only the child who has been sold, but society itself (1996, 139). The "elective gift of money serve[s] as a symbolic reminder that adopting a child is not an ordinary business deal"; indeed, the higher the gift one elects, the more precious and priceless the child (Zelizer 1985, 205).[22]

Although the distinction between the given and the sold child may make legal and cultural sense in some receiving nations, the assumption of free choice when the child is given and of being "induced or seduced" by money when the child is sold is problematic. It evokes a birth mother with the freedom to choose, as compared to one (as in the reports on Andra Pradesh, at the beginning of this section) whose choices are severely constrained. More affluent families have a greater range of options for reproduction (including adoption); for poor families, by contrast, "giving" a child in adoption can only with difficulty be construed as "voluntary," because of the conditions that surround this choice. There is a parallel with recent publicity regarding "reproductive outsourcing" of surrogacy to India, where clinics in Mumbai and in the eastern state of Gujarat report that they have been "inundated with requests from the United States and Europe, as word spreads of India's mix of skilled medical professionals, relatively liberal laws and low prices" (Gentleman 2008, A9). Surrogate mothers in India "sign away their rights to any children. A surrogate's name is not even on the birth certificate." From the surrogate's point of view, with the approximately thirteen thousand dollars she is paid for carrying a child, she can buy a house, or as one woman at a clinic in Delhi who is planning her second surrogacy in two years, explained, "'I will save the money for my child's future.'" Separated from her husband, this woman's monthly wage of sixty-nine dollars was not enough to raise her nine-year-old son (A9).[23]

Resources for Children

According to estimates made at the end of the twentieth century, 320 million of India's 1 billion people were "abjectly poor" (Crossette 1999a, A10) and more than half the children under five were malnourished and underweight (Crossette 1999b). Nina Nayak, a social worker in Bangalore who worked with street children and developed programs to promote in-country adoption throughout the 1990s, observed in 1997 that "an inordinately large population of nearly 30 million children are estimated to be in especially difficult circumstances and are in need of alternate care and services."[24] Just over a decade later, the picture has shifted only slightly. In a nation where economic growth has soared and where the government runs the largest child feeding program in the world (the $1.3 billion Integrated Child Development Services program), 42.5 percent of children under age five remain underweight, a critical indicator of malnutrition. The most vulnerable populations—pregnant women and children under age two—are barely touched by government feeding programs (Sengupta 2009, A1, A10).

Andal Damodaran, a former director of CARA in New Delhi and a long-time advocate for children's rights in India, argues that given the massive problems of poverty in that nation, the key questions are not so much which kind of adoption (domestic or international) should be sought for an abandoned child, but rather:

> How do you prevent abandonment? How do you prevent destitution? I feel all agencies—both placement agencies in India and receiving agencies abroad—have a responsibility to stop abandonment if it's possible. I'm not saying it's possible in every case. It brings me to a very basic thing: You don't grab children just because you want children. And I don't think placement agencies in India should keep finding children because they've got families and they can't run without doing a quota of intercountry adoptions. These are, I think, very wrong relationships to create. We're talking about children, not commodities. This is not an export market.[25]

Damodaran describes the 1985 Indian Supreme Court judgment as a turning point, when "we started looking at things in another way. We found so many cases of children being offered for adoption because people would—couples would—abandon them due to poverty. And I think that's unfair and unjust. Had the couple been told about what other options were available, or did the placement agency just take the child because it's one more kid? Then we started going into the agencies, and the social workers in the placement agency didn't themselves know about the alternatives [such as foster care, openings in children's homes for temporary care]."

For Damodaran and others, birth mothers are at the center of a reform program oriented toward what she describes as "the much wider issue of empowerment and of rights," an issue that includes, but goes beyond, the problems that surround child adoption. Pursuit of a wider program of this kind is entangled, however, in the relationship of child welfare activists in India with the very organizations that promote overseas adoption of Indian children.

One project related to the issue of empowerment is the Indian Council on Child Welfare–Tamil Nadu's Information, Documentation, and Research Center (IDRC), which was funded by Sweden's International Development Agency (SIDA) and completed in 1996. The IDRC is, in Andal Damodaran's words, "just a small office with a library." But, she notes, "it is really kind of seminal to lots of other things that are happening":

> The whole idea is to create awareness on children's issues, provide information for those who want more information on any of the children's issues. It

also follows that once we get this awareness, then advocacy, lobbying, group action is possible, because we are now trying to form a network of NGOs working for women and children in the state. We've already had about four meetings of people from NGOs all over the state getting together as a group to lobby for issues that concern women's rights and children's rights, because both are very close.

In Bangalore, Nomita Chandy, a strong advocate for transnational adoption when children cannot be placed in homes in India, includes a range of services at Ashraya, the children's home she directs. These encompass temporary care for children whose families need assistance, a program of crèches that provide day care for more than three hundred children in the Bangalore area, a strong domestic adoption program, and a foreign adoption program that specializes in hard-to-place children (older, disabled, sibling pairs, and so forth). In addition, in 1997 Chandy established Tara, a residential center for "distressed" mothers and their children (women who have been victims of domestic abuse, abandoned by husbands, or otherwise alienated from their families). Named Tara after her maternal aunt, Tara Ali Baig, and supported with Swedish development funds, the center is intended as an alternative to adoption, Chandy explains: "Every time a mother came to us [at Ashraya] with a child she could not care for, we felt we had to provide her with other options, not just adoption." A 2006 AC report on Tara notes that it has become self-sufficient. It accommodates twenty women with their children for a maximum of two years and provides counseling, support in finding a job, and assistance in setting up a savings plan.[26]

A third project supported by Sweden is the mother-and-child welfare project in Madurai District, Tamil Nadu, which was set up by Damodaran in 1987 following reports in the Indian media that female infanticide was prevalent in the region.[27] The aim of the project, which was partially funded by SIDA in 1994 as one of a series of projects administered by AC, is to counsel pregnant women so as to eradicate infanticide. The program operates in 286 villages in the Usilampatti and Chellampati administrative regions and by the end of 1995 had counseled 5,725 pregnant women and claimed to have "saved" 378 girl babies. There were 32 "unsuccessful interventions," and 16 babies had been abandoned at the Receiving Center set up by the program.[28]

The broader goals of the infanticide prevention program include advocacy and lobbying, socioeconomic development of the region, and

consciousness-raising. These goals are accomplished through the development of women's groups and by encouraging group economic projects such as erecting bore-wells to bring drinking water to a village and
promoting group saving funds from which individual women can draw
for horticultural, poultry, and other enterprises; by sensitizing the public
about issues relating to gender bias; and by organizing training programs
dealing with women's status, violence against women, and laws pertaining
to women. In this sense, as Damodaran points out, the program has made
possible "things which are much wider than . . . saving a girl-child or just
counseling the mothers."

The focus of these programs is on providing *resources for children* in an
environment of scarce resources, rather than on transforming *children into
resources* for the nation-state. But the programs depend on contributions
from Euro-American adoption agencies, and consequently they remain entangled in an exchange in which a crucial consideration is parents' needs
for and interests in particular kinds of (adoptable) children. The tension
noted in the 2003 SOU report on Swedish transnational adoption—between obtaining children for adoption and providing aid for development
programs in sending countries—is real, but I suggest that keeping the
two activities separate so they don't contaminate one another is not a solution to the problem.[29] Rather, *keeping them together*—that is, situating
transnational adoption in the context of a larger program for improving the quality of life of poor women and children in sending countries
so as to decrease child abandonment—forces both "the state" and organizations of adoptive parents to view transnational adoption from what
Nomita Chandy (speaking at a workshop for AC co-workers in 1995) calls
an "internal" perspective: "In India, the law now gives us a stable situation.
Adoption is reasonably inexpensive [for Indian families]. But according to
the [1990] UNICEF Report, there are 18 *million* destitute or abandoned children in India. There are 9 million orphans. India is nowhere near solving
its problem of finding families for these children. We are going to continue
to need intercountry adoption. Our task is to see where are these 18 million
abandoned children and to find services for them."

The internal perspective on transnational adoption is far messier than a
neat exchange of children between orphanage and agency, and it presents
nothing like "cleanness." It is a perspective in which the idea that the adoptive child has been relinquished freely (or is presumed to have been abandoned freely) can be maintained as a legal fiction only in a world where
everyone is equally free to abandon (or to adopt) children. As in the case of

the child presented to the AC representative during our visit to Ashraya, whose parents had planned to kill her because the lack of a forearm made her look "like a payment for past sins," child abandonment cannot be regarded as a process that is unconditional. Only by separating the conditions that produce abandonment from the possibilities for adoption in Sweden and other Euro-American nations, can an ethic of transnational adoption be imagined in which the central consideration is the question of whether there have been inducements (to the mother, to the orphanage), making what would otherwise be a clean transaction irregular, one that commoditizes the child.

For child welfare activists in India, by contrast, an internal perspective on transnational adoption means working *with* western European and U.S. agencies to broaden their concept of what adoption consists in. Such a policy is not dissimilar from that of broadening Indian parents' perspectives on the desirability of adoption. Adoption has the potential to become an ethical practice if it is understood as part of a program to support women for whom physical abandonment of a child may seem to be the only viable option in a world where the costs of raising a (female or disabled) child are too high for the woman, the family, or the community into which that child is born.

The work of Nomita Chandy, Andal Damodaran, and other child advocates demonstrates this more complex, less transparent approach to transnational adoption, one in which the ethical dilemma identified by the Swedish report—that Euro-American agencies want children for families, while child advocates in India and elsewhere want to prevent abandonment—is a central, productive contradiction. In the first half of this chapter I argued that the value of the destitute child at home took shape in the context of the desires of adopting parents in other nations and that legal decisions and conventions aimed at controlling the market in children (such as *Lakshmi Kant Pandey v. Union of India* or the Hague Convention) work in ways that expand, rather than constrict, this market. If that argument is persuasive, then the construction of an expanding range of children as desirable (for adoption) may contribute (in slow-working ways) to the empowerment of (marginalized) women and children: that is, contribute to processes that work over time toward their inclusion as "one of us" and not simply as "one of ours" (Sunder Rajan 2003, 55).[30]

Space-Blankets

Susan Wadia-Ells, who adopted her son Anil from Kolkata's International Mission of Hope (IMH) orphanage in the 1980s, reflected a decade later on the distortions that promote willful ignorance, among parents, of the conditions that surround the adoption of their children. In a short but powerful essay, "The Anil Journals," Wadia-Ells describes the journey she made with her husband to Kolkata to bring their child home and her sense of "nagging curiosity about the woman who had given birth to [him] a few months earlier. Who was she? Why had she become pregnant? Why had she decided to give up Anil at his birth? What was she feeling right now about her decision? Would I ever be able to find her, to thank her for this incredible gift?" (1995b, 117–118).

Seeking answers to these questions, Wadia-Ells accompanies a staff member from IMH on her daily tour of "'nursing homes'—doctors' offices containing a few hospital beds," which, she notes "are found throughout India." She meets the doctor who delivered her son. He explains to her that the women who come to him are "very, very poor," may have five or six children already, and cannot keep more. He is "happy to give the children to IMH." As they continue to the next "nursing home," Wadia-Ells asks Besanti, the IMH staff member she is accompanying, "Who are these mothers?" Besanti's response—"They are not mothers"—leaves Wadia-Ells puzzled and vaguely discomfited (1995b, 118).

It is only years later, back in Vermont with the eight-year-old Anil and visiting with a friend whose two children were also adopted from IMH, that Wadia-Ells understands the implications of Besanti's statement. Her friend explains that "these women, the widows and the unwed teens, deny that they're pregnant. . . . They can keep their pregnancy hidden under their saris until the seventh or eighth month, but then they begin to show. They have heard about several doctors' offices in certain sections of Kolkata who will induce the birth. So they go." Wadia-Ells recalls a statement by Cheri Clark, the founder of IMH, that "we rarely see babies who are over three pounds" and her comment that "we can't use incubators because the electricity goes off too often. Here if these babies live through the first day, we just hold on to them and don't let them die after that" (1995b, 119–121). "Suddenly a space in my mind cleared. Now I understood why many of these babies were not held by a mother's hands immediately after their birth. Now I understood why some of these infants were held only by space-blankets until Besanti arrived to take them. Was this 'saving' an act of human compassion, I wondered, or was this profound cultural arrogance?" (121–122).

This story underscores much that is left unsaid but that infuses the figuring of an adoptive child as "a gift" and specifically of the birth mother's consent as "freely given." It captures the power of the adoptive mother's experience of gratitude to the birth mother of her child and her fantasies about who this woman might be, while pointing to the silence into which the birth mother's experience disappears and the incalculable distance separating her circumstances from those of the woman who will raise her child.[31] Confronting this distance, and the limitations of a concept such as "cleanness" in bridging it, may be helpful for rethinking the relations between giving and receiving nations, between adoptive families and the birth parents or orphanages that supply them with children, and between adoptees and the children who were left behind, who "might have been me," had their adoptive parents not taken them to Sweden or the United States.[32]

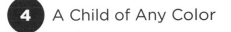

4 A Child of Any Color

They are playing a game, they are playing at not playing a game.
If I show them I see they are, I shall break the rules and they
will punish me. I must play their game, of not seeing I see the game.

   —R. D. Laing, *Knots*

The discussion of a child's adoptability as entangled in the relations of givers to receivers is not only a matter of orphanage and agency, or of representatives from giving and receiving nations at forums such as the Hague Conference on Intercountry Adoption in the early 1990s. It also involves the longings of adoptive parents such as Susan Wadia-Ells and their fantasies about the child they will claim as their own (chapter 3) or of birth mothers and the adoptive parents they imagine for their child (see "A Letter," at the beginning of this book; Kendall 2005; Borshay Liem 2000). My second chapter began with the story of Gunilla Andersson's journey to India in 1964 to fetch her new daughter, after years of writing to orphanages in the developing world. Presented with a baby who had "almost nothing on" and was "quite pathetic," she immediately accepted her as "my child," refusing to see any other.

In this chapter I return to the question of the adoptive parent's desire and the dream children who are simultaneously a focus of longing and of refusal. Once again, my grasp of this complex issue begins with the encounter of an adoptive mother with her new baby.

Saying "Yes" to a Black Child

On a trip to Colombia in 1996 with Birgitta Löwstedt, AC's representative for Latin America, I met a young Swedish couple at a small residential hotel in Bogotá. They had arrived in Colombia some weeks previously and were awaiting the completion of paperwork that would finalize the adoption of their third child, a three-month-old girl. Their two older children, boys adopted some years earlier from Cali, in southern Colombia, accompanied them. The parents, fair-skinned and blond, were a marked contrast to their two Afro-Colombian sons. Cradling the new baby in her arms, the mother commented that when she first saw the baby, she was concerned because her skin was so much lighter than that of her brothers. She had been told the child would "darken" (*mörkna*), however, and pointed to the dark folds in her tiny knuckles. She did not want color differences among her three children (she did not want "any" child, in this case a light child, one who might be perceived as a "white" child).

When she and her husband first began the adoption process with AC in the late 1980s, they had not thought about the issue of a child's color, she explained. But "in Colombia it works so that you get to choose the color [of the child]. It is one of the few countries where you can do that—you can choose not to adopt a black child. It's the Colombian authorities who determined that, not the authorities here in Sweden who came up with the idea." The color options they were given were "any color" (in practice, a choice *for* a black child), "moreno-mulatto," and "not black." Unfamiliar with what a black child might look like, they turned to the library:

> You must specially say "yes" to a black child or say "no" to a black child, because not everyone wants them. We got these papers in which you say "yes" or "no"—and it would never have worked with other colors [referring to the length of the wait for a light-skinned child]. So I borrowed picture books from the library and we looked at all sorts of different—how one looks— what a particular color *is*—which colors seemed relevant. And someone said, "Can you imagine Idi Amin or Harry Belafonte?!" What a comparison! But then we said, "Let's just put the book away, it is a child we want and whatever color it is, that's what it is" (*och den färg det är, det är det*). And then it went really fast, since there are so few who will—who can imagine—so I think that of all who apply in Colombia, there aren't more than 5% who will have black children. So in those cases, it goes really fast.[1]

Although this couple's adoption of their Colombian children took place almost thirty years later than Gunilla and Nils-Erik Andersson's adoption of Maria from the orphanage in Delhi, both (in effect) refused "to see the other child" (to make a choice), opting instead to "put the book away" (actually, metaphorically) because "it is a child we want and whatever color [condition] it is, that's what it is." The category "any color" allowed this refusal of choice and openness to being chosen *for/by* a dark-skinned child (a "pathetic child"), just as Gunilla's refusal to see the "other" child in the orphanage constituted acceptance of being chosen for/*by* the "pathetic" child. The pull of the pathetic baby on the adoptive mother was expressed in different words by a woman who adopted from Ethiopia in the 1980s and who described the black child as "my dream child" (*mitt dröm barn*). This phrase suggests the ephemeral quality of such a child, who materializes as "my child" in the very moment when she or he is bestowed on the adoptive mother as her own.

Other adoptive parents with children from Colombia or the Dominican Republic talk about the ambivalence accompanying such bestowals, even as their own sense that it is a child they long for, that color does not matter, becomes compelling. One man, interviewed in the mid-1990s by Kerstin Weigl for her book *Längtansbarnen: Adoptivföräldrar berättar* (Children of longing: Adoptive parents speak) (1997), explained:

> From the beginning it wasn't actually all that easy to imagine. I am a strong opponent of everything having to do with hostility to foreigners (*främlings-fientlighet*), but even so, deep down inside, there remained some feeling when confronted with blacks, which probably went back to my childhood, perhaps when I was in school and read about Black Sambo. A Negro (*en neger*) was something incredibly strange and deviant then. . . . We are still surrounded by all kinds of stereotypes about blacks, and I hear them almost every day. "Negro job" (*negerjobb*), people say. (67–68; freely translated)

This man spoke of his determination to oppose skin-color stereotypes when he encountered them but noted their pervasiveness and how easily, almost unobtrusively, they make their appearance: "We read about Pippi Longstocking's father who is a Negro king (*negerkung*)—Maria Cristina [his daughter adopted from Colombia] loves it. There is still a way of thinking, even in Astrid Lindgren's books, that originates in a colonial mindset about people with a different skin color, all those things that made slavery possible" (Weigl 1997, 68).

A third couple with two Colombian daughters described the responses of friends to their conviction that the skin color of their children was unimportant:

> People we knew were uneasy while we waited to hear about which child we would get: "Surely they won't take a dark one," and, "You'll of course take the lightest one possible." I have seen a figure that about 50% actually can't imagine [getting] a dark child. I can get very upset about that. That there are so many who say no.
>
> Others want to play it down, saying that of course people must be allowed to feel that way, that one needn't be a racist for that reason. Racist is too strong a word. But still. . . . At home we talk sometimes about how it

should be obvious that one shouldn't be able to choose by color. If one can't imagine having a dark child, then one isn't mature enough for adoption. And how can one stand in line for four years for a light child from Eastern Europe when one can get a dark child so much faster. *There is so much one chooses when one chooses a country.* (Weigl 1997, 65, emphasis added)

In a study carried out in the mid-1970s with adoptive parents, AC's president, Madeleine Kats, noted how sensitive parents were when asked to express preferences about national origin or skin color for their child. Many families in her sample refused a child "with negroid features" or added phrases to their application such as "doubtful about a very dark child." One person interviewed said, "Usch, I'll have a bad conscience my whole life for adding 'not a child with negroid features.' . . . But we didn't dare. Both of our parents were so opposed to our adopting a foreign child. And then there is something about the hair, also, when one cuddles the child, it's so rough—of course, I know it's idiotic, but . . ." (Kats 1978, 12, freely translated).

As these interviews suggest, "real adoption stories" complicated the utopian visions of Sweden's first adoptive parents.[2] The adopted child—a site where "desire's optimism and its ruthlessness converge" (Berlant 1998, 282)—not only embodies our own unspoken longings but announces them in ways that violate unquestioned assumptions about what makes a family (or a nation) one's own (and assumptions about equality, altruism, and compassion that are supposed to transcend emotions and deep-seated racism with logic and commitment). The drawing in figure 12 illustrates the sharp contrast between parent and child that could be found in official representations of the 1990s adoptive family in Sweden at the time of my research.

In the drawing, the black child (whose gender, unlike his or her racial configuration, is impossible to determine) constitutes the meaning of the parents as "fully Swedish" and of Sweden as a place of refuge for the adoptable (the black, the homeless, the stateless). The difference between child and parents is crucial to the layered messages of the picture. In text that accompanies a similar image in a publication of the Swedish Board for Intercountry Adoptions that was distributed at the time of my research, readers are informed that "our adopted children today most often have an appearance which differs from the prevalent Nordic appearance. . . . Adoption means that the child with its [different] appearance will trumpet out [*basonera ut*, literally, "bassoon out"] for those around it the fact that continues to be so sensitive: that the couple cannot have a biological child."[3]

FIGURE 12. An adoptive family. Pen and ink drawing by Finn Yngvesson.

Although the text that appears with that image underscores the parents' infertility (they cannot have "a biological child"), what is ignored in the text but leaps out in the drawing is the *racial* "fact" that "continues to be so sensitive," in spite of the efforts of adoption organizations, governmental adoption commissions, and many adoptive parents to overlook it: that in spite of its white parents, the adopted child "with its [different] appearance" can*not* become "fully Swedish," "fully Andersson" in its new home and nation (Andersson 1991, 2). The black child is a black *child*, with all the sentimental associations this conveys (desire's optimism).[4] But the black child is also a *black* child, whose "rough hair" makes her or him impossible to cuddle like a normal child: he or she is a "strange and deviant" child, with all the phobic projections and fears that accompany blackness in the imaginative social space where "white" (Euro-American) identity and belonging are discovered (desire's ruthlessness). This difference threatens to shake up those who adopt such a child, with unpredictable consequences for its family and adoptive nation. Its inappropriate exterior is also horrible for the child itself, who is placed "forever in combat with [its] own image," with what it sees in the mirror (Fanon 1952, 194).[5]

"Ethnical Complications"

The earliest Swedish transnational adopters were intent on a certain amount of shaking up (but not too much). They were reaching out to a *child* (a process that placed them in a familiar, increasingly global, tradition of child-saving). But they were no less intent on reaching out to *parents*, an extension that they hoped would transform the Swedish family in fundamental ways. The stark image of the black child with its hands held by those of its tall Swedish parents in figure 12 captures the intensity of the desire of the first adopters that "genetic heritage" would make no difference in Sweden and the concern that certain children—African children—might be "too different," creating "ethnical complications" for their new families and their adoptive nation. Gunilla Andersson wrote in a paper circulated by AC in 1991: "Although adoptions took place from Asia, Africa, Latin America and a few European countries, many adopters . . . didn't feel capable of raising a child with an African heritage. On the other hand, Ethiopia was early a favourite country for many adopters, because we had Swedish medical staff and missionaries there since many years, so Ethiopians were familiar to us" (1991, 2). Ethiopia became, in a sense, a test case for Sweden's capacity to incorporate the "different" child, a euphemism among the early generation of adopters for a black child, considered the most extreme form in which difference might be incorporated into Swedish society.

The first adoptions to Sweden from Ethiopia came about through the activities of Greta Svedberg, the wife of Nils Svedberg, a professor at Stockholm University's Business School who was invited by Haile Selassie in 1959 to take up the post of state assessor in his government and became a trusted adviser to the emperor. Selassie had actively recruited Swedish missionaries, and subsequently Swedish government advisers, beginning in the early decades of the twentieth century, when he embarked on a project of development and modernization in which Sweden, as a neutral country with no colonies and no political aspirations in Ethiopia, became an important ally (Norberg 1977). While Sweden had no explicit political interest in Ethiopia, the connection between missionary activities, modernization, and the potential for Ethiopia to emerge as a significant export market for Sweden was apparent throughout this period, and Swedish involvement in providing medical, educational, and technical support in Ethiopia continued in the period following World War II. Nils Svedberg's appointment

was a part of this ongoing relationship between the two nations.

Svedberg lived in Addis Ababa with his wife and three children from
1959 to 1973. In an interview published in the journal of the Swedish-
Ethiopian Association some forty years later, Greta Svedberg described her
feelings about this journey "to the end of the world," as she put it. The interview was conducted by Sara Nordin, a woman born in Ethiopia who was
adopted by Swedish parents during that period. Greta's words echo Gunilla
Andersson's sentiments about traveling to India a few years later ("It was
almost like going to the moon") and capture the combination of excitement and apprehension such voyages provoked for the Swedish women
who undertook them in the 1950s and 1960s. For Greta, her apprehension
was centered on the journey itself, since she had never flown before, even
as her excitement focused on the idea that she was traveling to the limits
of civilization as she knew it. But the sight of a familiar flower—the mul-
lein pink, with its bright crimson blossoms—growing in the cracks of the
asphalt at Bole airport in Addis Ababa when she stepped off the plane,
reminded her of home. "So perhaps they hadn't landed at the end of the
world" after all (Nordin 1999, 12).

For the first few years, Greta "was primarily mother and housewife, going to dinners and representing [Sweden], but after a while she found her
own area of work—adoption." In 1968 Greta made contact with a nurse
who worked at the orphanage Kebebe Tzehay in Addis Ababa. The children
there were doing well by Ethiopian standards, she said, but were poor in
Swedish terms, and "she was certain that [they] would have a much better
life in Sweden." Asked whether she had considered that "there might be a
problem in bringing to Sweden a child from a different culture by moving
him or her to a milieu where he or she would be in a minority in terms of
skin color and culture," she responded that this "wasn't regarded as a problem in the 60s and 70s." The only problem was in persuading the Ethiopian
courts that the children sent to Sweden would not be exploited and that
this was not a traffic in children.[6]

In the five years that remained of the Svedbergs' tour in Ethiopia, Greta
facilitated the adoption of sixty-one Ethiopian-born children by Swedish
families. A picture accompanying Nordin's article about Greta shows her
at Bole airport in Addis Ababa on November 5, 1970, surrounded by six of
her "wards." Ranging in age from an infant in a small basket to what appears to be an eight-year-old, they are about to depart from Ethiopia for
new parents and a new life in Sweden.[7]

Adoption Centre's Margareta Blomqvist, who adopted two Ethiopian children in the early 1970s, noted in the mid-1990s that the situation of Ethiopian adoptees in Sweden has been complicated because they share their physical appearance and cultural background with immigrants from that nation, making it harder for them to be accepted as "not" immigrants but instead fully "Swedish" people. She contrasted the situation of Ethiopian adoptees to that of adoptees from Korea, the birthplace of another of Blomqvist's children. Since there were virtually no Korean immigrants living in Sweden in the 1960s and 1970s, "everyone knew" that people who "looked Korean" were adoptees.

Blomqvist's own sentiments about the "Swedishness" of adoptees from Ethiopia, and their difference from Ethiopian immigrants, are suggested in her tendency to refer to all Ethiopian-born persons adopted through AC as "my children." One woman, who at the time of my interview with Blomberg was in her late twenties, found this representation disturbing. "It was fun the first time [she said it], perhaps, that she at least remembers you, but she has no right of ownership and sometimes it can be a bit much of that. She calls even those who *didn't* come through Adoption Centre that. *All Ethiopian children are 'her children.'*"[8]

Another woman who adopted from Ethiopia during this period hinted at the particular kind of investment in difference that surrounded the adoption of an Ethiopian child in 1970s Sweden. In an article titled "Mamma till två svarta pojkar i tonåren" (Mamma to two black boys in their teens), illustrated with a picture of Eivor Näslund, her husband, their biogenetic daughter, and their two Ethiopian-born sons, Näslund asked,

> Is it really the case that adoptive parents today [1982] worry so much about different countries? And that they are so afraid of an African child? . . . Of course there have been and continue to be problems with our boys—how could it possibly be otherwise with children who have had such a difficult time in their first years? But the problems aren't caused by the boys' coming from Africa, it would be just the same if it were Korea, or Chile, or even Sweden, for that matter. . . . The problems they have don't come from their hair. And one can't fixate on skin color.[9]

Näslund observed that in spite of the difficulties they had experienced with their adopted boys, "these children accomplish an important mission: to teach people that there is equality. . . . I think we have a special task as adoptive parents, to work against unconscious biases and ignorance— not give in to it. We have to stand firm" (Kats 1984b, 38).

The families who adopted Ethiopian children became a testing ground for the idea that with the proper (intimate) environment, the most extreme forms of difference could be absorbed as those of "my children."[10] This was particularly important at a time when questions were being raised about Sweden's capacity (and willingness) to become an immigrant nation. As the postwar economic boom came to a close in the late 1960s in western Europe, immigrant labor programs in Germany, Sweden, and elsewhere were terminated, concluding what has been termed Sweden's "gradual" transition to becoming a multiethnic, multicultural nation. In the following three decades, refugees from Allende's Chile, Kurdish nationalists, Somalis, and Bosnians replaced "economic" migrants, generating "the 'sudden' phase of the emergence of multiethnic Sweden" (Caldwell 2006, 56). As increasing numbers of refugees from non-European nations sought asylum in Sweden in the 1970s and 1980s, creating what one observer has described as "a media-induced moral panic," with images of Sweden as threatened by an "'invasion' or 'uncontrolled flood' of refugees" (Pred 2000, 43), the adoptee came to emblematize Sweden's vision (and its hope) to become a multicultural nation.

"Wild" Differences

Adoption of the child with a "non-Swedish appearance" took on complex political, psychological, and cultural meanings in this climate. It precipitated heated debate between officials at Adoption Centre (who became the most visible advocates for transnational adoption in Sweden from 1969 onward)[11] and some adoptive parents, as well as scholars who were critical of Swedish immigration policy.[12] The debate focused on the question of whether the adopted child was or was not an "immigrant child." Noting that the distinction between the two could be "very difficult, sometimes almost impossible to grasp for many," AC president Madeleine Kats argued nonetheless in a 1975 editorial of *Att Adoptera*, the organization's journal, that "adopted children are not *immigrant children*. Their problems and difficulties are of a completely different type than those of the immigrant child." It was troubling, she implied, that "in preschools, child care facilities, hospitals and state offices for child welfare, and especially in schools, people seem to find similarities between the older adopted child and the immigrant child" (Kats 1975, 124; emphasis in original). The differences were clear, she argued:

> The immigrant child comes together with its family—pappa, mamma, siblings, perhaps father's mother or mother's mother. If the child comes from Turkey, they speak Turkish at home, cook Turkish food, socialize with other

Turkish families, continue to live according to a Turkish pattern. The child's
family situation and home life don't change much because the family moves
to Sweden. The problems tend to arise when the child is torn apart (*slitas*)
by the difference between two cultures, living according to one pattern in
school and among his friends, and according to another at home and together with other families "from home."

The adopted child comes alone to a wildly different (*vilt främmande*) family, perhaps the first the child has ever had. The family doesn't speak the
child's language, it lives in a Swedish way, socializes with Swedish families,
usually knows very little about how the child lived before it came, which
values were applied in raising it—indeed, often the family doesn't even understand what the child is saying because it speaks an unknown language,
Korean or Marathi, or Amharic. . . .

The immigrant child's problems tend to be social. The family perhaps
lives in poor conditions, by Swedish standards. They have little money, the
parents must work hard just to get by and the children are expected to help,
take care of the house, mind younger siblings, and so forth. . . .

The adopted child's problems are seldom social—the parents generally
live in secure economic circumstances, take time off to be together with
their children, demand no work from the child at home, and support the
child in all ways so that it will blend in to Swedish society.

The adopted child's problems are not social, they are emotional. (124, emphasis
added)

The passion with which AC officials (who in the 1970s were all adoptive
parents) defended a vision of the adopted child as different from the immigrant child illuminates in painful detail the contradictions which "tore
apart" significant numbers of adopted teenagers and adults, as well as
their adoptive families, in the ensuing two decades. These contradictions
included the assumption that a "wild" *cultural* [read "racial"] difference between adoptive parent and child was bridgeable because the parents were
"completely Swedish." The Swedishness of the parents both underpinned
the child's difference and guaranteed the child's assumed capacity for assimilation in a family that simultaneously embraced and could contain or
control "cultural" (racial) difference. By contrast, the immigrant child's
difference was read as unbridgeable. Because this child inhabited an immigrant milieu (immigrant parents, other immigrant families), it would experience "violent cultural [again, read "racial"] clashes" upon its encounter
with "Swedish society" (Kats 1975, 124).[13]

As this discussion suggests, the adoptive family assumes a key transformative role in Sweden's multicultural project. Its task becomes, in effect, the twinned goal of absorbing "otherness" (understood as ethnicity,

or cultural difference) in the adoptee while maintaining "Swedishness" as the template for national identity and real belonging. The civic function of the adoptive family in Sweden is not unlike the civic function of Euro-American nations in the developing world, represented in the development discourse of the 1950s, 1960s, and 1970s as "a child in need of guidance" (Escobar 1995, 30). This representation of developing nations "was integral to development as a 'secular theory of salvation,'" and underpinned the system of relations (helping, exploitative, transformative) through which the forms and practices of modernization took shape in the Third World (39).[14]

These forms included a vision of the nation as an ethnicized (and racialized) community with a shared feeling of common descent (Swedishness, Ethiopianness, Indianness, and so forth) that is represented discursively through "familialist discourse," such as that used in chapter 3 to discuss India's relationship to "her" children.[15] In connection with this familialist discourse, the figure of the sentimentalized child that assumed such a prominent place in nineteenth- and early-twentieth-century Euro-American law and literature was circulated globally in the form of the "true thing" inhabiting the most private interior spaces not only of the family but of the nation also.[16]

The commitment to bestowing a childhood on every child—a commitment that was affirmed in Britain, Sweden, the United States, and other industrialized nations during the first decades of the twentieth century and was (implicitly or explicitly) affirmed on a global scale in the last decades of the twentieth century in documents such as the 1989 UN Declaration on the Rights of the Child and the 1993 Hague Convention on Intercountry Adoption—was simultaneously a romance of childhood and a "romance of nationhood" (Steedman 1995, 6).[17] The figure of the child, with its implicit need for parental and national protection, was symbolically central, necessary not only to an understanding of the adult the child becomes, but "necessary to our psychic and cultural life" as a nation, as well (8). In this project, the position of the transnationally adopted child is particularly fraught. This child represented a form of love that exceeded the boundaries of nations and the ethnicized and racialized exclusions through which national identities are constructed. At the same time, this child hinted at the contingency of national identity on incorporating such excess and at the key role of the adoptive parent (and especially the adoptive mother) in such incorporations.

Ann Anagnost, in an article focusing on the adoption of children from China by U.S. parents in the 1990s, argues that "becoming multicultural through adoption is central to the constitution of a cosmopolitan subject-hood, a citizen capable of living at home in the world." Her frame of reference is the American adoptive parent project of constructing a specific cultural identity (e.g., "Chinese") for the adopted child, and she reflects on the implications of this process of cultural construction for subjects whose assumed belonging to one "culture" or another situates them in a global hierarchy of embodied value that is coded in racial and ethnic terms. She also suggests that the cultural mission of adoptive parents contributes to the circulation of "culture" as a powerful discursive tool with real-world effects, not only for the adopted child but for her or his "ghostly doubles . . . the illegal migrant, the indentured laborer . . . the infants left behind in the orphan home," and so forth (2000, 412–413; see also Yngvesson and Coutin 2006).

In Sweden, the multicultural challenge in the 1970s and 1980s (and arguably in the 1990s and the first decade of the 2000s) was to produce an adopted citizen-subject who would be fully Swedish in thought pattern and life style but would *look* "Ethiopian," "Korean," or "Chinese." Unlike the perspective of the more recent U.S. parents of transnationally adopted children who are the subjects of Anagnost's article—people "whose biggest fear is that their children could grow up to be Chinese, Korean or Mexican on the outside only" (Zhao 2002, A27)—the mission taken on by Swedish adoptive parents was for their children to be fully Swedish under the skin.

Adopted Nation/Immigrant Nation

Insistence on the distinction between adopted and immigrant children became increasingly hard to sustain as transnationally adopted children became teenagers and young adults. In a 1981 article in *Att Adoptera*, Lise Blomqvist, press liaison for the Swedish immigration authority and herself an adoptive parent, cautioned other parents about their use of the concept "immigrant," noting its negative connotations in everyday usage. "It is equal to 'those others,' blackheads, those who shouldn't be here, those one doesn't like. . . . In everyday speech, immigrant is a very subjective concept which is often used with a subtext of contempt and racism." Blomqvist pointed as well to the common interests of adoptive children and other immigrant children vis-à-vis Swedish society as a whole: "If racism and hate of foreigners is allowed to increase in Sweden, it is hard to believe that an exception would be made for adoptive children" (1981, 16). An article written a year later in the same journal, reporting on a study of immigrants' views of discrimination in Sweden, notes: "Adoptive children are immigrant children. They are treated in a particular way and they are at risk of discrimination. But adoptive parents deny this and suppress the child's difference. The result is that the children must bear the burden alone" (Anderfelt 1982, 10, quoting Bo Swedin). In a third article in *Att Adoptera*, under the title "Svenskheten är inte alltings mått" (Swedishness is not the measure of everything), the then president of AC, Johan Lind, who took part in a demonstration against racism in Stockholm on March 17, 1985, pointed out: "There are many reasons that Adoption Centre engages as we do against racism, prejudice, and discrimination. One is that it involves our children. They are foreign-born Swedes, like immigrants and refugees. We must expect that all of these will be treated in the same way as we, who are born in Sweden" (Lind 1985, 3). Finally, another 1985 piece, by Madeleine Kats, titled "Oroliga barn oroar oss" (Unsettled children unsettle us), noted that "our children are often not at all like us, not like the people we socialize with, work with, or have as neighbors, not like the children we see around us. *Not in the sense that there are no children and adults who are like them—but often they are not around us, in our nearest surroundings*" (1985, 13, emphasis added).

By the early 1990s, AC was holding seminars on prejudice and discrimination. In an article in *Att Adoptera* in 1993, printed under the cartoon in figure 13, Eleonore Park-Edström, a 25-year old Korean-born journalist who was raised by adoptive parents in Sweden, asked, "Do we assume our responsibility as an immigrant family?"

Commenting on the widespread belief that "in Sweden there is no racism," Park-Edström noted in a series of conversations on racism with adoptive parents during the fall of 1992, "Your unease has been no less obvious than your propensity for simple solutions to complex problems.

FIGURE 13. The words in the frames read (1) Kapil, 5 months old; (2) 15 years later: "NIGGERS OUT OF THE COUNTRY"; (3) "I am guilty of descent, you of deeds!" Reprinted from *Att Adoptera* 24 (1) (1993): 6. Marianne Bergström; courtesy of the artist.

In your eagerness to be liberal-minded—we who adopt internationally are of course uniquely color-blind—you resort to the same simple concepts as the 'enemy haters' you so sincerely despise." She pointed out that parents ask, "Why do adoptive children suffer? Our youngsters are Swedish children." She responded: "The question is absurd. Why shouldn't we suffer? Why should we be spared when the skinheads do their purifying among the handicapped, the refugees, and the gay. . . . Why do the Danish national socialists want to force adoptive children to be sterilized?" (Park-Edström 1993, 6–7).

The ambiguous position of the adopted child during the period of Sweden's transition to becoming an immigrant nation in the 1960s, 1970s, and 1980s is echoed in other ambiguities, such as laws passed in the 1970s giving immigrants "a choice" regarding "the extent to which they adopt a Swedish cultural identity or maintain and develop their original identity" and guaranteeing ethnic minorities a right to "express and develop their cultural heritage" (Pred 2000, 45). As ethnic minorities, adopted children during this period were guaranteed the right to study the language of their country of origin (e.g., Amharic, Korean, or Spanish) as part of a policy of providing such instruction for immigrant school children. Regardless of AC's position to the contrary, officially speaking, the adopted child *was* an immigrant child, with all the social and legal rights made available by the Swedish welfare state to such persons in recognition of their "cultural" difference, a difference that was signaled, both officially and publicly, by their "non-Swedish appearance."[18]

In a stinging critique of Swedish immigration policy written in the mid-1990s, Mauricio Rojas, a Chilean-born economic historian, argues that Sweden's immigration policies generated "the worst possible type of ethnic fragmentation a nation can have, one that gives birth to increasing conflicts between different population groups, one which produces a sense of disdain and fear in the majority, and a bitter sense of resistance among minorities" (1995, 92; freely translated). Rojas attributes this fragmentation to the very emphasis on preservation of culture—the "ethnic, religious and linguistic minorities' possibility to retain and develop its own culture and social life"—that was a cornerstone of Sweden's plan for a multicultural society.[19] He argues that "after fifty years of very intensive immigration and when at least 1.5 million of the nation's inhabitants have a foreign background," there is still no understanding of what a multicultural society consists in (93–94). The fundamental assumption is that Sweden, with its carefully cultivated "middle way" between communism and capitalism, is the ideal society, one to which any newcomer—the product of a "less developed society"—would *want* to adapt, and that the fundamental institutions of Swedish society would remain unchanged (97). Immigrant policy in the 1970s was modeled on a pattern more suitable to an adopted child, Rojas suggested, in which adaptation was assumed to flow in one direction and to be controlled by the parents and the state (98). Multicultural, for Swedish policymakers at this time, meant pizza places, kebab bars, ethnic markets, and immigrant associations. None of these were imagined as disturbing the taken-for-granted, the deep and unchanging level of cultural values, which "were assumed to coincide with the Swedish, with Swedishness" (99).[20] Swedishness, unlike the multiculturalism brought by the immigrant, involved the capacity to welcome difference while keeping it controlled (segregated, insulated, taken care of by welfare or by adoptive families) until it became "like us."[21] Sweden's approach to this problem provides a particular response to a common European dilemma of how to absorb difference while remaining the same. Jane Kramer noted in a comment on "Difference" in the *New Yorker* at a time when France was confronting violent immigrant protests:

> Every country with an influx of migrant workers had to scramble toward some sort of social formula to absorb them (or, as often as not, pretend that they weren't there). . . . There was the British "multicultural" model—or, to put it perhaps more accurately, the "You will never be us" model. There was the "We'll support you, but please be invisible until you *are* us" Scandinavian model. There was the "integrated but not assimilated" oxymoron called the Dutch model. There was the "You're guest workers, so you'll be going home" German model—which, until the late nineties, put off even the possibility of citizenship for most immigrants and their children. . . . The French model could be called the "You will be us" imperative. (Kramer 2005, 41)

The debate among Swedish adoptive parents in the 1980s and 1990s about what might be termed the "immigrantness"—the not-Swedishness—of their children simply displaced the public debate about Sweden's capacity to absorb difference and still remain "the same" onto more intimate terrain. In doing so, it revealed even more starkly the real issues that were at stake: Swedish "identity" and the inseparability of "Swedishness" (that deepest, most ineffable, and most authentic dimension of Swedish identity) from the longings and transgressions that were provoked by the rough hair, dark skin, strange smells, and Amharic tongue of the "child of any color" that lived within their midst yet could not be cuddled, could not be completely assimilated into the "me."[22] The adoptive child with the not-Swedish appearance was *neither* completely Swedish (on the inside), *nor* not-Swedish, like the immigrant, but embodied the problems of such a dichotomy at a time of radical and inevitable change in Euro-American nations where formerly colonial subjects were coming "home."

In her insightful critique of the view, ubiquitous in the Euro-American world, that it is possible for "a life" to unfold "intact within the intimate sphere," Lauren Berlant argues that "virtually no one knows how to do intimacy" (1998, 281). She suggests that it is important to interrogate intimacy by "track[ing] the processes by which intimate lives absorb and repel the rhetorics, laws, ethics, and ideologies of the hegemonic public sphere, but also personalize the effects of the public sphere and reproduce a fantasy that private life is the real in contrast to collective life. . . . [Intimacy] poses a question of scale that links the instability of individual lives to the trajectories of the collective" (1998, 282–283).

I suggest that the construction of transracial, transnational adoptive families in Sweden in the second half of the twentieth century was, in a sense, an experiment in "doing intimacy." By locating difference in the midst of the adoptive family, in/on the body of the dream child, the racialized world order that produced transnational adoption could be made invisible (it could be contained in "the immigrant" with her "mighty fine culture") while leaving Swedishness intact.[23] By examining the failures and successes of this project, I suggest some of the ways that the persistence (and ineradicability) of racism reveals itself: in private fantasies for overcoming it, no less than in public efforts to eliminate race by controlling the discourse in which it is (not) mentioned. The potential for unsettling racism is located not only in the *inability* of adoptive parents to "contain" the impact of the adopted child within their family sphere, but also in the struggles of the adopted to change the meaning of "belonging" in Sweden—that is, to transform the fiction that it is only *they* who are unable to become "completely Swedish."

5 Early Disturbances

Do you remember the story about the little frog who would be transformed into a wonderfully handsome prince if one only kissed it. . . . But what happens if we kiss and kiss and the frog *doesn't* change into the prince or princess we dreamed of but stubbornly goes on being a frog and moreover insists that it isn't the frog's obligation to change, but ours, if we want to be the same . . .

—Madeleine Kats, *Adoptive Children Grow Up*

If we fully negate the other, that is, if we assume complete control over him and destroy his identity and will, then we have negated ourselves as well. For then there is no one there to recognize us, no one there for us to desire.

—Jessica Benjamin, *The Bonds of Love*

Sameness and Difference

Madeleine Kats, whose insistence on the distinction between the "adopted child" and the "immigrant child" spoke to widely shared assumptions about the ease with which adoptees would assimilate into Swedish society, as long as they were placed in a loving home (chapter 4), raised questions about these assumptions in her popular book *Adoptive Children Grow Up* (1990a). Troubling reports from parents and teachers suggested that some children adopted from abroad were experiencing a range of emotional and social problems at home and at school.[1] In the context of widespread concerns about racism directed against immigrants in 1980s Sweden, and the gradual realization that transnational adoptees were no less subject to racist incidents than (other) immigrants, it would have been surprising had there been no difficulties.[2] Yet Kats, describing a situation specific to Sweden in its details, but one that replicated patterns reported in professional literature from other adopting nations on both sides of the Atlantic, explains these problems as follows:

It is surely worth contemplating why we in Sweden who adopt more foreign-born children—all with a very difficult start in life—than any other nation, at the same time regard problems and difficulties as a sign of failure and something which should not happen. . . . If it is the case that *we adopt foreign children with damages that can be traced to lacks that go back to earliest infancy (utländska barn med tidiga skador och brister)*, with the unspoken assumption that the child will eventually "recover" and "catch up," and be just like all other children who received all they needed from the first moment— yes, in that case it is time to rethink adoption, both foreign and domestic. (1990a, 8, emphasis added; freely translated)

Kats, trained as a psychologist and herself the adoptive parent of a child born in India, hints here at complex issues that may underpin the "problems and difficulties" of adopted children in Sweden, even as she seems to attribute these problems to a single cause: the "difficult start in life" of the child. Issues include her depiction of Sweden as a nation that adopts "more foreign-born children . . . than any other nation" as well as the representation of the transnational adoptee as "damaged" from "earliest infancy." She asks: What happens "if just *we* get a child who isn't like us and who doesn't become like us—a child who doesn't just look different but in fact *is* different and will always be so?" (1990a, 9, emphasis added).

For Kats, difference is a function of "early disturbances" (*tidiga störningar*) (1990a, 11), "early emotional deprivations" (*tidiga känslomässiga brister*) (12) that derive from the lack of a continuing mother figure, someone for whom the child is "a completely *special* child, 'my child'" (13). Drawing on the work of John Bowlby, D. W. Winnicott, Margaret Mahler, and others, Kats argues that "insufficient motherly care" can produce such serious deficits that children "will only sometimes, partially, and with great effort be able to overcome them" (13). While it seems clear that Kats did not mean to suggest that all or even most adopted children would necessarily have serious deficits, she nonetheless underscored the potential risks to the adopted child of a "very difficult start in life," arguing that the "early disturbed child will grow into an early disturbed teen-ager and an early disturbed adult. We give them different names depending on the angle from which we look at them: borderline personalities, psychopaths, grave personality disturbances, 'the worst ones' etc." (8).[3] Kats asks that parents rethink "*on what terms* we adopt?" (9, emphasis in original).[4]

Epidemiological research on Swedish transnational adoptees published in the first years of the twenty-first century seemed to confirm concerns about "grave personality disturbances" and was received with alarm by adoption organizations, while viewed by critics of transnational adoption as supporting their argument that transnational adoption was detrimental to the welfare of the child (Lindqvist and Ohlén 2003).[5] One such study reported that the cohort of 11,320 Swedish adoptees born 1970–79 had "a high risk for severe mental health problems and social maladjustment in adolescence and young adulthood," particularly suicide (Hjern, Lindblad, and Vinnerljung 2002, 443; also see Hjern and Allbeck 2002). According to the study, transnational adoptees, compared to other children in Swedish society living in similar socioeconomic circumstances, are three to four times as likely to commit or attempt suicide or to be admitted to psychiatric care, five times as likely to be drug-addicted, and two to three times as likely to abuse alcohol or commit crimes (Hjern, Lindblad, and Vinnerljung 2002, 446).

Hjern, Lindblad, and Vinnerljung argue that because the odds for mental health disorders and social maladjustments in biological children in the adoptive homes is low, "factors related to the adoptive parents are less likely to be important in understanding the problems of the adoptees as a group." Like Kats more than a decade earlier, they point instead to "circumstances in the country of origin for the mental health and social adjustment of intercountry adoptees" (2002, 447). Similar concerns have been raised in studies of transnational adoptees conducted in the United States and elsewhere.[6]

To their credit, Hjern and his colleagues caution that interaction patterns between adoptive parent and child may differ from those between biological parent and child. Specifically, they note that there is higher risk for social maladjustment among adoptees in white-collar than in blue-collar families, a difference they attribute to "coping with high expectations of performance in school and other competitive arenas" (447). Moreover, they note that as a group, adoptees in their study "were more or less equal to immigrant children, with slightly higher odds ratios for mental health disorders and slightly lower odds for social maladjustment," a finding they describe as "surprising, in view of the low socioeconomic positions held by many immigrant families" (447). Finally, they suggest that "discrimination and prejudices against children and youths with a non-Swedish appearance could be important in accounting for these similar odds ratios" (447).[7] On a more positive note, Hjern and colleagues point to the 82 percent of 4,340 adopted boys and 92 percent of 6,980 adopted girls who did *not* show up in Swedish records of psychiatric disturbance or social maladjustment and conclude that these statistics could be interpreted as "further evidence of resilience in children who start their early life in adverse circumstances" (446–447).[8]

My aim here is not to dispute the importance of a caring parent or parents for the adopted child, nor to deny that early separations may prove difficult and possibly traumatic for young children. I draw attention rather to the caution voiced by Triseliotis and Hill (1990, 115) almost two decades ago, about the implications for the adopted child of being "held hostage to adverse early childhood experiences," a perspective that they argue is "too deterministic."[9] The rhetoric of early deficits and ensuing disturbances recalls Ann Anagnost's discussion of Internet exchanges in the 1990s among U.S. parents of children born in China. Noting their "need to envision and memorialize the loss of an affective bond they would like to believe had been there," Anagnost suggests the key role of such imagined bonds for constituting the child as able to transfer its love elsewhere. By reassuring themselves "that affect *was* there, at the origin," the adoptive parents can also believe "that the child will be capable of delivering fully on its promise of love" (2000, 400).[10]

In Kats's account, the early-disturbed child—the child for whom affect was *not* there "at the origin"—will turn out to be "'less affectionate' than other children" (1990b, 2), a deficit that demands "an excess of emotional capacity [känslomässig överbegåvning]" (1990a, 11) on the part of the adoptive parent, particularly the adoptive mother.[11] In a parallel account of adoptive parenting, Anagnost notes how the "affective labor . . . culturally identified with 'the maternal,' lying within the deep interiority of family life . . . becomes more urgent the more the link to the child appears to be tenuous" (2000, 391–392). In this sense, the figure of the transnationally adopted child with its special need for (maternal) love constitutes "a dense locus of desire and value" for adopting families and adopting nations (403). The more "needy" the child (the more tenuous its link to a mother, the greater its potential for disturbance), the more powerful it becomes as a locus of desire.

I suggest that the displacement, in the 1990s, of emotional deficits in the adopted child onto the birth mother and onto nations that have "nothing but children to give away" (chapter 2) is not unlike the displacement of "wild cultural" difference from the adopted child onto the immigrant child in the 1970s and 1980's (chapter 4). In the 1990s, "emotional" difference is explained by the child's abandonment in early infancy and distanced from the child's lived experience of racism in the adopting nation. In the 1970s–80s, the adopted child's "immigrantness" is displaced onto nonadopted children who lack a Swedish family. In both cases, there is no middle ground. The adopted child is either the same as me (completely

Swedish), or it is completely different (an immigrant child). Indeed, the observation of Hjern and colleagues (2002, 447) that "intercountry adoptees in our study were more or less equal to immigrant children," in spite of the difference in socioeconomic circumstances of the families, hints at the (racialized) ways that radical otherness takes shape in someone who, as Madeleine Kats writes, "stubbornly goes on being a frog [regardless of how much we kiss it] and moreover insists that it isn't the frog's obligation to change, but ours, if we want to be the same" (Kats 1990a, 8).

Kats does not expand on her provocative idea that it is *"our problem [as parents] to change* if we [parent and child] are to become like one another" (1990a, 8, emphasis added), a formulation that calls for a more dynamic approach to parent-child relations than the theory of early disturbances, an approach in which both adoptive parent and child are actively engaged over time and well into the child's adulthood. This requires a shift in focus away from a unilinear trajectory in which "disturbance" is understood to reside in the child (the birth mother, the birth nation), predates the child's arrival in Sweden, and can be transformed into the Swedish only by the emotionally resilient; it calls instead for a relational perspective that attends to the tension between sameness and difference and "a continual, dynamic, evolving balance of the two" in parent-child relations (Benjamin 1988, 25). It recalls the increasing engagement of adoptive parents in the 1980s in protests against racism in Sweden and their dawning awareness that by adopting a foreign-born child *they, too, had (to) become "different."*[12]

If it is incumbent on the *parent* to change (for the Swedishness of the parent to be transformed) in order for the child to "fit in," then the very Swedishness of the parent (that intangible essence that constitutes Sweden as being a fertile ground for the adoption of children "with a very difficult start in life") may be a factor in producing the adopted child's "disturbance." Likewise, "the Swedish" may take shape through and be provoked by the parent's response to the child. Swedishness, in other words, "names the detour through the Other that provides access to a fictive sense of self" (Fuss 1995, 143).[13] For the parent, this detour is enabled by the child's exterior (his or her "rough hair" or black body, the purple silk dress that seems "horrible" in Gunilla's story in chapter 2 of adopting Maria), but is contingent on the association of these visible signs with (imagined) settings of deprivation from which the child "comes" and to which the child "belongs." This dimension of the child—symbolized most broadly by his or her condition of being "abandoned"—takes shape "inside" the parent (as a fantasy of the child) and is powerfully provoked by imaginaries related to the child's "origin," as embodied in the "birth mother," the "orphanage," or the child's "native ground."[14] Such journeys (or detours) "constitute the very entry into [Swedish] subjectivity" for the parent (143).[15]

"Excess of emotional capacity" refers to the imagined capability of the parent to overcome the child's radical difference, that is, to transform her or him into a completely Swedish child in spite of the "disturbances" produced by the child's environment before the child went to Sweden. But *what if this excess exacerbates difference, becoming the detour through the parent in which the child's subjectivity as "not Swedish" takes shape?* More hopefully, in what ways might such detours have the potential to transform *both* parent and child, disrupting the "completely Swedish" (and the hierarchies this identification represents) in the process?

If, following psychoanalyst D. W. Winnicott and others, parenting is (at least in part) about *differentiation*—that is, about "the initiation of the . . . state of separateness" of parent and child and the construction of "a world of shared reality . . . which the subject can use and which can feed back other-than-me substance into the subject" (Winnicott 1971, 97, 94), the task of differentiation begins (for the adoptive parent) from the first moment that the parent begins to imagine himself or herself as "adoptive." Psychoanalytic theorist Jessica Benjamin describes this imaginative process as "mental holding," in which "adoptive mothers, like biological ones, hold their baby inside their minds before birth" (1988, 13). Recall the young Swedish couple who were given color options when they adopted an Afro-Colombian child in the late 1980s (chapter 4) and turned to "picture books from the library" to help them imagine what this might entail: "And we looked at all sorts of different—how one looks—what a particular color *is*—which colors seemed relevant. And someone said, 'Can you imagine Idi Amin or Harry Belafonte?!' What a comparison!" Another adoptive parent, interviewed in the mid-1990s, explained how adopting a black child had not been "all that easy to imagine," a feeling he attributed to patterns established in his childhood when "a black person was something incredibly strange and deviant" (Weigl 1997, 67–68). In a similar way, imagining the adoption of an orphanage child (a motherless child) also shapes the parent's experience of the child's difference and may affect the child's potential for "disturbance."

I suggest that the differently charged meanings of adopting a "black," "Ethiopian," "Indian," "Chinese," "Korean," or "Russian" child are part of the process of producing a child who is "adoptive" and are forged in the potential space that opens up between parent and child from the first moment that adoption of a particular child, from a particular nation, is contemplated.[16] Such meanings can establish "an imagined history of cultural and family pathology even before the child enters the home"[17] and in this way may constitute the particular forms of "early disturbance" that take shape in the child. At the same time, fantasies of what it means to adopt a child with a specific (imagined) ethnicity become a measure of parental worthiness, and learning the child's name a potential moment of anxiety about belonging and erasure (or anchoring) of identity (Anagnost 2000, 406–408).[18]

The meanings that accompany particular "kinds" of adoptive children are neither conscious nor easily measurable, but they may nonetheless be visible in the earliest postadoptive interactions between parent and child. Research in the Netherlands with new adoptive mothers and their children suggests that video recordings of nonverbal interactions between parent and child may provide clues to parental perceptions and responses, allowing the parent who views the recordings a greater degree of awareness regarding her or his unconscious reactions to the adopted child (and the child's reactions to the parent).[19] These reactions and interactions, in which both parent and child are engaged, create an emotional foundation for the adoptive family and for the capacity of the adoptive child to experience himself or herself as belonging (or not belonging) in that family.

Jessica Benjamin's analysis of early exchanges between parent and child as a "struggle for recognition" (1988, 38) in which the fantasy child must be continually destroyed so that the (adoptive) parent can develop "a relationship with a real—outside—baby" (13) is helpful in exploring the intersubjective context for the adopted child's experience of belonging or not belonging in the adoptive family and the transformative possibilities of the project of transnational adoption. Destruction, Benjamin argues (building on Hegel and Winnicott), "is an effort to differentiate" (38) and is crucial, paradoxically, to the "survival" of the *real* child (the child who is not simply an object of the parent's fantasy). But the fantasy child (the "pitiful" child) is not so easily disposed of: it is precisely the attractor that is compelling for the adoptive parent and must be preserved (must be continually produced in fantasy) if the adopting parent (the adopting nation) is to remain "the same." It is this paradox—that the measure of parental (maternal) worthiness is (her) capacity to overcome the child's difference, a difference that must be preserved if the parent (the nation) is to retain its autonomy—that constitutes the potential for "disturbance" in/by the adopted child.

To me, Ethiopia would just be chaos.

—Sofia Berzelius

The inseparability of the child's value for the adopting parent (and the adopting nation) from her radical difference, and specifically from the "early disturbances" she or he has suffered—abandonment by the mother, months or years spent in an orphanage, separation from a native soil where he or she "really" belongs—is captured in the narratives of desire of adoptive parents such as Gunilla Andersson, Annika Grünewald, and Ann-Charlotte Gudmundsson. Grünewald, who adopted her daughter Kanthi from an orphanage in Bangalore when she was five years old, keeps a picture in her office of the crying child she brought to Sweden in 1975. In an article written for AC's journal, *Att Adoptera*, in 1980, she describes Kanthi's first journey back, when she was ten years old, accompanied by her mother and another adoptive mother, Siv Nygren, whose daughter Anya was also born in India. Grünewald represents Kanthi's memories of India as "mostly negative. . . . She remembered hungry children left on their own, with matted hair, begging for food, 'but no one had any to give.'" Kanthi wanted to go back to India, Grünewald explains, but was afraid of meeting such children, who "didn't even have an orphanage to be in" (Grünewald 1980, 3; freely translated).

Recounting their visit to the orphanage where Kanthi once lived, Grünewald describes "children who sat with crossed legs and did nothing. They were between 1 and 5 years, but the size of a 1-year old. One was developmentally disabled. Kanthi once sat in just that place." She notes the small supply of rice to be distributed among the children, the dirty mattresses stacked in a corner. Kanthi and her friend Anya immediately focused on the one baby who seemed healthiest, a strategy, Grünewald suggests, for coping with their own complicated response to the children and the place. That evening, in Grünewald's words, Kanthi said to her: "Imagine if I had been left there and you had adopted another child and you had come back with her and looked at me" (1980, 4).

This portrayal of the orphanage, recounted in the words of the adopted child but written by the adoptive parent and published in a journal intended for other (prospective) adoptive parents, illuminates the power of the abandoned child in the fantasy of the adoptive parent, while targeting India as the imaginative geography where such radical impoverishment is to be found.[20] Kanthi's words "Imagine if I had been left there . . ." underscore the difference that materializes between parent and child in this situation, while emphasizing the power of the adoptive parent. Her mother, Annika, can only imagine what it would be like to live in the orphanage; her ability to mother is contingent on this distance from Kanthi's lived experience, a distance that is confirmed in her capacity to "come back" and "look at me" in the orphanage. By contrast, Kanthi situates her "self" both inside and outside the orphanage. She is simultaneously the orphanage child (the child with crossed legs who did nothing, who might have been me) and the Swedish Kanthi, who can gaze at this child because of a chance encounter that took her to Sweden.

Likewise, Gunilla Andersson, describing the trip she made with her daughter Maria to the orphanage in Delhi from which she had been adopted ten years previously, asked Maria, who was present at the interview:

> Do you remember what you said when you went into the orphanage and saw those statistics on the wall? They have these statistics of how many babies died and were adopted. Almost 60% died. Very few were adopted, some left for other institutions. You pointed to the [figure on] dead babies and said, "That would be me if you hadn't come for me, I would be dead, I would be in that column if you hadn't come." And then we went to see the orphanage, and then we got back to the car, and you said: "When we come back to Sweden, to Daddy and Jan [her brother], then I'll have a big glass of lemonade." She had to tell herself [turning from Maria to address the interviewer] the world she had in Sweden was still there. Daddy, brother, and water (she wasn't allowed to have water in India). The one, little, random possible opportunity [turning again to Maria] which came out and made us a family, I mean, you were a thinking person. That was so shaky and scary that you had to grab what was reality at home.[21]

Like Kanthi's response to the children at the orphanage in Bangalore, Maria's reaction to the statistics on the wall situated her simultaneously inside and outside the orphanage, both "dead, in that column if you hadn't come" and "back in Sweden" with her father and brother, where she could have "a big glass of lemonade."

In both cases, the difference between parent and child, a difference that shapes them in their "innermost depths," is constituted in the experience of the child's abandonment vis-à-vis the parent's capacity to travel "to the ends of the earth" (Serrill 1991, 42) to find her. How does this difference structure the relationship of parent to child? How does it enable an "excess of emotional capacity" in the parent, while producing emotional deficits in the child—a reality "so shaky and scary that you had to grab what was reality at home"?

To begin to answer this question requires returning to a point that may get lost in an approach that focuses too narrowly on early disturbances (the child's abandonment by a birth parent) and too little on the ways an "abandoned" child, as a social, legal, and culturally powerful category that demands political and personal attention, calls forth a "needing" or "desiring" parent or nation who or which can provide "a family" for the child. To return to the moment in the Delhi orphanage in which the baby Renu became the Swedish child Maria (chapter 2), the process of becoming was not simply a choice by the parent but involved (in Maria Brunn's words) "a co-work," a labor in which both parent and child were caught up.

This labor of producing parent and child is a part of any parent-child relationship, but the absence of detail about the early history of so many transnationally adopted children and the powerful presence of media images representing the nations from which adopted children come imbue the child with particular kinds of value for the adopting parent and may generate equally powerful responses in the child.[22] Former AC president Madeleine Kats underscored the significance of the complex circumstances surrounding a child's adoption in a 1981 editorial in AC's journal, noting that "even though it is so hard for us here in Sweden to even imagine the previous history of a child, that history is crucial. It was just *these* circumstances that led to just this child becoming our child. It is just *these* events that mean it can never be exactly the same thing to take charge of an adopted child of three weeks, three months, three years . . . as to take charge of a newborn, three seconds old biological child whose history is one's own, known and experienced in every detail" (1984a, 17; freely translated).

What Kats observed about the adopted child's (largely unknown) pre-adoptive history and its potential impact on the child's life is an undeniable presence in the life of the child and the adoptive family. But the parent's fantasy of the child (and, for somewhat older children, the child's fantasy of the adoptive parent) is surely no less important in the labor of making the Swedish child Maria, or Sara, or Anna and the work of producing the adoptive parent. Here I suggest that in the case of children adopted transnationally in Sweden in the 1960s, 1970s, and 1980s, the very concept of an orphanage child and of the nations (and mothers) that produced such children became a central part of the adopted child's history, a part that could prove an obstacle to a process described by social worker Ingrid Stjerna as "giving [adopted] children their own life" (Stjerna 1976, 101; freely translated).[23]

In exploring this obstacle and the importance of Stjerna's concept of

and others, but especially on a phrase that Gunilla Andersson used in describing her desire to adopt a child in the early 1960s—that she wanted to
"make a family with an orphanage." This phrase caught my attention when
I first heard it, perhaps because of my own experience in trying to make a
family with the birth parents and siblings of my son Finn, at a time in the
early 1980s when domestic adoption practices in the United States were
only beginning to "open up" in ways that allowed the birth parent(s) to
figure in the adoption process (chapter 1). In my own case, in which there
was relative parity in social and educational, if not in economic, circumstances, the endeavor proved sufficiently challenging (Yngvesson 1997).
But what does it mean to make a family with an orphanage? How does
the labeling of the mother of a child who is placed for adoption as having
abandoned her child situate her vis-à-vis the adoptive parents (and specifically vis-à-vis the adoptive mother)? And what does it suggest about the
identity of the adoptive child? Likewise, how does the characterization of
a child as "coming from an orphanage" or "coming from Ethiopia" or India
situate him or her vis-à-vis the adopting parent or adopting nation?

Sara Nordin, who was adopted from Ethiopia in 1969, at age one and
a half, describes how hard it was to speak about her adoption as she was
growing up. When she was very young, her parents told her a "wonderful
story" (*en jättefin historia*) about why she was adopted:

> That story was about how my mother had gone to the [Kebebe Tzehay] or-
> phanage and left me and then I had had a great time at the orphanage. Every-
> thing had been really, really good, and then I came to Sweden. But then they
> forgot to tell me the real adoption story, because I never wanted to talk about
> the adoption. I never wanted to talk about coming from Ethiopia. . . . The
> few times we tried, mamma and pappa got really sad. Mamma was on the
> verge of tears, each time. And then I thought: "No, we just won't talk about
> it. We'll talk about something else. You shouldn't have to feel this way." My
> parents tried, but I refused. Now I realize that their efforts were a little naïve,
> or somehow mistaken, because they should have forced me or made it more
> positive, because it was always negative: "Yes, it is so poor in Ethiopia." They
> had never been there, so they only knew what they read in the newspapers,
> and that was just garbage.[24]

Nordin described her first visit to Addis in 1997 and her relief in discovering "that it wasn't just awful. But that was the image of Ethiopia we got
in Sweden. And then there are the questions when one comes home and
talks with those who haven't had contact with Ethiopia: 'Did you see a lot

of starvation? It's so poor there, it must be really hard.' Those weren't the thoughts I had while I was there. I've been in India and there it was much poorer. People were dying on the streets." This sense of Ethiopia as terribly poor places a burden of guilt on the child, a burden "I took on very early, from people on the street, as well as from friends and relatives: 'Oh, how lucky you were! Oh what wonderful parents you have, to have brought you here. You would have died had you remained in Ethiopia!'—until at last you are living in debt [man lever på lån] and you have to go around feeling grateful for everything and feeling that you have no right to what others have, or to what you want to do, but live instead thanks to the kindness of others." In an interview three years later, Sara talked about her complex relationship to Ethiopia as she was growing up, caught between the Swedish sense that "we don't have problems the rest of the world has" and her own sense of her need to "prove, both for yourself and others, that you are Swedish, because you have this 'Ethiopianness' [det här etiopiska] that is such an irritating presence."[25]

Sofia Berzelius, who was also born in Ethiopia and adopted by Swedish parents, elaborates on this complicated dynamic of the "Swedish" and the "Ethiopian." Her story begins with her parents' description of their first encounter with her at the Haile Selassie orphanage in Addis Ababa, while they were on an official visit to Ethiopia as part of a delegation from SIDA, the Swedish International Development Agency, in 1971. During a lunch at my house in Amherst in 2002, Sofia's mother described being taken to the crib of an undernourished, sickly baby who was being bottle-fed by an older child. Compelled by the baby, they decided to adopt her, although they had not planned on an adoption when they began their trip. They left the baby at the orphanage while the paperwork was completed, then returned to get her before their departure for Sweden three months later.

Her parents' account of seeing Sofia at the orphanage is filled in with details provided by Greta Svedberg, who arranged for her adoption and those of more than sixty other Ethiopian children sent to Sweden in the 1960s and 1970s (chapter 4). Sofia was told that her mother had died in childbirth at St. Paul's Hospital in Addis, a hospital for the "very poor" where (in Sofia's words) "people who died were just put outside and were picked up by some truck in the morning and were dumped somewhere." Sofia says she "had always imagined that my mother had been unconscious and she'd been picked up and she died all alone." She was also told that the hospital had been torn down in the 1970s. But when she visited Addis in December 2000, she found the hospital still standing:

I had this picture of this hospital that would be so poor. . . . And here comes
this midwife and she is about 60 and she has got something very elegant in
her appearance. She has got this very nice lipstick and she has done her hair
in a pretty elegant way and she wears ordinary clothes. She says, "Hello!" and
she speaks fluent English. She says, "Oh, I am sorry you come here now. This
place is such a mess. We are rebuilding it. I could show you around." This
is so crazy, we have just been at the place where I found the files [relating to
her adoption] and it is maybe one hour later and we are standing here in this
hospital that doesn't exist.[26]

Sofia was taken to the maternity ward and then to "the operation the-
ater, and that's where I was delivered. And there is this really, really amaz-
ing feeling, because suddenly it's like I touch ground, as if I had been living
maybe 4 or 5 millimeters above the ground for my entire life and then suddenly I just touched ground. It was fantastic just to see. It was like, 'Yeah,
ok, so this is where I started.'" The midwife offered to check the hospital
files for details about her birth. Sofia asked, "'Files?' This was not according to my picture of Ethiopia. To me, Ethiopia would just be chaos."

She discovered that "for every day they had made little, little records."
There had been thirteen deliveries on the day Sofia was born, and she
found her mother's name, that she was twenty-six years old, that this was
her second delivery, and that she had died in childbirth, from complications surrounding the delivery. She had come in regularly for check-ups.
"We could see what time of the day I had been born, and how long I was
and what the name of the doctor was. . . . It just felt so good for me to find
out that this place that I had heard about, and the stories that I had heard
about this country and the place where I was born, it was so different. It
gave me a completely new picture."

Sometimes an adoptee's "completely new picture" can seem far less reassuring. Maria Brunn, whose return when she was ten years old to the
Delhi orphanage from which she was adopted was described above, wrote
about the value of this visit in an article addressed to adoptive parents, six
years later:

> What was most important to me the first time I was in India was to visit the
> orphanage I come from in Delhi. It was with mixed feelings that I realized
> I had actually lived in this home for ten months. What I most wanted from
> the visit to the orphanage was some information about my background. I
> was a so-called foundling, so I know only the date when I was taken into
> the orphanage. Nothing about who left me there or why. And just that, that
> one knows nothing, is really hard when one then wants to search for one's

identity, it's better if one's parents at least have a little they can tell the child when it asks.

What I gained most from the orphanage visit, even though we found no information about me, was that I finally understood that it isn't strange that no one knows anything about me. I knew only about Swedish record-keeping and couldn't imagine until I visited India how badly any kind of record-keeping would function in this swarm of people everywhere. . . . But now it is just for me to accept and learn to live with that fact, that my early origin is and will remain unknown (Andersson 1984, 35, freely translated).

Maria, whose brother Jan is the biogenetic child of her parents, added: "I think also that it is really important that parents and child be able to talk openly about the differences that actually exist between adoptive children and biological children. Adoptive children don't look like their parents and that means that the child's identity will be questioned many times, even if this isn't done in a negative way. If both parents and child haven't accepted that the child LOOKS different . . . then it is hard for both parents and child to answer questions about where the child comes from and who its 'real' mother is, tolerantly and in a friendly manner" (Andersson 1984, 36).

It Doesn't Show on the Outside that One Is Adopted

In commenting on her parents' effort to present a positive account of her preadoption history and on her own skill in reading between the lines, Sara Nordin speaks to the power of "real" adoption stories that haunt accounts of "really, really good" birth mothers and happy orphanages, no less than they haunt narratives of dying people who are thrown into the street and picked up by a truck the next morning. The theory of early disturbances, whatever its limitations in explaining the inability of a child adopted from abroad to adapt to Swedish society, forces attention to what "it requires hard work *not* to see."[27] What required the most work "not to see" about the transnational adoptee growing up in Sweden in the last decades of the twentieth century, and what has only slowly emerged as a focus of concern in response to the memoirs, the research, the social activism, the performances, and the narratives of adopted adults during the past decade, is their *connection* to immigrant populations in Stockholm and elsewhere, a connection that is inscribed on their bodies, however "Swedish" they might feel themselves to be. This connection evokes an experience of "Aha!" when they glance in the mirror (Nordin 1996, 4). It produces the revulsion Hanna Wallensteen describes in her autoethnographic monologue *Know Your Place*: on the first day of preschool the teacher put Wallensteen's

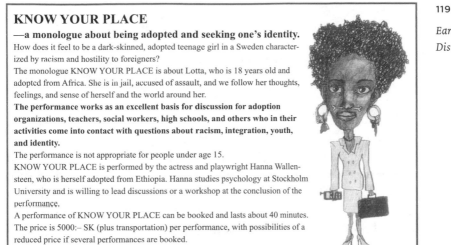

FIGURE 14. *Know Your Place. NIA Informerar* 4 (1999). Illustration design by Synnöve Magnusson.

protagonist, Lotta, "in the middle of a circle of kids, so everyone could touch my hair with their dirty, snotty little fingers. 'Let me feel! Let me feel! It feels weird. Oh, I can feel. Look, look! It looks like worms!'" (Wallensteen 2000, 4).

The ambiguities of adoptive identity in Sweden are suggested in the advertisement for Wallensteen's monologue, with its caricature of a black woman in the garb of a Swedish professional woman but with an afro and a bone through her nose (fig. 14). It was displayed in an issue of *NIA Informerar* (the newsletter for Sweden's National Board for Intercountry Adoptions) in 1999; the text reads in part: "KNOW YOUR PLACE—a monologue about being adopted and seeking one's identity. How does it feel to be a dark-skinned, adopted teenage girl in a Sweden characterized by racism and hostility to foreigners? The monologue KNOW YOUR PLACE is about Lotta, who is 18 years old and adopted from Africa. She is in jail, accused of assault, and we follow her thoughts, feelings, and sense of herself and the world around her."

In one passage from the monologue, Lotta reflects on why she is "a good example of a newcomer in this country":

I have been here since I was nine months old so I know how to behave in a civilized society. I don't wipe my ass with my hands and I don't eat with my fingers. But just imagine if I had been left down there. Then I would have had cowshit in my hair and breasts sagging to my toes. . . . Sometimes I think the reason why I was chosen, of all those children in the orphanage, to be sent off to Sweden, is that I'm supposed to show people that Africans can become intelligent too. Because we can. As long as we grow up in the right environment. Like me. When my parents saw all those abandoned children in developing countries on TV, they just couldn't bring themselves to deliver a new child to the world. So they adopted me. (Wallensteen 2000, 1–2)

The adoptee who can't blend in, in spite of her educated and socially blessed Swedish parents, becomes a "point of contact with invisibility" (Cheng 2001, 16). As "black," she or he embodies the highest ideals of the Swedish nation for social justice and international solidarity and hence is a symbol of Sweden's (parental, national) goodness—of its capacity to stand as a model for the rest of the world. But the adoptee's blackness must disappear in the fantasy that color makes no difference in Sweden. If she sees someone "exotic" in the mirror, is disgusted when other preschoolers want to feel her hair, or is terrified when anti-immigrant sentiment seems threatening (because "it doesn't show on the outside that one is adopted," to quote a Chilean-born adoptee who was raised in Stockholm), it is attributed to "early disturbances" that shaped the adoptee's psyche long before arriving in Sweden, rather than to the ways the adoptee encounters and is encountered by her parents, classmates, and fellow citizens.

Marianne Cederblad and her colleagues in the Division of Child and Youth Psychiatry at Lund University in southern Sweden reported in studies published in the 1980s and 1990s that there were risks in the eagerness of parents to transform their transnationally adopted children too rapidly into Swedish children; the scholars cautioned them to show "great respect for the child's identity, when it comes" (Cederblad 1984, 34, freely translated). Building on earlier bodies of research in the United States and elsewhere and following Erik Erikson's approach (1968) to identity development as an inherently interpersonal and transactional process, Cederblad and her colleagues draw attention to John Triseliotis's argument (1973) that "the adoptive parents' most important task is to help the child integrate and identify with both its sets of parents" (Cederblad et al. 1994, 23, freely translated).[28] This task of integration is hindered, Cederblad and colleagues imply, both by Swedish law, which specifically identified adoptees as immigrants until a change of policy in the 1990s, and by the efforts of adoptive parents and others to draw a bright line between adoptive children and immigrant children, a distinction that had been taken on by a majority of the adopted subjects of their research (only one-third of 181 identified themselves as "a type of immigrant)" (1994, 77).

Swedish adoptees, Cederblad and her colleagues suggest, are faced with the "special dilemma of belonging to the majority culture but of often being met as though they do not" (1994, 78). And they noted that adoptees in their study overwhelmingly supported the following statement: "There should be control over the stream of immigrants to Sweden" (87% of the younger group studied, 92% of the older) (75). They suggest that the tendency to downplay the significance of origins and to emphasize adoptees' difference from immigrants is arguably related to the "increasing hostility to immigrants" during the 1980s and 1990s in Sweden, as well as to adoptees' official classification as immigrants by Swedish authorities. "If [this hostility] has to do with real racism, it doesn't help to say 'I am an adoptive child, not an immigrant,' since the attack is directed to the deviant appearance, not to other characteristics of the individual" (97).[29]

In her talk "Adoptive Families and Racism," delivered at the First Global Conference on International Adoption in Copenhagen in 2005, adoptive parent and researcher Anna Rastas describes what she terms an "injurious strategy" deployed by adoptive parents in response to their children's encounters with racism. "I have heard adoptive parents saying things like: 'But you can always tell people that you are not a refugee (or an immigrant).' That, as a strategy, is to support unequal racial hierarchies, and one way or another it will turn against our children. If nothing else, it is teaching them racism. And a racist victim of racism is a very lonely and a very confused person" (2005, 5).

Rastas points out that as long as working definitions of racism in the family and in the surrounding society "are so narrow that only open and intentional racism is discussed (and understood as racism)," children will have difficulty talking about experiences (of racism) for which they lack appropriate words and parents will assume that "racism is not a problem for us/for our child. Even though it definitely is" (2005, 3–4). Rastas adds:

> Most parents with older children that I have interviewed or met, have learned that racism is part of not only their child's but also their own everyday life. They have learnt, that their child is always seen as a "non-white," wherever s/he goes. They have also learned, that being "non-white" becomes an important part of their child's identity. For example her or his relationship to her or his own body is different from the way her/his peers process these things. . . . How to support a child who knows that the culture in the surrounding society "makes a difference" and distances itself from "the non-white" body. How to teach the child to love her or his own body, and to tell the child that there should be no need to "get rid of" that body? (2005, 5).

Insistence on the "set apartness" of the adopted child (insistence that he or she is not, or is not like, an immigrant) undermines the possibility of seeing and potentially working against everyday racisms that underpin a global economy in which adopted children circulate as relatively privileged "goods."[30] By contrast, embracing their likeness to immigrants opens a space in which adoptive families can unsettle rather than secure the hierarchies that mark their children's bodies as outside belonging, whether in Sweden or other adopting nations.

6 The Body within the Body

The law is baffled by a body within a body. . . . The law
has to kill off this disembodied personality.

  —Marilyn Strathern, *Kinship, Law, and the Unexpected*

Forum '97

In April 1997 Adoption Centre hosted a series of workshops, collectively
known as Forum '97, for transnational adoptees living in Sweden, Denmark, and Norway. Held in conjunction with AC's annual meeting of adoptive parents, the workshops were attended by some 120 young adults in
their early to mid twenties, adopted from twenty-three nations in Asia,
Latin America, and Africa. At a time of increasing attention in Sweden and
other adopting nations to what AC described as *"resor och rötter"* (roughly,
roots and returns), the workshops were of a piece with intensified concerns
in the 1990s about the meaning of origins for the transnational adoptee
and the implications of increased attention to origins for the project of
transnational adoption in Sweden and elsewhere. On the second day of
the workshops, the group of adoptees, wearing identical white T-shirts
with a large Swedish flag printed on the front, staged a carefully planned
entrance into the meeting of adoptive parents (figs. 15 and 16).[1]

When they had all filed onto a platform where they looked out at and
down on the parents, they turned in unison to reveal, on the back of the
shirts, the words MADE IN INDIA (COLOMBIA, NEPAL, CHILE, ETHIOPIA,
KOREA, ECUADOR, BOLIVIA, SRI LANKA . . .) and so forth, through each
of the twenty-three birth countries where they were "made." The parents
burst into laughter and everyone applauded enthusiastically. This was an
insider event, where the audience could read its tonalities of irony through
the playfulness of its enactment. With its parody of the prototypically
Swedish as made in developing worlds, the performance spoke to the paradoxes of identity that are embodied in the transnational adoptee. Never 100
percent Swedish in Sweden, a confusing presence in his or her country of

FIGURE 15. Forum '97: March onto stage. Photograph by Stig Dahlstrand.

FIGURE 16. Forum '97: Display of shirts. Photograph by Stig Dahlstrand.

birth, the transnational adoptee is always slightly out of place, a dislocation captured in the moment when the group turned and revealed their
"hidden" identity (an identity that resided both "outside" and "inside" the
flag-decked Swedish shirts) as products that were made elsewhere, in a
place where they "really" belonged (figs. 17 and 18).

FIGURE 17. Forum '97: "Made in . . ." on backs of shirts. Photograph by Stig Dahlstrand.

FIGURE 18. Forum '97: Close-up of a shirt back. Photograph by Stig Dahlstrand.

Two years after this event, when I was talking with several adopted adults who had participated in the workshops, one of them told me that not everyone had liked the T-shirt idea and some had refused to wear one, on grounds that it made light of an issue that was painful for the adoptee but hard to resolve without fundamentally unsettling adoption practice.

As one woman explained, alluding to the commitments of the earliest Swedish adopters, "We were some kind of token. 'For heaven's sake! We can at least show people that one can have a child that doesn't look like oneself!' And so one should be some kind of means of social change." She added, "When I think about what I've had to tolerate, or become, or not had, then I can feel: 'No, why should that be?'" Referring to what she described as the way adoption works at "the emotional level," she described herself as "deeply split about adoption in general," while stressing that it was important to acknowledge what organizations such as AC have done. "There are two levels for me—the organizational level, but also the emotional, egotistical, level, having to do with one's own identity. Sometimes it's hard to keep those two things apart."[2] Another participant, Sara Nordin, describes the identity issues she has confronted as follows:

> I am not against adoption but I don't want to embellish the conflict that it produces. I could never say to a child who needs help that it is better that you stay where you are, when there is the chance for another life. I could never say to a child who must grow up without love that he or she must try to live without it.
>
> It is hard to look at oneself in the mirror and feel that one is exotic. It is hard to look at oneself and wonder about what it is that one sees. Is one a story or is one a reality? It is hard to walk in the city and be met by hurtful stares and comments. And how many people can actually define "Swedishness"? . . .
>
> Those who know me well have tried to understand, tried to comfort me. By saying that origins make no difference. That I am Swedish. That I don't belong in Africa. That I would just feel like a tourist there. That all I have is a different skin color. (1996, 4–5)

Although *black* is applied broadly to people of color in Sweden, it is most clearly embodied in persons whose skin color and physiognomy signify their African origins. As another Ethiopian-born adoptee noted in an interview with Anna von Melen, as part of a study conducted in the 1990s by Sweden's National Board for Intercountry Adoptions, there is a hierarchy of belonging, and in Sweden, at least, "it is worse to be '*neger*' than to be '*chingchong*'" (von Melen 1998, 67).[3] Likewise, it is worse to be "immigrant" than "adopted." A second woman interviewed by von Melen explained the nuances of these linked hierarchies:

> I believe that it is definitely easier to be adopted from South Korea than from Ethiopia, for example. A Korean appearance is not connected with refugees. If one sees an Iranian, one thinks immediately, "refugee." Everyone who sees

me understands that I am adopted, or a voluntary immigrant who works and

does her part. That can feel really nice, because otherwise one is standing
in a sense outside. *I feel uncomfortable in the proximity of immigrants, which I
think is because they in some sense unsettle the picture I have formed of myself as
Swedish. They remind me that I, too, am a kind of immigrant, even though I feel
that I am not, because I don't want to see things that way.* Today I can handle it.
It was worse 10 years ago, when immigrants first began coming to Skellefteå.
(1998, 63; emphasis added)

This quotation illuminates the complex ways in which being adopted
works at the emotional level for adoptees in Sweden, where the figure of the
racially different adoptee serves as a marker both of the true Swedishness
of her or his parents and of what it means to stand outside of civil society
in that country. At the same time, the adoptee's comments hint at the dependence of full Swedishness on being surrounded by people who are not
too much "like me," even as it reveals how discomfiting the proximity of
(other) immigrants are to the Korean-born adoptee, since they remind her
that she, too, is "a kind of immigrant." The adoptee, with his or her Swedish "inside" and an outside that ties him or her to the foreigner, simultaneously secures and unsettles what "the Swedish" is imagined to be.

The Meaning of Color

It is an afternoon in late August 1999, and I am sitting with Sara Nordin
and Daniel Rosenlind in Nordin's comfortable Stockholm apartment. Nordin has been visible in Stockholm's community of transnational adoptees
since the publication of her article "More or Less Black" in 1996; Rosenlind is the founder and was the president (in 1999) of the Association of
Ethiopian and Eritrean Adoptees in Stockholm. I am there to interview
them about their experiences growing up adopted in Sweden, but as we
settle down with coffee in Sara's living room, our conversation turns first
to issues of racism and the different ways that racism manifests itself in
Sweden and the United States.[4] Both Sara and Daniel have spent time in
the United States, first as eleven-year-olds and then, for more extended
periods, as young adults. Sara observes:

You can think that in the United States, since there are so many who come
from different countries, that they should be more conscious of it. And just
in Sweden or Scandinavia, it is blue eyes and blond. But if you look in Sweden and Stockholm, it just isn't so. But when you are in the USA or other
countries, that's what they think we are like, and so it is really strange.

Sweden hasn't had immigrants in any significant number for very long, so it has been a pretty homogeneous population for quite a long time. Now it is really beginning to change. But it is a relatively new phenomenon, I think, that you can look like we do and be Swedish.

I ask Sara and Daniel: Can you say a little more about the differences you experienced between being black in the United States and in Sweden? Sara responds:

I have been in the United States twice, the first time for only a month, when I was 11 years old. There were 7 Swedish students and we lived with 7 different American families. But I was the only black Swede. We were in Ohio, in Cincinnati, and I lived with a black family. That was really weird. That was when I became aware of the meaning of color. You were always conscious of it, of course, but there it became so palpable, because [in the United States] there is a whole history that accompanies it. So we couldn't socialize with the others in the group in the same way. We couldn't be in all the places they could. We couldn't drive and visit with all of them, because they said: "No, that isn't a good area for us." For me it was really strange.

Daniel's experience of race in the United States is more positive, but he was nonetheless "very sensitive" about being black:

Well, I think it is definitely different to be black in the United States and in Sweden. Here there are immigrant Ethiopians and then there are adoptees. It doesn't feel so strange in Sweden to be adopted. But there it felt strange to be Swedish. I also speak quite good English. Often they could hear that there was something that didn't sound quite right, but they thought that I was American. But later I heard that they thought I spoke as though I was a white American. I didn't talk like a black person. But I've often thought about this—and I've lived there before—that I felt special there, in a different way than I did in Sweden. Because partly I am African there, which I thought gave me some status when I was there the first time, in 1988. And then in addition I was European, which felt kind of trendy: "Well, I live in the States right now, but I grew up in Europe, although I was born in Africa." I was Ethiopian, African, and European. It felt very special. But at the same time, I noticed that I was very sensitive. For example, I was at a Christmas party and I was speaking Swedish with a Swedish woman and she was responding in English. She didn't understand that I was speaking Swedish with her. She just didn't grasp it. In a situation like that, I could feel—I realized that I wasn't quite so tough.

Sara adds:

The second time I went to the United States, I was 17 and went to a high school in Minnesota. I remember that I was invited to a class to talk because there was a black teacher there who became very upset when I said that I lived in a white family in Sweden. So he said: "You have to come to my class. Then you can hear what we think about that here." Everyone said: "That isn't possible. You can't do that [have a black child in a white family]." Everyone thought it was very strange and very wrong. And he [the teacher] said: "Yes, you know, we blacks, we don't like that. It isn't good. You'll understand when you are older." He was a real pain because he didn't want to discuss it, he just talked about how things should be. "That's the way it is! That's something you'll have lots of problems with later." And I had been so happy, because he was the only black teacher in the school. And I had thought: "How neat!" It was really hard, because I hadn't really begun to think about these things, or rather I had, but not consciously. I didn't know what else to say except, "Well, but it works fine in Sweden." I thought it was super hard.

"I hadn't dared to think it all the way through"

We turn from the discussion of race in the United States and in Sweden to Sara's and Daniel's stories of growing up in Sweden in the 1970s and 1980s. Sara begins:

SARA: I was one and a half years old when I came, more or less. I don't know, exactly. I know nothing about my biological parents. What I learned was that I was found on the street. Then I was in an orphanage in Addis until I was adopted. My parents knew Greta Svedberg, who brought lots of children here later. She was there primarily as a wife, but then she became interested in children and went around to different orphanages.[5] My parents made contact with her and then she brought me to Sweden. That was in 1969, and I was her first child. After that she got a number of inquiries about whether she was interested in helping families here get children. And then I have a brother who is my parents' biological child, who is three years older than I am.

BY: So they didn't adopt because they couldn't have children?

SARA: No, but because they wanted to help. And that is what I came to think about later—I was told a wonderful story about how everything had come about, which I later learned hadn't really happened, when I was able to read my papers. It wasn't as nice, although it was OK, but it wasn't the story I had been told.

BY: And did your parents talk about Ethiopia?

SARA: No, they tried, but I didn't want to. . . . I never wanted to talk about it.[6] My thoughts about that kind of thing began when I was about 14 or 15, because there were lots of race problems in school. It was also a school with lots of immigrants. So there was a lot—the police were there, there was lots of fighting. *So then I got into a strange situation, because I became almost an immigrant although I felt myself to be very Swedish (jättesvensk). And the immigrants thought I was like them. And my Swedish friends thought I was like them. And I couldn't really decide myself where I belonged.* And I thought that was really hard, because then people ganged up on me a lot. When I was little, people could be punished. But in high school it became more serious. . . . And then I began to think about all of this, but they were pretty depressing thoughts. It wasn't fun. The first time I really began to come to grips with things was in 1995, when I began talking with Anna [von Melen, a South Korean–born adoptee]. We were working together doing home visits for the elderly. And she told me that she had been asked if she wasn't interested in writing about adoption. And then I thought that sounded really interesting. I had a whole lot of thoughts. So then we started [with the special issue of *Svart/Vitt* (Black/white) on adoption]. And that was the first time I had really thought about it. *You think about it of course, because it is obvious that you are black. But I hadn't dared think it all the way through.* And not about doing something interesting with it, either.

"But I am also called Haile Selassie!"

For Daniel, the process of "thinking it all the way through" and of "doing something interesting with it" also came in his midtwenties. He describes a parallel, but seemingly less fraught, process of becoming aware of what it meant to be black in Sweden:

OK. I've always had those papers at home, related to my adoption. There was a folder with my adoption papers, and I sometimes leafed through it. Even if I wasn't all that interested, I still would go in now and then and look through them. And they say that I was found when I was about three months old outside an orphanage in Addis. And when I was about a year old, I came to Sweden with that woman we mentioned, Greta Svedberg. And in the folder there were copies of the letters that my mother exchanged with Greta, back and forth. My mother had heard about Greta from acquaintances, and wrote to say she would like to adopt. And Greta wrote: "Today I have seen a beautiful boy in the orphanage, whose name is Daniel. Perhaps that could be something for you?" And my mother responded: "Yes, that sounds good." And so, back and forth. And that was more or less what I knew, that I came here when I was about a year old. My parents adopted because they could not have a child together.

Daniel's parents divorced when he was two years old, and he lived with his mother in a suburb about two miles south of Stockholm. She remarried when he was ten years old, and Daniel says of her new husband that "it is he who has been my pappa, really."

During the time I was growing up, I was quite protected. Many areas of Brandbergen were very ghetto-like, with many social welfare cases, but we lived in an area where people had ownership rights and people owned their own apartments, they didn't rent. So it was really quiet there. My mother was chair of the [apartment] owners association, so I had a little status. I was a bit of a leader in the neighborhood, I was best at soccer. So I lived very comfortably and very protected. The only times anything came up were when guys from another neighborhood came, and there were some who would yell: "*Neger . . .*" It was really strange. I was basically never teased as I was growing up, although I was the only black person in my school. I was completely accepted because we grew up together.

When I was 12 years old my friend Håkan began listening to Bob Marley, to reggae music. He introduced me to it and noticed that they were singing about Africa, about Ethiopia. That was the first time that I felt kind of proud. I thought: "But I come from Ethiopia." They were singing about Haile Selassie and rastafari. I looked in my passport: "But I am *also* called Haile Selassie!"[7] And I began to fantasize that I was a distant relative. And then my friend said: "I think you should get dreadlocks." So when I was 14 years old I made small braids and then I had them for 7 years. They grew and became longer and longer. On the walls at home I began to put up a big flag with Ethiopia's colors and Bob Marley. But I wasn't really interested in Ethiopia. I just thought it was cool to be from Ethiopia. It made me feel special. The longer my dreadlocks became, the more popular I became with the girls, which I hadn't been before. And then I was quite good at soccer. Everything was good. Sometimes it happened that if one went into the city [Stockholm] someone might say something like "*Neger!*" as they walked by. It was pretty unpleasant, but no one ganged up on me.

In high school I met another boy who was adopted and also came to Sweden through Greta Svedberg, and after high school I ran into him one day and we decided we would visit her. I was perhaps 22–23 years old. So I found her address and went to her apartment. But when I stood outside the door of the building, I thought: "What will I say when she opens the door?" And so I left without ringing the bell. And then I didn't think about it for several years. I just wasn't ready. *It wasn't something real for me yet.*

Daniel explains that it wasn't until he was twenty-five years old and reading developmental psychology as part of his academic program in social work that it became "something real":

At first I didn't understand what was going on. I found it really difficult to talk about the first year and the importance of the mother. And suddenly I realized that the reason was that I know nothing about my first year. I know that I was about 3 months old when I was found. I have no clue about those first 3 months. I know nothing about the orphanage, either, what happened there. And then this strong feeling came over me that "*I have to go down there and try to find out as much as possible.*" So then I thought, "I have to find this woman, Greta Svedberg." I sat on the subway and thought about it as I was taking the subway home from school. And when I got home, I looked up her number in the telephone book and called. When I said that I was Daniel Rosenlind, she immediately remembered my father, and I thought, "She remembers, after all this time!" So that's the way it was. I asked if I could come and visit, and she said I could. It was really emotional and I was very moved. She was very warm, and showed me pictures. She had two albums with pictures of adoptees. And then I began to feel that I wanted to go to Ethiopia and visit the orphanage, and wanted to meet other adoptees who had been there and could give me advice.

"There is a negative charge in black"

It was through Greta that Daniel began to make connections with other Ethiopian adoptees and eventually decided to organize AEF (Association of Adopted Ethiopians and Eritreans). He and Sara talk about the importance of the organization and what it meant for different members. At first, Sara says, it was just a wonderful feeling that "one didn't need to explain, present, and tell, but one could just be in it. Plus one could hear other experiences and could see variations on the same theme." Daniel says that for some in the group, their interest is principally in Ethiopia, while others are more concerned with the problem of being black in Sweden:

> When I think about "black" I think that I have more in common with people from Colombia. And then I think that there are different kinds of black, with different status. I think about black Americans, for example. They are cool, they are Americans. There are many whites that look up to them, especially young people. But if one is from Gambia, for example, it isn't nearly so cool. If you are from the West Indies, it can also be pretty cool. You might have dreadlocks. *There is a scale distinguishing different kinds of black.* But at the same time, I feel that I have quite a lot in common with all blacks, although there are differences between adoptees in this regard, I suspect.

Sara adds:

There are biases that go along with the culture or ethnical belonging one has. Whether one believes in those belongings or not, one has to struggle with them. *That's how one becomes a "color," when one meets the same biases.* That problem is what creates a sense of commonality, because in reality I have very little in common with someone from the West Indies. But because one meets the same problem, then one becomes interested or curious about how one copes and reacts. Some people just shake it off, some are sunk by it, and I think it is incredibly interesting. I thought everyone felt the same, until we began to talk about it.

Daniel agrees. Recalling that for a long time he felt, "I am Swedish. My friends accept me," he says that there are things he repressed that he doesn't remember. He adds, "There is racism here, I have met it also. But one way I handle it is to shrug it off and then I forget that anything even happened. . . . But I am becoming more and more conscious of it." Sara says:

SARA: But as a human, I think, one can't go around and be conscious of these things the whole time. One just can't manage. Shrugging it off is a way of surviving. And throughout my childhood, I just kept the lid on. I just didn't want to think about it. *But now as an adult I can acknowledge that there were lots of really sad things that I—I don't know where I put those things. Mainly I thought it was my problem.* I never told my parents. I never told my friends, I just held it in. That was my role. I was strong enough to handle it. That's what I think about now: How good was that? What did I make of it? How did it affect me, really? Now I am really conscious of things, even if I don't always know what to do, nothing just passes over me. On the contrary, I am paranoid. That's because I am really infuriated over the naive mind set that still exists.

BY: Can you give me an example of the naive mind set?

SARA: For example, I remember that when I was little, I was actually offered instruction in Amharic, in Ethiopian, in school. And I said "No," and absolutely didn't want it. And my parents thought: "Alright, then we won't." It was such a pity that they didn't understand that I was little, that I had no idea what I needed, but thought that I should make those decisions myself. You don't always know what's best for you. It wasn't just my parents, but happened especially in school. They didn't know how to handle it when something happened, but thought, because I was tough and could talk, that I could manage. But that doesn't mean that you know what to do. In that sense I can think that people trivialize things that are very serious. You need a safety valve. In our case, it is obvious that we don't look like others, but then there must be something positive, and that's what I felt I missed, that my parents understood that I needed something but they thought at the same time [the adoption] was a failure. And they thought they could cover up all the holes with love—"You are special. It is fun. This whole culture." Instead of doing something positive.

It can be a problem when the whole family is involved in making it sound nice and friendly this way, but one is actually just this little child. . . .[8] It has taken some time. I could wish that it had been there earlier, and that's unnecessary to think about now, but I feel that it is important, when one adopts, that one realizes: "*I didn't give birth to this child, but the child had a history already and must have its own history the whole time, without my attempting to transform this into our history. It is the child's, and that is fine, it is something positive, not something tragic.*"

Returning to the issue of racism, Sara says:

There is a charge, a negative charge in "black" that actually is not related to appearance. Some people can be black and beautiful and some can be black and ugly and some can be black and look funny. *But there is still a charge in black.* And it is to be found here and it is to be found in most countries. And it is so hard, because people say: "It is up to you. If you can't handle it, then you are the one who has failed. Then you have a problem." It is so dangerous. And that's what I think is so great about the group [AEF], when one hears that several have the same experience. *It affirms that one isn't paranoid, but that there really are racist tendencies. There are biases or there are stupid people, but it is nothing that exists simply in my head.*

"The good black man and the bad black man"

In May 1999, on a visit to Stockholm to attend a celebration of AC's thirtieth anniversary, I was asked to speak at a workshop on roots, where I met Mattias Kollberg, who had recently returned from a visit to Agua Blanca, the neighborhood in Cali where his birth mother, siblings, and extended Colombian kin are living. He spoke with me at a coffee shop in town a few days later about his experiences growing up black in Sweden.[9] Born in 1978, Mattias went to Sweden as an infant. But he explains, "As long as I can remember I have always thought that I would travel back one day." When I ask if his parents talked about Colombia with him as he was growing up, he says they didn't speak about the country, though they sometimes spoke about the people they met there—for example, Carmen, the woman who arranged for his adoption. However, he says, "I have always been interested in African Americans":

MATTIAS: I grew up in a suburb of Stockholm called Täby, a middle class suburb, one could say middle class/upper class, but I am middle class. I live in a row house. When I grew up—Täby isn't a community where there are so many immigrants, or at least not when I was growing up. Now there are beginning to be more because more immigrants have come to Sweden. But I've never had any problems with being black. I have always spoken Swedish. My friends—I don't think they gave that much thought to the fact that I was black.

BY: And there were no problems in school?

MATTIAS: No. Most often it would be this way, that if one got in a scuffle, as one often does as a child, then it could easily happen that someone yelled: "Damn nigger!"[10] But it was more or less the same as if they yelled "Damn idiot!" or "Damn coward!" *It was an obvious point of attack. There was nothing racist in it.*

Mattias added that his interest in things African American intensified when he entered junior high school, "maybe when I was around 13–14 years old." A friend of his had a *Public Enemy* tape, which he copied, and from there his interest continued to develop. "Since then I have become really interested, read a lot. I read almost exclusively Afro-American literature. It is much easier here in Sweden, which is so influenced by America, to find that than to find Afro-Latin literature:

MATTIAS: And then, Afro-Latin literature is much less—how can I put it—it isn't quite as offensive [as Afro-American literature]. That has influenced me a lot. It has helped me, too.

BY: In what sense?

MATTIAS: In the sense that one has felt one could find examples and relate to people and events. One could relate to a lot, even though one lives in Sweden and is black and, even so, Swedish, one could relate to so much of what one finds in Afro-American music and literature. . . . Here in Stockholm, people in suburban communities where most of the immigrants live—communities like Botkyrka and Norsborg, south of the city, where socially they have it a little worse—listen to it. What influenced me most was that I read Malcolm X's autobiography. Then I felt that now it is time to be consciously a black man. I saw the film for the first time a few years ago, when I was 16 and then I thought I should read the book, because books are usually better than the film. I thought that in that way one could perhaps get a more accurate picture.

BY: Do you have many friends who are Afro-Swedish or Afro-Colombian?

MATTIAS: I don't have any adopted friends. The thing is that as a black man, especially in Täby, where I live, there aren't so many. . . . I spend most of my free time with Swedes.

BY: And your strongest sense of identity, as you mentioned the other day [in a workshop held by AC on roots trips] is as a black man?

MATTIAS: Yes, as a black man.

BY: And is that different from being Swedish?

MATTIAS: *Nja*[11] . . . it is as I said, apart from whether I am a black Swedish person or a black Colombian or a black African, one encounters the same things where racism is concerned and the way people respond to you. For me it doesn't feel much different, whether I am Swedish or Colombian. One runs into the same racism, but in different proportions and different strength. For me it has been an advantage by virtue of the fact that I am Swedish. I have grown up as Swedish. It is after all the culture that I was raised in and that I know best. It belongs to me, even though I am really interested in Afro-American and Colombian culture. It's an advantage that I know perfect Swedish and I know everything, *so if people try to attack me because I am black or because I am adopted or because I am an immigrant, they become really irritated, because they have no point of attack.* They can't attack me because I speak bad Swedish. Swedish is my best subject in school. . . . As an immigrant, if you are attacked and you don't speak correct Swedish and have no job and have social problems, then you turn to violence or something to protect yourself. Then you simply strengthen biases, which are only biases, really, but you strengthen them. And I don't need to do that.

Mattias said his perspective varied from that of some other adoptees, who felt conflicted about being Swedish and Colombian, or Swedish and black: "I have felt clear, I haven't felt this split."[12] Rather, he has felt a split between "the good black man and the bad black man. For example, if you go into a store and you feel that the security guards are watching you all the time, then eventually you think: 'I might as well snitch something, just to get back at them.' But then you only confirm the biases. That is the split I have felt." He described these feelings as being "more patriotic about my origins than other adoptees."

The distinction drawn by Mattias Kollberg between "good" and "bad" black men is a variation of the tension between adoptee and immigrant that was experienced by other adopted adults I interviewed, with an important difference. His self-positioning as "consciously a black man" gave him a certain room for (imaginative) maneuver beyond the Swedish-black or adoptee-immigrant dichotomy, in that it allowed him to imagine himself *as if* he were the "bad" (immigrant) black man, even as he knew himself to *be* the "good" (Swedish) black man, in this way facilitating the integration of the "black" and the "Swedish" in ways that had the potential to transform both.

By contrast, for a Chilean-born woman, described by her friends as having a more "Mapuche-like" appearance than other Chilean-born adoptees, the opposition between "Swedish" and "immigrant" was reinforced. She

explained to me that her first awareness that she might be seen as an immigrant came in second grade, when "some people came up to me and began speaking Spanish, and at first I couldn't figure out what they were saying. And then I began to realize that they saw me as an immigrant, when in fact I am Swedish." She recalled an incident some years before our interview, when a man in Stockholm shot four immigrants, three of whom were Somalis and one of whom was Chilean: "I remember because I was terribly afraid, since it doesn't show on the outside that one is adopted. And I thought, 'No, I don't dare go into the city.' I remember that I worried about it a lot. It gives one this sense of unease, that others see one as a dark person, those around one, those one knows, but one knows oneself that one is completely Swedish. . . . And you see, sometimes I forget that I am dark-skinned. When one sits with friends and chats. And then when one looks in the mirror: 'Aha! Just so!' "[13]

"It had to do with needing to see myself in the other person"

The "terrible fear" of the Chilean-born woman that she would be identified as an immigrant when she herself was completely Swedish manifested itself quite differently in the experience of Anna ChuChu Petersson, one of the organizers of the Forum '97 workshops that are described at the opening of this chapter. ChuChu explains that she had no real interest in visiting Ethiopia as she was growing up; her concerns about that country began "when there was the huge famine—in 1984."[14] She asks me, "Do you remember that?" and continues,

> It had a powerful effect on me—it was really difficult. I thought that all the people they showed on TV were my parents and my brothers and sisters. I became terribly upset that they had such a terrible time and I thought that my family had all died. It was a terrible sadness and I became ill because of it. So then I got involved in making sure that people in the world should not starve and I became involved in the Red Cross, in SIDA [Swedish Agency for International Development], in all kinds of causes. But I wasn't at all interested in Ethiopia and my origins. That came later. *It began with the feeling that it was my family that suffered.* I was afraid of my biological mother. I was afraid that she would come and hit and scratch me. I had some strange ideas. . . . In any case, that's the way my teenage years were.

ChuChu was adopted from Ethiopia in 1975, when she was one year old. Her new family lived in Västervik, a town on the Baltic coast in southern

Sweden, where, she explained in an interview in 1999, "I was alone in being black. Västervik has about 30,000 inhabitants, more or less. Little, though it is big enough that you'd think there should be some black people, but there weren't. So I was alone. And everyone knew who I was, though it made no difference at that time, when one was small. There were no problems. When I began the fourth grade there was a little boy who began at the same time who was also black. So people thought we should play together, but we didn't. People asked, 'Have you spoken to him?'"

By the time she was in her teens, ChuChu says, the experience of being black began to affect her much more deeply.

> I can make really sharp—I can draw boundaries for myself, and the boundary I drew was that I shouldn't be together with any white men, because I wanted someone who looked like me. Perhaps also a feeling that one was never, that is to say, as a black woman, one isn't a woman that someone can be together with, you know, when one begins to date, when one is that age. It was actually really hard, and I thought myself that it was hard. But people never ganged up on me, there was none of that because I was quite strong myself.

Mikael Jarnlo, another Ethiopian-born adoptee, in whose Stockholm apartment we were sitting at the time of this interview, responded:

MIKAEL: I have no boundaries at all. No, that's something I haven't thought about specially. When I was so young that I was in high school, there were no black girls. That was what created boundaries. It was more a question of, not emotionally so that "I only want to be with blacks because I want someone who looks like me," but it was more a question of being fascinated with the black because it was something exceptional, something different and something unusual and exciting. I was just like any white guy in that regard. Because there's this attitude among white guys here in Sweden that meeting a black girl is something that one longs for in fantasy. It's exciting. So of course, I felt that way also.

BY: So you think there is something specific about the way white guys experience black women in Sweden?

MIKAEL: They are something exotic. Black girls or black people in general, in the white world, are experienced as sex objects. And that isn't so nice, actually. There is a negative side to that way of looking at black people. I didn't realize that until later. Of course it is there, if one thinks about it that way. So I can understand a little the resistance to being with a white guy, so that one won't become this object that fulfills their fantasies, but one should be liked for oneself. As a guy I've also felt that way with white women, that they think that's what it's all about. Then I've somehow been able to see beyond it and see if I feel it's ok. "Let them think that, if they want." So I haven't felt myself set apart in that way.

Amanda Fredriksson was a third adoptee who was taking part in this conversation.

AMANDA: We've talked about this in the association (AEF). I can have a feeling that guys relate to this in a completely different way than women do. You can transform it into something positive, where it can almost be, "Wow! She wants me!" While many of the other women, and I, I think, experience it more . . . I despise it![15] If I notice that a guy begins to play on the fact that I am black, I lose interest immediately. It doesn't work with me. No, I don't like it. It's really interesting.

BY: Yes. And have you had the same feeling Anna had, that it would be better or that you absolutely prefer being with a black guy and not with a white one?

AMANDA: No, not up till now. Before it was the opposite. I should never be with a black guy. It wasn't even part of my way of thinking. I thought it was awful. I thought it was "Usch!" It had to do with needing to see myself in the other person. That's what I was afraid of. Now, on the other hand, I feel as though that would be the ideal. It may also be, and I wish that one didn't need to think that way, that he should be black or he should be white, but that that shouldn't have anything to do with it. It is part of this whole process of identity.

MIKAEL: With black guys in the association as well as other black guys I know, it's a little bit as though one should have a black girl. It's almost as though one is a traitor if one is with a white girl. I don't go along with that.[16] It isn't really possible, of course if you decide on that and it's the only thing you're after, but it really isn't possible here in Sweden. Most people are white. If you exclude all of them, just for that reason, it would be really strange.

AMANDA: It's an incredibly difficult situation. *I get so angry when I think about it because I didn't get myself in this situation of having to choose* [a white or a black man], *or whatever. I can think about my children. I can think: "Jaha, will they,"* or rather, *will people in general say: "But it's so nice with a mulatto child!"*[17] I've heard many white women say that they would like to have children with black men because they would like to have a mulatto child. I think that's completely awful. It makes me furious.

MIKAEL: That's the only reason I'd like to have a black woman, because they are so beautiful. That's not something I'd say openly, but it's the way I feel.

AMANDA: Well, but they are.

CHUCHU: I also feel how nice it would be to have a family where everyone looks the same. That would be so nice, in a way. And that I shouldn't have to—for my children's sake—I wish it could be that way. But then I think in any case that I do myself a disservice if I consciously seek out a black man. That isn't the solution to my problems. Perhaps it seems that it would be. I'd long for a family like that.

I look at other families where it is so obvious. Everyone is alike and it isn't necessary to get sidetracked by conflicts on another level. It would be nice. But that isn't going to happen.

"Grief's dilemma"

Several years ago, a friend who was by training and profession a violinist suggested that the experiences of racism described by Swedish adoptees and (in quite different ways) by their parents, were a dimension of "the instrumentation of the white soul." What I understood her to mean by this was that complex histories of race relations, structured by colonialism and paternalistic attitudes toward the developing world, contribute to the orchestration of people's longings and belongings, both pulling parents to the "different" child *and* transforming the child into a racialized "other." I had just returned from a visit to Colombia, where I had met several European and American adoptive parents at the Pension Stein, a small hotel in Cali frequented by adoptive parents. Some (including a Swedish couple) were concerned that their new child's skin was too light and would not "match" that of their darker, older children; others (including an American couple) were upset that they had not been permitted to adopt a black child, although European couples, including a husband and wife from the Netherlands who were just leaving Cali with their new baby, were permitted to do so. My friend's observation helped me to see the connections between adoptive parent stories of longing and ambivalence when confronted with a black child, on the one hand, and the anguish, anger, bravado, and fear that form a recurrent theme in the stories of adopted adults whose origins are understood to tie them to Africa, Asia, or Latin America but who were raised by parents in Sweden, on the other.[18]

In *The Melancholy of Race: Psychoanalysis, Assimilation, and Hidden Grief*, Anne Anlin Cheng underscores how *Brown v. Board of Education* expanded the notion of justice "to accommodate the 'intangible' effects of racism," specifically in its attention to the effects of racism on the "*hearts and minds*" of raced subjects (2001, 4, emphasis in original). Cheng adds an important cautionary note to her argument: that attention to hearts and minds— what she describes as "the psychical" and what my friend captured in the imagery of the tuned "soul"—not be mistaken for essentialization. Rather, she asks: "*How is a racial identity secured? How does it continue to generate its seduction for both the dominant and the marginalized? And what are the reper-*

cussions, both historical and personal, of that ongoing history?" (7; emphasis added).

Drawing on Freud's seminal essay "Mourning and Melancholia" (1917), Cheng describes the "chain of loss, denial, and incorporation through which the ego is born" and the import of melancholia as pointing "not to loss *per se but to the entangled relationship with loss,*" a relationship that generates "profound ambivalence" around the incorporated/lost object (2001, 8, emphasis added).[19] It is this ambivalence that Cheng describes as "grief's dilemma" (9). While Cheng is referring specifically to race relations in the United States, her discussion of a "white national ideal, which is sustained by the exclusion-yet-retention of racialized others" (10) is equally appropriate to an understanding of the position of the transracial adoptee in Sweden and other Euro-American adopting nations. Recall the words of the South Korean adoptee who was interviewed by Anna von Melen: "I feel uncomfortable in the proximity of immigrants, which I think is because they in some sense unsettle the picture I have formed of myself as Swedish. They remind me that I, too, am a kind of immigrant, even though I feel that I am not, because I don't want to see things that way." Likewise, Sara Nordin explains, "There is this image of the adoptees as a group that does not stand out, because they are, after all, Swedish. But we look like any other African. So of course we cannot help but stand out."[20]

With a Swedish identity that is tied to an egalitarian ideal of embracing the refugee and the immigrant and an adopted identity that is premised on difference from (rejection of) the immigrant, if he or she is to become completely Swedish, the transnational transracial adoptee is in an impossible bind. The premise animating a racialized national identity— the "completely Swedish" that so many transnational adoptees take on as who they fundamentally "are" on "the inside"—is an ideology of cultural difference (manifested on the skin, on the tongue, and in multiple ways on the body) that is imagined to be superficial. The adoptee stands (out) as a token of the capacity for such difference to be overcome, revealing the potentially Swedish (potentially governable) human subject within. But as Nordin's statement above suggests, her difference *cannot* be overcome—she looks "like any other African." Indeed, it is (only) because her difference cannot be overcome, as I argue in chapter 5, that it is possible to imagine such a thing as the *"helsvensk"*—the "completely Swedish"— which demands the presence of an incorporated but excluded other in "the Kingdom of Sweden."[21]

Using words that recall Sara Nordin's description (chapter 5) of being "compelled, both for yourself and for others, to prove that you are Swed-

ish, because you have this Ethiopianness that is such an irritating presence," psychoanalytic theorist Jessica Benjamin argues that "the negativity
that the other sets up for the self has its own possibilities, a productive
irritation, heretofore insufficiently explored" (1998, 85). In Nordin's case,
this negativity manifested itself when others (in Sweden) defined her as
"Ethiopian." She explained, "It makes you crazy and you don't know where
you are."[22] Likewise, Sofia Berzelius, when asked why she decided to go
"back" to Ethiopia in December 2000, when she was twenty-eight years
old, explained:

> Well, I think one important thing is, to me it was important to go back, very
> much because so many people kept telling me about Ethiopia, and what
> Ethiopia is like: "It's awful. It is wonderful. It is great. It is horrible. It is
> poor. It is beautiful." I had heard so many different versions. And people kept
> asking me also if I had been back and I always had to answer: "No." And then
> they came, so many people who knew, mostly like people who would see me
> maybe on the bus and who would come up to me and say:
>   "Are you from Ethiopia?"
>   "Yeah."
>   "I could tell by your looks." And:
>   "Where are you from?"
>   "I'm from Ethiopia."
>   "I was almost going to guess, because you look very Ethiopian. Have you
> been to Ethiopia?"
>   "No, I haven't."
>   "Oooohh!"
> And then there came this long story about what Ethiopia *is*. And I could
> never say: "Yeah, right!" or "No, I don't think so, I disagree!" because I didn't
> know. I was beginning to get rather bothered by that actually. I couldn't ar-
> gue, I couldn't say anything. I just had to say, "Aha, really! Oh, is that so?"
> And it felt as if they knew something about me that I didn't know, because
> they were talking about my origin and they all attributed some importance
> to this. . . . It was really difficult to relate to, because they were relating to
> something I couldn't relate to.[23]

Arguing that "violence is the outer perimeter of the less dramatic tendency of the subject to force the other to either be or want what it wants,
to assimilate the other to itself or make it a threat," Benjamin suggests
that violence "is simply an extension of reducing difference to sameness,
the inability to recognize the other without dissolving his/her otherness"
(1998, 86; citing Irigaray 1985). Violence, in other words, is an effect of the
failure to "give the child its own life," in this way circumventing the child's

potential for psychic agency.[24] By "attributing some importance" to "my

origin" even as "I" cannot relate to that because "I am" completely Swedish, interlocutors of adopted children or adults allow no space for a more
complex form of the Swedish (or the Ethiopian) to take shape, one in which
(to anticipate the discussion in chapter 7) *"I can have Ethiopia here (in Stockholm), not as 'Ethiopia,' but I no longer have to feel that 'Ethiopia' exists only in
Ethiopia."*[25]

To be able to "have Ethiopia here in Stockholm" involves a more nuanced sense of what "my origin" might mean to the Ethiopian-born Swedish adoptee. It suggests a connection to Ethiopia that is not simply based in
the representation of Ethiopia as impoverished, of hospitals there as places
"where they sort of dumped dead people outside, and where people were
thrown in and thrown out" (chapter 5), or of orphanages such as Kebebe
Tzehay as places so dreadful that one's adoptive mother can only cry when
they are mentioned (chapter 5). Rather, to have Ethiopia in Stockholm requires a lived experience of what pulls "Stockholm" toward Ethiopia, just
as Stockholm has become a draw for Ethiopians who are not adopted. It requires some understanding of the history of Sweden in Ethiopia—of why
Greta Svedberg "happened" to live there with her husband in the 1960s
(chapter 4)—or of the history of the United States in Korea and how American missionaries Harry and Bertha Holt "happened" to choose Korean "war
orphans" as an object of their attention in the 1950s (J. R. Kim 2006). More
generally, it requires a narrative of Anglo-European colonialism in Africa,
Asia, and Latin America and the record this provides of *connection* rather
than separation between the "Swedish" or the "American" (or the "Dutch"
or the "French"), and their others in the developing world. It is this connection that pulls Ethiopia (and its children) to Sweden and that continues to
constitute an "irritating presence" for the adopted child (and the adult she
or he becomes) in the adoptive nation, pulling them to a "back" to which
they must return so that they can become "Swedish people."[26]

7   Return

Part 1

re-turn *vi* 1a : to go back or come back again (as to a place, person, or condition). . . . b : to go back in thought or practice : REVERT.

—*Webster's Third New International Dictionary*

The individual can be said to be "tangled up in stories" which happen to him before any story is recounted.

—Paul Ricoeur, "Life in Quest of Narrative"

"People do go back, but they don't survive."

Sara Nordin experienced "a kind of panic attack" when she returned to Addis Ababa in her early twenties: "I had come to Sweden and then returned to Ethiopia, and perhaps I wouldn't come home [to Sweden] again. I thought, 'One can't make these trips several times. Maybe I will die here.' I don't know why I felt that way, but I did." In Ethiopia, she tried to shut off those feelings, just so she could manage. "But when I came home to Sweden it caught up with me and everything seemed unfathomable: 'Why just me?' And all the children one sees. It feels very strange. One wonders: 'What would have become of me if I had stayed there? Who was I while I was there?'"[1]

Sofia Berzelius reports having similar feelings before she embarked on her first return journey to Ethiopia in 2000:

> I was so frightened, I was very, very scared. I really haven't liked traveling ever. I just had this feeling that I would never, ever come back to Sweden. I was completely convinced. And I called everybody before I left just to say "Goodbye." I didn't tell them I was panicking. I think I told Marianne and my Mum and Dad, but the rest I didn't really tell. And I remember I went out jogging that day. I was so scared. And then I sort of, on the train to Arlanda [Stockholm airport] I was like, "OK, now I'm going." And then I remember we changed planes in Copenhagen and I thought, "This is my chance. I could

leave here. I could leave here, I could go back to Sweden." And then when the plane lifted from the ground, I was sort of sad. I thought, "This is stupid, I shouldn't do this. I am too young. I will never return. I like my parents." So it was strange.

As these narratives suggest, journeys "back" by adopted adults to a place or a person (a native land, a hospital, an orphanage, a foster mother, a birth mother) that is associated simultaneously with their coming into being and with the death of that being may provoke powerful mixed feelings of longing and fear. The experienced proximity of death involves more than Maria Brunn's matter-of-fact statement that "it might have been me" in the death statistics of the Delhi orphanage, when she returned there at age eleven with her mother (chapter 5). It includes Kanthi Grünewald's uncanny sense, when she visited the orphanage in Kolkata from which she had been adopted eight years earlier, that she and the child left behind had changed places: "What if you had adopted one of them instead and she had been standing there today looking at me?" she asked her mother that evening. It is implied as well in Sara Nordin's question "Why just me?" and in the anxiety expressed by a nineteen-year old woman adopted from Chile, after we had returned from a "roots tour" on which adoptive families visited orphanages, hospitals, and courts in which their children were abandoned and became adoptable. "How are the children chosen?" she asked, hinting at the arbitrariness of choice and some intuitive sense that her adopted self was intimately connected to (exchangeable with) the abandoned self that pulled her back to Chile.

Each of these questions touches on the ways that returns by the adopted to an imagined point of origin where they may hope to "find" themselves can be profoundly unsettling. As social theorist Slavoj Žižek (1989, 20) argues, the very concept of a "self" that is continuous over time is "*defined by its blindness to this* [originary] *place: it cannot take it into consideration without dissolving itself, without losing its consistency*" (emphasis in original). It is in this sense, as Jeanette Winterson suggests (1991, 158), that "people do go back, but they don't survive." The experience of dissolution is suggested in Deann Borshay Liem's autoethnographic film *First Person Plural* (2000), in which she documents the terrifying dreams that finally led her back to an adoption process that transformed her from Kang Ok Jin, born June 14, 1957, into Cha Jung Hee, born November 5, 1956, and finally into Deann Borshay, who was born "the moment I stepped off the plane in San Francisco on March 3, 1966."[2] As Borshay Liem indicates in this powerful and insightful film, her reunion, some two decades after her departure from Korea, with the mother and siblings who were left behind when she was sent to California as Cha Jung Hee could not restore her mother to her. Rather, "The only way I can develop a relationship with my mother is to realize that she is not my mother" (and by implication, that she herself is not—did not remain—Kang Ok Jin).

This insight points both to the impossibility of return to an origin or ground of identity and to the identifications, ruptures, and instabilities that continually pull identity toward that impossible ground (Fuss 1995, 2).[3] This dynamic is not simply an issue for the adopted. It is fundamental to the logic of identity as an *existential* reality, a self-conception that is inseparable from cultural and political discourses that are "spatially organized" and distinguish self from other, individual from society, the "inside" from the "outside" (Hall 1997, 43) (or birth nation from adopting nation). The dynamic of identity is "driven by a perpetual tension 'between the demand for concordance and the admission of discordances'—by the need, in other words, to find threads of continuity in the face of 'diversity, variability, discontinuity and instability'" (Antze 1996, 6, quoting Ricoeur 1992, 140–41) over a lifetime.

What distinguishes adoption narratives, and specifically narratives of return by adopted children and adults, is the tension between a *legal discourse* of adoption focused on closure—legal abandonment is irrevocable; the adoptable child comes "home" from the orphanage or foster parent to "the only family s/he has ever known"; the child has no other parent than the adoptive parent—and a *cultural discourse* of adoptive families as "as if" (genealogical) families (Modell 1994). As philosopher Hans Vaihinger (2001, cited in Riles n.d., 13) argues, "as if" knowledge is knowledge that is "*neither* true nor not true . . . but . . . is itself the tension between what is true and not true." The "as if" family of adoption is constituted by this form of knowledge: it is simultaneously the only legal family of the child *and* it presumes a "real" (family, nation, birth mother, self) pulling the adoptee "back" to a place and time before the legal declaration of abandonment and the production of the child as adoptable. This foreclosed "back" is shrouded in mystery: *Why was the child abandoned? How did the child become adoptable? And what kind of life (and self) did he or she leave behind?*

Adoption stories, and especially stories of search and reunion by adult adoptees, illuminate the longing for a secure ground of identity, even as they expose the tenuousness of a concept of identity as more than "as if." The adoptable child (and "the adoptee," who always retains the "trace," the "remainder" of the process of symbolization that created her or him)[4] cannot be contained either by conventional adoption narratives of absorption, adaptation (full incorporation and belonging in a new family and nation), and a "clean break" from the past (Duncan 1993, 51); or by stories of (illicit) search, reunion, and return to an originary place. Each adoption points to the contingencies of birth, to the arbitrariness of choice (which family, which nation), and to the fact that any adopted child could have had a different story: there is no "meant to be" in adoption stories, although *this* reality is also misrecognized in the closures toward which adoption stories incline as they "tell themselves" (White 1980, 3).[5]

The following account from an interview with Sara Nordin, whose "panic attack" on first returning to Ethiopia is described above, reveals the sense of uncanniness that accompanied her visit to the Kebebe Tzehay orphanage in Addis Ababa, more than three decades after her adoption from the orphanage in 1969:

> The first time I was there [in Addis Ababa] I was curious, but didn't dare, but this time, since I was with Amanda . . . I mean, I didn't know how I would react, so I thought that it was comforting to be with someone in case I started to cry and fell apart completely. So we began to ask about the orphanage and it turned out that it was very close to the place where we were staying. It was so weird. It's a big city and the only place I had spent any time was just in that area. I couldn't believe it. I had thought, "It can't still be here," or "It will be really hard to find." But it was incredibly easy. It was just a matter of looking on the Web.
>
> So we went. We just walked in through the gates and there it was. I have pictures from the time I was there, and I recognized the building. It was right there, but at the same time unbelievable. One can't grasp it. Then we met the headmistress and she had a huge file, which she looked in. And she asked when I had been adopted and what my name was. She had only been there a few years, so she didn't know personally about my adoption. And she began to leaf through the file. I thought you would go down in a cellar and bring up some files. But it just stood on the top of her desk. And she just kept leafing and leafing through the pages, and then she said: "Here you are!" And I began to sob. It was the first evidence that I had actually been there, even though I knew that it was so.
>
> And then she [the orphanage director] said that there was a woman at the orphanage who worked there when I was an infant. So then we went out and there were lots of nannies and then this woman came. She didn't recognize me. But I remembered that I had brought pictures with me, and we went back to the place where we were staying and got the pictures. Then she recognized me. I was very chubby and like a baby. And she just said, "Oh, oh, oh!"

I was in shock. With this knowledge, it was as though all the older people I saw could be my mamma or pappa. I would get these feelings every now and then: "Think, I could actually walk by my parents without even knowing about it." Before that, I thought: "I'll never find my parents, and that's OK." And that's how it felt, and still feels, even though you can wonder.

Nordin's recounting of her experience captures both the power of the conventional narrative in which there is no return from an adoption (her conviction that the orphanage would not be there), and the transformative power of discovering "herself" in the orphanage registry, with the "as if" knowledge this discovery conveyed: "It was as though all the older people I saw could be my parents." Her experience of splitting (*sedan blev det schizat*) into a Swedish and an Ethiopian self also had a paradoxical effect, in that she was finally able to "relax" (*slappna av*) in her sense of being Swedish. She explained: "I think that before you develop a relationship to Ethiopia, there is a part of you that you know is a part, but you don't know what it is. But when you begin to find a way to relate to that, then you can also take [for granted] the other, the Swedish, because then it is up to you whether you want to be Swedish or Ethiopian, or whatever you want to do about that." Here Nordin moves toward a more complex story of agency and identity in which the moment of self-identification as Ethiopian—a moment that was dreaded as instantiating the death of a familiar Swedish self—transforms the geography of the self, placing the Swedish in relationship to the child who was discovered in the orphanage registry and allowing her to "choose" where she is "from" in a different way.

Her capacity to do this was facilitated, she felt, by the fact that although the orphanage found the record of her being there, no record specifically of her birth was found. She explained to Amanda Fredriksson, who was present at the interview and accompanied her on the visit to the orphanage:

> Even though in one sense I can feel envious of [those of you who have found your birth parents], I also think it is a really difficult situation you have, since the physical and cultural distance is so great. I can feel that I like Ethiopia, but what I like about it is the people, while the culture isn't exactly—if I could choose—it isn't the country I would choose to be from. . . . But for those of you [who have found birth parents] it is harder, since you have those ties. It is a kind of luxury [for me], even though it has a price, as well.

Sofia Berzelius expressed related sentiments when she commented on her decision not to pursue information she had discovered, on visiting the

> I just felt it was too much already. Also I figured there must have been some
> reasons for this grandmother not to want to take care of me, so I thought
> I needed to think about this. For instance, if I would find out who they are
> and if I would find out that they are extremely poor, what would I do with
> that? How would I handle that? Do I have any obligations? Do I want to have
> those obligations? Can I handle it? What does that mean? Is it important?
> So therefore I have not followed up on it, but I might.

In both of these accounts, the more familiar story of search and reunion
as a journey toward self-completion (or alternatively, as expressed in Nordin's and Berzelius's fears about return, as a form of death) presents itself
instead as an opportunity for each of these women "to become the *nar-
rator. . . of [her] own story*, without actually becoming the *author of [her]
own life*" (Ricoeur 1991, 32). In this way, returns illuminate philosopher Paul
Ricoeur's argument that "the story of a life grows out of stories that have
not been recounted and that have been repressed in the direction of actual
stories which the subject [can] take charge of and consider to be constitutive of his *personal identity*" (30, emphasis in original).[6]

"The reality I live in"

The work of discovering what Ricoeur (1991, 32) describes as "the narrative
identity which constitutes us" presents particular challenges for adoptees
who develop ongoing relations with members of their birth families. In
each case, the dynamic of identity—a dynamic in which "what we call the
subject is never given at the start" (33)—involves the adoptee in a kind of
balancing act between a "past" that has been foreclosed, but in which he or
she is increasingly entangled through journeys "back," and his or her everyday life in the adopting nation, which also becomes a "back" in repeated
returns from the birth country (Yngvesson and Coutin 2006). The complications of negotiating this space between nations that send and those
that receive children in adoption were addressed in all of my interviews
with men and women who searched successfully for birth kin. Among the
issues that were brought up were tensions created in an adoptee's relations with her or his adoptive parents (however supportive they might be
about the reunion), profound emotional distress about the unbridgeable
gap between birth parent and child, a sense of economic responsibility

for impoverished birth parents or siblings, concerns about the inability to stay in touch and expectations that the adoptee should do so, and rage over the conditions surrounding the adoptee's relinquishment. In each case, the adoptees were confronted with what Stuart Hall (1997, 50) describes as "the really hard game which the play of difference actually means to us historically" by inhabiting "the constantly shifting frontier—irreducible to the frontiers between states—between two humanities which seem incommensurable, namely the humanity of destitution and that of 'consumption,' the humanity of underdevelopment and that of overdevelopment" (Balibar 1991, 44).

For Amanda Fredriksson, the difficulties of straddling this frontier made themselves felt as repeated visits to her family in Ethiopia became a "charged" (*laddat*) topic for her Swedish family, especially for her Swedish mother. The third time she went, her mother asked: "'Why do you want to go?' She didn't really understand why I should continue to make these visits. She said: 'Why do you want to go there again? What is so good about it?'" Only after Amanda's fourth journey did her mother explain that she had assumed the first trip back, when she was a teenager and was accompanied by her adoptive parents, would be the only one. When she returned again after five years, her mother told her, she began to fear "that I would become transfixed by my feelings and by Ethiopia (*att jag skulle fastna fast i mina känslor och Etiopien*). But I told her that I can't be transfixed by it. It is a reality I live in. It isn't that I create something that doesn't exist."[7]

For Anna ChuChu Petersson, this "reality" includes a mother, a father, and ten siblings in Addis Ababa and an adoptive mother in Sweden (her adoptive father died when she was twelve years old). Anna ChuChu made contact with her Ethiopian family in 1992, when she went to Addis Ababa as part of her job with the Swedish Red Cross. The Red Cross was scheduled to make a field visit and the only country they could go to was Ethiopia: "I thought that was really hard, because I didn't want to go there at all, though in fact I really wanted to do so. I was really scared. That's the way it was. In any case, we went, a good friend of mine and I. I was seventeen then. My mamma Ulla thought I should take my papers with me. I thought, 'No, I won't do that.' But she succeeded in convincing me. So I took with me this little description and through the Red Cross, they found my family."

What changed Anna ChuChu's mind about searching, once she arrived in Addis, was the sight of "people who sit on the street and beg. For me, that meant that all of them, the ones who were most sick, must be my brother. So I became almost worse from not knowing [compared to the

fear of knowing], and then I tried, and it went really fast. They found my
family. I met my mother and my father, since my father [who she had been
told was dead] is alive and was healthy."

When I first met Anna ChuChu, at a gathering of adult adoptees in 1997,
she told me about the phone call she made home to her mother in Sweden,
just after meeting her Ethiopian family. "'Mama, I met my mama,' I said."
Like Sara Nordin's experience of splitting when she found her name in
the orphanage registry, Anna ChuChu's encounter with a shadow self that
came to life in meeting her family was very difficult. Asked how she felt
about the meeting, she replied:

> I couldn't afford to have any feelings, because it was too much. And when
> I came home from there, I became really sick. It was partly physical, but I
> was entered into the hospital. I think it was mostly psychological, actually.
> But it was wonderful just to lie there in the hospital when I came home, in
> a completely white room, no impressions, nothing and it was completely
> quiet. Then I could begin to think a little. So I lay there and cried maybe for
> two days. I hadn't dared to have any feelings down there, it was too much for
> me. My mamma Ulla here at home didn't become stressed. When I was in the
> hospital, she came and just lay next to me in the bed, without speaking. She
> didn't try to ask me a whole lot of things. She didn't try to draw conclusions
> from what had happened. By contrast, others came and asked me: "What
> does your mother think?" But she herself wasn't that way, it didn't feel that
> way with her, although she may have spoken with someone else about it.

Here the issues of splitting and of continuity of the self that emerged
in Sara Nordin's narrative are intensified and seem intimately tied to ruptures (or potential ruptures) of the parent-child relationship, as understood in the exclusive forms of Euro-American parenting and specifically
in the expectation that there can only be one "real" mother. In a subsequent
conversation with Anna ChuChu and two other adopted adults, Amanda
Fredriksson and Mikael Jarnlo, I asked about what they call their mothers
in Ethiopia:

CHUCHU: I was told to call her mamma Besanech.
BY (to Amanda Fredriksson): And you?
AMANDA: Mamma Almas.
MIKAEL (who has searched but has not found his birth parents): I was think-
ing about that when you asked that question, what one calls one's mothers.
Because "mamma" for me carries so many feelings. I never call my mother
anything other than mamma, hardly even when I talk about her. When I
say "mamma," then there is something very strong emotionally. And when

I address them [his parents], even today, I think a little more about it. As a child one doesn't, because one is with one's parents so much—for example, if one is out shopping and she is some distance off and I call her, it is pretty loud and people look. But it is so special that I would never dream of calling her by her given name. Not my father either, for that matter.

CHUCHU: But perhaps it is a little like it would be if one grew up in a homosexual family, that one can have two mothers. For me just now, it isn't more complicated than the fact that I happen to have two mothers.

AMANDA: But it is like you say, Micke, that it is very emotionally charged, this business with "mamma," because I feel as though after our trip I've had a really hard time saying "mamma" to my mother Maggan. I've tried to say her name instead, but that feels strange too. So it's just: "Hey, mamma!" even though it feels like I can't really say it as easily as I did before, and I know that is directly linked to my feelings. It is really an emotionally charged thing. And my father in Ethiopia, I have a special relationship with him that I can't explain. In that way I can also feel, this was the first time that I thought, "What if they should die? That would be terrible." It would feel as though, "Now everything has come to an end." I think it has to do with their being so far away and that I have just found them *and so if they should disappear, then it would be as though they had never existed.* (emphasis added)

Anna ChuChu's second trip to Ethiopia, together with Amanda Fredriksson in 1999, was provoked, she said, by her fear that her parents in Ethiopia would die: "I became panicked, because I had heard that the average life span in Addis Ababa was 47 years, and I figured out what their ages were, and I became really nervous that they would die. Then I thought, "No, now I have to go."[8] Amanda, who planned to make a second trip back to meet her own family, suggested that they travel together, and so they did, spending two weeks living with Anna ChuChu's family and a week visiting Amanda's. For both women, their second visit was easier than the first, at least in part because they were together.

At Anna ChuChu's, they spent time with her family of ten brothers and sisters, who also have children. Her parents, who are divorced and both have new partners, "are anxious that when I come they be seen together with me. And there are all kinds of rules about proper behavior. If I take a picture of my mother, then I must take one of my father. That kind of thing was important." I asked how she spoke with them, and she explained that one of her brothers speaks English and could interpret. "But sometimes it didn't matter, because talking was just too much. They don't say so much, because one doesn't talk about the same things." Our conversation continued:

CHUCHU: But the biggest thing for me was that we went to them and I slept there at my mother's house. To wake up in her bed and that she tucks you in (*stoppar om en*) at night, and strokes your cheek. That was a huge thing for me (*jättestort*). They treated us like sisters the whole time. She [Mamma Besanech] said [about Amanda]: "This is my child too. I will take care of her." Both Almas, Amanda's mamma, and Besanech, my mamma, took on the mother role in a way that one perhaps doesn't expect, that they care about what one is wearing, they ask if one has a boyfriend and care—well, perhaps Almas didn't ask about that, but my mother did. She asked and wanted to be sure that I—for I said: "In Sweden it is ok to have lots of boyfriends" and then she thought I had lots of boyfriends at the same time. Then she was really upset. And when we were going somewhere, she cared about it like a mother. Although it felt as though both Almas and Besanech gave enough space so that you didn't feel overwhelmed. So I think that both of them did really well.

AMANDA: What I felt so strongly and have more or less understood intellectually, is that one is their child, that is just the way it is. It doesn't matter that we have been away from them for more than twenty years, because they gave birth to us and we are their children. And that can be a little difficult because sometimes it involves certain expectations that are placed on us as well.

BY: What kinds of expectations?

AMANDA: Well, having to do with money and helping them out. For my part I like that feeling.

CHUCHU: It is so self-evident for them.

AMANDA: That's right. There is nothing strange about it.

CHUCHU: And it's really cool (*jättehäftig*), because it is so abstract for me here. And here in Sweden there is no one who encourages one to feel secure in that feeling. Here, the feeling is scary.

The "scariness" that Anna ChuChu refers to here is the flip side of Sara Nordin's experience of splitting when she found her name in the registry of the Kebebe Tzehay orphanage. It alludes to the risk (to a familiar Swedish self) of accepting "certain expectations" about belonging *both* in a relatively affluent family in Sweden *and* in an impoverished one in Ethiopia, and to the complex (and nonidentical) subjectivity that takes shape in this (dis)location. This subjectivity is in tension with the legal fiction that there is only one "real" family (and with the cultural fiction that a family that is "only" legal isn't real) and only one "real" (Swedish, Ethiopian) self. It requires a capacity to tolerate the longing for such a "real" and the closure it promises, even as "the reality I live in" demands a different kind of story, one that takes shape "outside belongings" in what Elspeth Probyn, in her book on this topic, describes as "the slip between being and longing" (1996, 44). Probyn suggests that the slip between being and longing is propelled by a politics of surfaces and involves "proceed[ing] along the skin—skin which is both surface and redolent of certain orders and ordering of sociality" (15). Surface, then, is not simply "superficial" but is always figured by "the deep historicity of why, how, where, and with whom we may feel that we *belong*" (35, emphasis in original).

Two Different Identities

These issues are central in the story below, which was recounted by Jaclyn Campbell Aronson, together with her adoptive mother, Barbara Rall, over a nine-year period between 1996 and 2005.[9] As was true in the stories of the Ethiopian-born adoptees quoted above, my own position as an adoptive mother and my involvement in an "open" adoptive relationship with the birth family of our son Finn contributed to the telling of the tale. During this same period, our relationship with Finn's birth parents (and in particular, my relationship with his birth mother) was developing in response to Finn's own emerging sense of himself as he matured and as I began coming to terms with what Ingrid Stjerna (the Swedish social worker I have quoted at numerous points) means when she says that parents must "give the adopted child its own life" (1976). Negotiating this process, in a relationship that (minimally) involves the adult adoptee, the adoptive mother, and the birth mother, is a central theme in Aronson's narrative.

Jaclyn Aronson was born in Korea in 1975 as Kim Hyo Jin. She lived for eight years with her mother, Kim Mi Young, in Pusan, until she was placed by her in an orphanage in 1983. She remained in the orphanage, Angel Babies Home, until she was adopted by American parents five months later. Aronson reunited with her birth mother when she was twenty years old, just after completing her second year at Hampshire College. In interviews and in her senior thesis, as well as in a workshop on search and reunion that she conducted with her adoptive mother in 2005, Aronson, speaking sometimes alone and at other times together with her adoptive mother, describes her complex relationship to her birth mother and to Korea, a nation that she spent her late childhood and adolescence rejecting:

> When I first came to this country, I wanted so much to be American. I feel that assimilation is really so different from what an adoptee has to go through. I had to assimilate on a certain level, like I had to learn the language very quickly in order to communicate, in order to survive. I had to adjust to American culture and my family culture very quickly. I had to figure out a lot of things just for my survival alone. But so much of the little things you

do as a kid, like playing certain sports or playing with certain dolls or having

the desire to do something meant for me a kind of rejection of something else. Like I rejected Korean culture school and language school for soccer. Because in Korean language school I felt so alienated from that setting, because these were all Korean-American kids that had Korean parents to go back to. They could practice with their parents, eat Korean food *and I was different in that situation*. Whereas outside I looked different but inside I was just like everybody else in white society. And so for me to voluntarily place myself in Korean-American culture, I just couldn't deal with . . . I didn't want that. I think in a lot of ways people don't want anything to do with their birth mother and birth mother and Korea is synonymous. Your birth mother and Korea did the same thing: they rejected you. I think a lot of it is fear of being rejected again, fear of, oh my god, *I'm nothing like Korea or Korean people, and I'm not like Americans.* Who the fuck am I supposed to relate to and associate with? Who am I supposed to fully connect with? And the reality is, I don't think anyone fully connects with anybody. I think it's a basically human experience. (emphasis added)

Aronson's decision to return to Korea after her sophomore year in college was prompted by the experience of being part of Hampshire's most "diverse" class to date (in fall 1993) and of beginning to come to terms with the split between an "inside" that she experienced as "just like everybody else in white society," and an outside that set her apart:

That was the first time that I actually knew that I was *different*. I mean, the first year was quite a shocker, in terms of—*my* identity. A lot of my friends my first year were of color, and that was really the first time—I mean, even in high school, my best friend was half Asian. . . . but *I personally* just identified as—"I'm not like them, but there's no specific name for what I am." And I was fine with that. So it was really a shock that first year, and there was an incredible amount of tense stuff going on. That was the year that they had that black—African American—male artist who came with the basketball installation at the gallery that caused a huge debate about race and identity, and all of it just went over my head. And I didn't—I went to meetings with the Asian-American students' association at that time, and I didn't really understand that, and I didn't understand why people were so insistent on *naming* people and saying who should sit with whom and blah, blah, blah. So that was a very confusing year because I had never been in a situation where I had to claim and take responsibility for what I perceived as someone naming *me*. (emphasis Aronson's)

The issue of "someone naming *me*" (as Korean) was a recurrent source of tension as Jackie was growing up. Hers was not unlike the experiences

of adoptees in Sweden, whose parents' determination to *overlook* their resemblance to immigrants, even as others claimed that they were not Swedish, placed them continually outside belonging in what was legally their
only family and nation. While the experience of each adoptee—whether
American or Swedish—is unique to the circumstances specific to his or
her adoption, the proliferation of culture camps, language schools, and
other institutions for developing a child's "national" (assumed to be her
or his "natural") identity in the United States (Zhao 2002; Volkman 2005b)
is a marked contrast to the concern of Swedish parents with what one psychologist (Cederblad 1984, 34) described as "Swedishizing" the child (*att
försvenska barnet*), that is, making sure the child becomes fully Swedish
on the "inside."[10]

In Jackie's case, her adoptive mother, Barbara Rall, felt strongly that she
should maintain her connection to Korea: "Some things, I really twisted
her arm to do." These included attending Korean language school on Sat-
urdays and eventually Korean culture camp, where Jackie served as a coun-
selor. Rall explains: "I have always felt that to be bilingual is an incredible
gift. Here was somebody who was totally fluent in Korean, and to give that
up would be terrible." In hindsight, Rall views Jackie's rejection of these
activities as having less to do with language school or culture camp than
with "really wanting to be American."

Similarly, Jackie had no interest in traveling to Korea with her mother.

RALL: I was really eager to go and see the orphanage, travel around the country
and all, and I thought it would be wonderful for the two of us to go. And I
thought that the whole key to going was—well—it wasn't even so much
about searching—but you [addressing Jackie] just didn't want to go. And we
talked about it all through high school, and I campaigned, diligently. I kept
saying, "You need to think about this, you need to think about one of those
homeland tours, and you need to think about searching."

BY: Why did you feel this way?

RALL: Well, because by that time I was studying with Joyce MacGuire Pavao.[11]
At least three summers I went to Cape Cod [where Pavao holds adoption
workshops]. The new thinking was that children adopted internationally
shouldn't wait. The longer you waited to search, the higher risk that the trail
would be cold, and be more difficult to find. And I felt that we had a really
good chance of finding because Jackie's mother had signed off herself. A lot
of these kids were found in the street, at the bus ticket kiosk or something
like that, but Jackie, her mother brought her and signed off, so I thought we
had a good shot at finding her. And finally, in the middle of [Jackie's] sophomore year at Hampshire, she agreed she would do it.

BY: Let me ask you one thing. This may seem obvious to you, but why did you think it was important for her to find—to search and find?

RALL: Because I thought it would answer some questions and because I think that, among other things, one of the pieces of work that Jackie has had to do has been to bring her two halves together. And I think all of these kids, who come from a different country, from a different culture, or as a different race, have this work to do. . . . I think particularly, being a minority in America and growing up in a white family, that there is some kind of work that needs to be done about integrating your two halves, and I felt that searching for her birth-mother and going back to Korea might be helpful in doing that work. And I felt that once she got to Hampshire and she was struggling with all this business of the Asian students' organization and so forth that going to Korea might accelerate this process. So finally she agreed to go on this homeland trip.

Jackie explains her desire to return to Korea in slightly different terms, as a process of "placing the eight-year-old Korean child within myself," noting that she regards Kim Hyo Jin, the Korean child who was dropped off at Angel Babies Home orphanage in 1983, and Jaclyn Campbell Aronson, the woman who returned to Korea in 1995, as "two different identities":

> When I say that Kim Hyo Jin and Jaclyn Campbell Aronson are two different identities, I am serious. They are not one and the same. Symbolically, Kim Hyo Jin is "within" me. . . . I think what she experienced in Korea and how she was raised and her understanding of her circumstances has influenced the way I am now. But I speak of her in the third person. For me, I often see Hyo Jin as the little girl who never got the chance to grow up past eight and a half years. I don't know if her growth was stunted when I became Jaclyn Campbell Aronson or when she stopped being Kim Mi Young's child. Or in the orphanage when she was no one's child. But my memories of life in Korea are vivid.

With her parents' encouragement and support, Jackie contacted the Children's Home Society of Minnesota during her sophomore year and signed up for their homeland tour, as well as for the "option" of having them initiate a search for her birth mother. She remained deeply ambivalent about the journey, however, and when she heard a month before the trip that Mi Young had been found and wanted to meet her, her initial reaction, as she explains in her 1997 senior thesis on Korean transnational adoption, was "rage at the news" (1997, 49). Her sense that at an emotional level she was "trapped" into following through with a meeting about which she was deeply conflicted expressed itself in nightmares: her birth mother appeared as a disfigured hitchhiker who tried to grab Jackie from the car in which she was traveling with her adoptive mother. The nightmares "made me wake up in a cold sweat." They captured "all my fears and feelings of ambivalence" about a woman "who I felt did not belong in my world" (50).

In the end, Jackie decided to go through with the meeting, and in doing so she was able to confirm memories that she had previously been able to narrate only as though she were "writing about someone else's life." In addition, reuniting with her birth mother gave her more of a perspective on why she had been placed for adoption and allowed her to see Mi Young as "a three-dimensional person with feelings and thoughts and outside things affecting her life," not simply as an "evil bitch who was an alcoholic and who used to abuse me": "She told the whole story about . . . that she was really sick with tuberculosis. I contracted it from her. But the stage of her tuberculosis was to the point where she really thought she was going to die. And her friends all said to her, 'You have to make a decision about her [Hyo Jin] now.' And she did."

Even as Aronson's understanding of her birth mother's situation deepened, the reunion was deeply disturbing for her, as she explained at a workshop that she led together with her adoptive mother in 2005. Describing a brief, but intense, shopping trip on which her birth mother insisted on buying her presents, Aronson observed:

> The thing that I noticed when we were shopping is that the things that she bought me were . . . she still thought of me as an 8-year-old. She's bringing me these barrettes that had like cartoon characters. It was just frozen in time for her. What was upsetting for me at that point was literally, I realized, *literally*, everything had kind of frozen because she was still, again, sick with tuberculosis, she could only kind of afford medicine up to a certain stage, and so then she would have bouts of tuberculosis every two or three years. She was still incredibly poor. And when I was growing up with her I knew that we were poor. But twelve years later, for her to be in basically the *same* place, and I had been adopted to a much better and happier life. So I felt incredibly guilty, and leaving her at the bus stop and realizing *nothing had changed for her*—she was still illiterate, she was still poor, she was still drinking heavily, and sick, and I just—got very angry. . . . I almost felt a kind of rage at Korea: why they couldn't make room in their society for our family, why, when the country was developing and kind of getting better, why they couldn't take her along, and why she had to kind of remain in a place, to me, was just so awful.
>
>   I came back from Korea and I was just obsessed with working. . . . I just wanted to work, so I could support her. *I can't live with this.* It was too much

for me to try to process that. And I was so angry with her for buying me things when she was so poor. I remember one of the adoptive parents [on the tour] saying, "It makes her feel better. She's your mother. She wants to do things for you." But I just couldn't make the connection back then.

After her graduation from Hampshire in 1997, Aronson returned to Korea on a Fulbright fellowship and spent a year and a half there studying Korean and reacquainting herself with her birth mother. During this time, her adoptive mother visited and they spent ten days with Mi Young. Barbara Rall describes this meeting as "extraordinary" but extremely stressful. She wishes, on the one hand, that she could have had more involvement with Mi Young and had been less dependent on Jackie to translate for her. But before the visit was over, she was "just totally strung out" and longing to go home:

RALL: I couldn't communicate with Mi Young, I had to say to Jackie, "Tell her this, tell her that, tell her the other." And I really felt that that also was a burden on Jackie, and I was very much torn between my two roles, my role as the adoptive mother and my role as a social worker. And it was very clear that this woman has never processed any of the painful feelings around surrendering, and all. And I was unable to help her. Maybe I wouldn't have been able to help her, even if I spoke fluent Korean. But I felt so constricted, so unable to do what I do, that it was *very* difficult.

There were two points that were just so extraordinary. At one point, we were in a Korean BBQ restaurant, and it was an odd hour because there were no people in the restaurant, and she had had a couple of beers by then, I think, and she got up and she went over into the center where there was an open space, and she did this whole bowing thing to me, all the way down to the floor, in gratitude. And that was [voice becomes husky] a very—emotional moment. And then there was another time, the last day, at the train station . . .

JACKIE: When we were saying goodbye, yeah . . .

RALL: She sobbed, she sobbed, she sobbed. And I held her—and everyone else in the train station—I mean, this is not a Korean thing to be hugging people in the train station [laughter]. And everyone else—I mean Jackie wanted to drop through the floor, and here I am holding her and patting her back and she just could not stop sobbing. *It was awful.*

JACKIE: You don't remember?

RALL: I wanted to say goodbye earlier.

JACKIE: OK, this is something that's important to understand, because it's important not to kind of put a rosy shade to this visit, because it was extremely stressful . . .

RALL: Oh, no, no, no, I know it was, such a stress—yes . . .

JACKIE: But because there were two times when my mom said, "Maybe I should go home."

RALL: No, I don't think . . .

JACKIE: How long were you there?

RALL: I was there for 10 or 11 days.

JACKIE: You don't remember this. Twice, you got me to call the airlines.

RALL: No, I don't remember that. I remember saying, the last day we were with Mi Young, and I was just totally strung out by then, and we had to go someplace and she had to go someplace, and I said to Jackie, "Do you think we could say our goodbyes to her now? Because I'm just saturated, I can't do another minute." We had an hour or two to go till the train. And Jackie said, "No."

JACKIE: Because there was no way. She was going to watch us get on that train. I knew that she was going to stay at that station until she basically saw us boarding that train and at that point, mom had . . .

RALL: I was on overload . . .

JACKIE: There was too much, there was just too much.

RALL: Then we went back to the hotel to get our bags, and I had gotten her this basket of flowers. It was gorgeous. And when we came back to the hotel to get the bags, I wanted to present her with the basket of flowers and say goodbye and go to the train station without her. And she took the basket of flowers and she just got hysterical, absolutely hysterical. And it ended up that she's only gotten flowers twice in her life, and then she just couldn't stop sobbing, and I just couldn't wait to escape from her because I just couldn't help her in any way, and I couldn't communicate with her, and then the next day, you [Jackie] were really angry with me . . .

JACKIE: I was, because, *I wanted her to be stronger* than she had been and I felt, I was very conscious of the both of them [begins to cry] and I wanted both of them to be—*my whole role that I saw was to make sure everybody was stable, and no one was gonna go crazy, or insane* [BY emphasis], because I was very aware of how guilty my birth mother felt and how overly, kind of, embarrassingly grateful she was to my parents. So I wanted it to be as much of a controlled situation as possible. And so when my mom, kind of broke down, and she said "I can't take this!" it was a very emotional—I mean, for me . . . So when my mom said—you said—"I want it to be over"—those were her exact words. She said: "*I want this to be over.*"

RALL: It was the truth.

JACKIE: Right. I mean, we were all speaking truth. She [Mi Young] was sobbing, you [Rall] were saying you want it to be over, and I said, "We have an hour and a half until the train leaves." It was all a very, very, emotional time. But I think we could have gone without that afternoon.

RALL: But I have never regretted for a moment that I went, oh absolutely. I have never regretted for a moment. I am so glad that I met her, and I'm so glad that we have that photograph with the three of us together. And I'm hoping—we had wanted her to come for Jackie's graduation from Hampshire, but she didn't seem up to it. And we just couldn't bring it off. She showed little enthusiasm, so we didn't press. Maybe she'll come for Jackie's wedding.

BY, to Jackie: How do you feel about that?

JACKIE: I think I would like her to take part in a major life event, like that. I think about, you know, one day if I have kids, her involvement and my kids' involvement, and their relationship to Korea, whatever it may be, probably depending on who I marry and what that person's relationship to Korea is, if there is one. And, so, I think about those things. You know, a lot of people have said—um—I have a friend who is Caucasian who is adopted, and she just reunited with the birth-mother about a year and a half ago. And her parents, who are also Caucasian, when they found out she had reunited, and so on, they were very interested, and they said, well, "Why doesn't she just come live with you?" And several people have said, "Why don't you just bring her [Mi Young] over?" And you know, the bottom line is that, this woman has never been on an airplane before, she's never been outside—it's like traumatic for her to be in Seoul. And so for her to pick up and move to an entire new country is just something that I'm not . . .

RALL: I just feel that we could probably take better care of her is she were nearby, but who knows, she might not be amenable to the kind of care we might want to take of her.

Subsequent to the Fulbright, Aronson has returned twice to Korea (as of 2005). Her birth mother's health has improved, and she has found employment; in addition, Aronson sends regular remittances to Korea to help support her, something she has felt strongly about doing since her first journey back in 1995. Aronson explains: "She's by herself and the whole thing in Korea is, your family is everything, they take care of you, and they make sacrifices. *She doesn't have any family over there—we're the end of the line*" (emphasis added).

Barbara Rall, ambivalent about this decision, comments about the time when they began the search process in 1995, "Our fantasy, and we had this fantasy early on, was that part of why she had surrendered Jackie was so that she could marry, because, you know, in Korea, a woman cannot . . ."

JACKIE, interrupting: Maybe it was *your* fantasy, because I remember thinking about that possibility, and I remember thinking that there was some sort of miscommunication that my birth mother had gotten married . . .

RALL: No, I never thought she got married. I thought she had a boyfriend . . .

JACKIE: There was some sort of story that had come from the agency that she had gotten married, and, like, had a child, or something. And I was *enraged* by that story. Because for her to pick up and be able to—have a life—without me was . . .

RALL: Well, that's one side of it, but the other side is that if she had picked up and had a life without you, we, you know, we, I have a strong feeling about how Jackie feels really responsible for her, and I find myself, often, not often, but when it comes up, *more* when we first found her, less now, but when it comes up, it still irritates the hell out of me that Jackie feels responsible for her and I wish that she had moved on as well *so that Jackie could be free to be her birth daughter and not have to kind of be her caretaker* [BY emphasis].

JACKIE: Right.

RALL: Because I think it's a burden, and it upsets me that my daughter has to deal with this burden. But this is what it is.

BY, to Jackie: Do you feel it's a burden?

JACKIE: I feel like it's my responsibility. And you know, she's not—whereas I understand where my mother is coming from, in that, in the best possible scenario [my birth mother would have moved on], she's always survived. In the 12 years that I didn't know her, she's survived. She's survived repeated bouts of tuberculosis, she's still an alcoholic but she's managed not to have it kill her, and she's, she's very poor. She was illiterate up to just a few years ago. Um—you know, the kind of work that she can find is extremely physically demanding, and I do think it's a responsibility of mine to help her out. Obviously, I'm not in a position to completely take over her financial needs, but . . .

RALL: Jackie sends her sums of money, yearly.

BY: And you're uncomfortable with that as a responsibility?

RALL: No, that's Jackie's judgment to make. But I'm just—I'm just angry and sad that Jackie has to be saddled with that responsibility. You know, it's so interesting, because I've worked with a lot of people [in her role as a social worker with adoptees and their parents] who have searched and Jackie will tell you from her own experiences with friends that—*searching is always double-edged, always* [BY emphasis]. And some of Jackie's friends who have searched unsuccessfully are envious of Jackie, and they don't really understand all of the ramifications.

JACKIE: *The thing with money is, I feel very comfortable with the money situation because it doesn't demand that I be there* [BY emphasis]. I'm able to help her, but I'm not having to completely give up what I want in life by being there. I mean I could very easily find a job in Korea, live with her, and take care of her, and make sure that she's in a place where she doesn't even have to work, you know, I could very easily do that. But I don't want to. I don't want to live in Korea, I don't want to have a professional life there. So sending her money is really the most comfortable thing for me to do because I'm not asking her to disrupt her life, and I'm not demanding for myself that I disrupt my life.

In its stark engagement with what Jaclyn Aronson describes above as "speaking truth" about the ten days she spent with her mother and her birth mother in Pusan, this narrative illuminates the powerful pull of a discourse of identity and the "returns" (to an origin) that identity requires, while at the same time pointing toward a more complex story of movement between (temporary) locations, of desire that is shaped by hegemonies of race, blood, and nation, and of the impossibility of ever fully belonging in the places where we find ourselves.[12] A central theme—echoed in the narratives of Sara Nordin, Sofia Berzelius, and others whose stories appear in this chapter—is the tension between *identification* and *identity*, and what Aronson describes as being placed in the position of having "to claim and take responsibility for what I perceived as someone naming *me*."

As Diana Fuss (1995, 2) explains, "Identification is a process that keeps identity at a distance, that prevents identity from ever approximating the status of an ontological given, even as it makes possible the formation of an *illusion* of identity as immediate, secure, and totalizable." Powerful moments that disrupt identity include Aronson's meetings with the Asian-American students' association in her first year at Hampshire College and her experience that "I'm not like them, but there's no specific name for what I am"; Sara Nordin's frustration, as she was growing up, when others in Sweden told her that she was Ethiopian or that she was Swedish—"It makes you crazy and you don't know where you are"; and the experience of the Korean-born adoptee quoted in chapter 6: "I feel uncomfortable in the proximity of immigrants . . . because they in some way unsettle the picture I have formed of myself as Swedish. They remind me that I, too, am a kind of immigrant." But these disruptive experiences also include the "very emotional moment" described by Barbara Rall in the BBQ restaurant in Pusan, when Jackie's birth mother "did this whole bowing thing to me, all the way down to the floor, in gratitude," a moment that compromised her sense that Jackie was "free to be [Mi Young's] birth daughter"; and they include Jackie's sense that "Kim Hyo Jin is 'within' me," even as Hyo Jin and Jaclyn Campbell Aronson "are not one and the same."

Returns are both provoked by and generate such experiences, and recall Elspeth Probyn's image (1996, 42) of the in-betweens in which identity is entangled as like "the moment when the trapeze artist has let go of one ring but hasn't yet grasped the other." At the same time, returns provoke and are provoked by fantasies of closure: Barbara Rall's fantasy that Jackie's birth mother had "moved on" so that Jackie would not be burdened with sending remittances to her, or alternately that Mi Young could move to the United States, where it would be easier for Jackie (and Barbara) to take care of her; and Jackie's fantasy "that my mom was strong enough to deal with all this" during the visit with Mi Young and that she herself could mediate the expectations of her mother and her birth mother in such a way as to "make sure everybody was stable and no one was gonna go crazy or insane."

These fantasies of closure and the experiences of dissonance that interrupt them —"*I can't live with this*"; "*I want this to be over*"; "*It makes you crazy and you don't know where you are*"—open up the symbolic order of lineage, blood, and nation (and the legal narratives of adoption that secure this order) to rifts through which real adoption stories can be pieced together.

Part 2

¹re-turn *vi.* . . . . 2b : To bring in or produce (as earnings or profit): YIELD.
²re-turn *n.* . . . . 4a : A quantity of goods, consignment or cargo coming back in exchange for goods sent out as a mercantile venture.
b : the value or profit from such venture.

 —*Webster's Third New International Dictionary*

"They are nationalistic, in a way"

In 1998, a group of twenty-nine adopted adults born in South Korea and raised in Anglo-European homes was invited by President Kim Dae Jung for an all-expense-paid tour of his country. The high point of the tour was a reception and ceremony at the Blue House, where the president formally welcomed the group and offered them a formal apology for their de facto exile.

> It's been eight months since I became President. During this period, I've met countless people. But today's meeting with all of you is personally the most meaningful and moving encounter for me. Looking at you, I am proud of such accomplished adults, but I am also overwhelmed with an enormous sense of regret at all the pain that you must have been subjected to. Some 200,000 Korean children have been adopted to the United States, Canada, and many European countries over the years. I am pained to think that we could not raise you ourselves, and had to give you away for foreign adoption. (Kim 1999, 15)

Kim referred to the adoptive countries of his visitors as their "home," but described Korea as their "homeland." He concluded his address by urging them to "strengthen your identity": "The world is becoming a single sphere. Globalization is the trend of the times. No nation can live by itself. Cultural exchanges are important. So, nurture your cultural roots, and try to harmonize that with your national identities, wherever you are from" (16).

Kim's implicit inclusion of transnationally adopted adults as part of Korea's far-flung diaspora is regarded by some as less a way of undoing a wrong than as a means of "benefiting from westernized overseas Koreans as intermediaries for economic expansion and investment" (Hübinette 2004, 21). The Overseas Koreans Foundation, a division of South Korea's Ministry of Foreign Affairs and Trade, was inaugurated by the South Korean government in 1997. Its activities include developing summer programs that will "wed" Korean adoptees to Korea by offering "motherland tours" on which adoptees are presented with a "folklorized vision of Korean culture" as they are transported from one location to another on what one woman referred to as "the orphan bus" (E. Kim 2005, 50). Adopted young people or adults who return to South Korea, either on motherland tours, for broadly based "Gatherings" attended by hundreds of Korean-born adopted men and women from Europe and North America (such as the ones that took place in Seoul in 2005 and again in 2007), or on more private journeys, become both "spectacles of national and cultural alterity" and economic support for South Korea's capitalist transformation (72). Since 1999, Koreans adopted overseas have been eligible for F-4 visa status, which allows them "to stay in Korea for up to two years with rights to work, make financial investments, buy real estate, and obtain medical insurance and pensions" (E. Kim 2003, 59).

The ambiguities confronted by the two thousand young men and women who return each year to South Korea are specific to the history of that country and its economic transformation. But similar questions have emerged elsewhere, as adopted adults increasingly go back and find that it is they, not the country that gave them away, who are expected to be (or feel that they should be) doing the giving. Sara Nordin, whose return to Addis Ababa in 2002 is described in an earlier section of this chapter, was ambivalent about being welcomed "back" to Ethiopia when she made her first trip there in 1997:

> They are nationalistic in a way, so that they take you in. If you have some aspect that is Ethiopian then you *are* Ethiopian. "We need you. You should be here. This is your country. You should live here and learn the language." It makes it easier to feel at home, while here [Sweden] you can be questioned

even though you have lived here your whole life: "How Swedish are you? Blackhead [*svartskalle*]!" There is also racism there, but another type of racism. Especially all that business of taking you in even though you don't know the language, don't know the culture. You can feel like an alien, even though they don't regard you that way. . . . They can get upset if you don't want to live there.[13]

Sara and her friend Amanda Fredriksson described related concerns that took shape in the context of implicit or explicit expectations of economic assistance from (officially nonexistent) Ethiopian kin. Some adoptees, Sara related, simply rejected such claims out of hand: "What?! I don't get it. Why should one help them?" But, she explained, "I feel this way—why not? They are terribly poor." Amanda described her (Ethiopian) father's tentative approach to requesting help:

AMANDA: He didn't ask. He has never asked himself, but through the interpreter. He hasn't asked me. And first I thought: "Jaha, why doesn't he ask me? Doesn't he want to?" Perhaps it isn't so easy to ask your child for money. And I think he didn't want to appear to be begging. So I just indicated through the interpreter that it was ok.

SARA: But then, I think it has to do with your family. It feels as though you have known each other for some time now, because there are a lot of feelings and you are very close, because it would be bad if one met only every 5 years or so, and the relationship were odd and tainted, and then there is a request for money. But in this case, it's more like, "Now we have been able to live here, we have been here."

AMANDA: I spoke with another girl in our association [the Association of Adopted Ethiopians and Eritreans] and I think that in her relation to her family she has become a kind of bank. She is supposed to help them with money. She has regularly given them quite a lot of money, which you also have to be careful with, because they possibly haven't had so much and so all of a sudden to get a whole year's salary—! And here's what she said: "I have to keep track of what they have done with the money, so they don't do things they shouldn't." It's a bit like playing God. I don't like it. . . . I think she is treating her mother like a child.[14]

To ease such uncomfortable transitions, the siblings of Ethiopians adopted in Sweden have formed an organization called The Bright Star in Addis Ababa. Bright Star helps adopted adults find their birth families and provides support for emotionally complex reunions. It also seeks to inform Ethiopian-born adoptees about their birth country and works toward helping Ethiopian families keep their children or place them in domestic adoption in Ethiopia, one of the goals of the 1993 Hague Convention that has been the most difficult to implement.[15]

The founder of Bright Star, Gizachev Ayka, is the brother of eight children who were adopted in Sweden before he was born. In an article written about the organization in Sweden's official journal on international adoptions, *NIA Informerar* (2003), Ayka explains that as he was growing up, his parents talked about his adopted siblings and showed him photos. He suggests that because Ethiopians whose children are adopted abroad are poor and have been told that having their children adopted overseas will give them a better life, when children who have been adopted return (as seven of his adopted brothers and sisters have done), their parents "want to know that they did the right thing for the child. They expect to be rewarded. It is a cultural question. They expect the same from my adopted siblings as they expect from me. Logically speaking, it is correct that the parents have done the right thing for their children. They have planned for them. It is hard for the adoptees. After they have met their families and feel happy about the reunion, the next step is that they must help their family" (quoted in Sammarco 2003, 6).

Bright Star has established a close connection with Stockholm's Association of Adopted Ethiopians and Eritreans, whose chairman, Mikael Jarnlo, I first interviewed in Stockholm in 1999. Jarnlo described his positive experience the first time he visited Ethiopia in 1992, noting how quickly he was accepted as if he were "Ethiopian": "Just the fact that one has chosen to make contact with them and shows one's interest, they think it is so great, and then they think 'Well, you are of course Ethiopian and you should learn to speak the language and you should marry an Ethiopian woman.'" Jarnlo explained that while he felt that he was Ethiopian, that didn't change the fact that he was "first and foremost Swedish." In an interview that was included in the *NIA Informerar* article above about Bright Star, Jarnlo, who has not been able to find any information about his birth family, stated that he disagreed with Gizachev Ayka regarding the expectation that children adopted abroad should support their birth parents: "To have been abandoned and then to expect that you will help the abandoning parents, that is a lot to expect from an adoptee" (quoted in Sammarco 2003, 7).

Choosing "away" Ethiopia

The differences in expectation voiced by the adult adoptee and the adult who was left behind are not easily reconcilable. Adoption policies that encourage poor and marginalized populations to give their children away, laws that mandate a clean break between the adoptee and his or her past, and receiving nations that situate adoptees outside "natural" belongings— neither immigrants nor native-born—locate the adopted in what Tobias Hübinette, who was adopted from South Korea as a child and raised in Sweden, describes as a "third space" created by the conditions of European colonialism (2004, 23, citing Bhabha 1994).

Occupying this uncharted space means different things for different people. Mattias Kollberg was adopted as an infant from Colombia (his account of growing up in Sweden appears in chapter 6). When Mattias returned in 2002, he experienced the connection to Colombia and the mother, siblings, and maternal kin he discovered there as no different from that of other emigrants to family left behind. They live in Agua Blanca, a vast, very poor area of Cali known for crime and drug trafficking. Mattias began sending money back to his family in Agua Blanca after he returned to Sweden. In an account that recalls Jaclyn Aronson's explanation of why she is supporting her birth mother in Korea ("She's by herself and the whole thing in Korea is, your family is everything, they take care of you, and they make sacrifices. She doesn't have any family over there, we're the end of the line"), Mattias explained:

> It isn't because I feel some kind of obligation out of gratitude, or that I have a bad conscience. It is more that I know they are poor and I feel that this is my family. It isn't any different than a rich Swede who works in the United States and sends money home to his family in Sweden. I also feel that it is mostly for my brothers. One of them will be getting out of school next year, and has high ambitions. He wants to be a data programmer or data engineer. This could be a chance for him to have a better life. If I can help with that, then that is good, because it can help the rest of the family also, since they have such a strong collective bond.[16]

This young man commented that the staff of Adoption Centre were opposed to such remittances. They felt the funds sent would only go to drugs and would entangle him in commercial transactions that he would subsequently regret.

Daniel Rosenlind, who was adopted from Ethiopia when he was one year old, and whose account of his Swedish upbringing also appears in chapter 6, had the powerful feeling that he "must go to Ethiopia and learn as much as possible." As a result he traveled there in 1996 and again 1997, when he was in his late twenties, but the feeling seemed to abate when he returned to Sweden after his second trip. He had found no trace of his

birth family. The woman who was his girlfriend at the time, however, successfully searched for hers and he participated in that reunion, an event he describes as "incredibly powerful." That girlfriend subsequently moved to Ethiopia with her (white) Swedish partner and their two children. Today, Daniel lives in Stockholm with his partner, who was also adopted from Ethiopia, and their two children. He works as a family therapist and is writing a memoir about growing up adopted in Sweden.[17]

For Sara Nordin, several return trips to Ethiopia have transformed its "irritating presence" in her life. During one of our last interviews, when she was anticipating the birth of her first child, she explained, "It is a good thing, for now, with the situation I have. I can choose in a different way. I can choose 'away' Ethiopia (*jag kan välja bort Etiopien*) without feeling that I lose by doing so, even though I have friends there."[18] On her most recent trip, in January 2009, accompanied by her husband and two daughters, she described her relationship to that country as "still ambivalent":

> I have been received with such warmth and have made such fine contacts in the country, and hope I will be able to maintain them. It is really the people who make this country for me. They make it more real and more alive, and through them I have been able to approach some kind of everyday, which perhaps is a sign that you have come somewhat . . . closer to something. . . .[19] It has also contributed to my acquiring a taste for more (*att jag har fått mersmak*). But since it is a country with such enormous problems that affect the population in different ways, there are always shadows, and this means it is not a simple relationship.
>
> It has also meant a lot to share many of these experiences with my husband and now even our children. After having children it seemed important to try to present the country where I was born for them in a more or less graspable way, since it is a country that they too are a part of (*de har del av*). . . . And since their father is from Finland, we are also a part of (*har en del i*) that country and travel there fairly regularly. . . . It feels good that Ethiopia is no longer so strange for me, even though there is still a lot that I neither understand nor know about it.[20]

For Sofia Berzelius, who lives in Stockholm with her partner and three children, her positioning between Sweden and Ethiopia no longer seems as impossible as it did after her first trip there in 2000. Following that trip, she returned to Sweden just before Christmas feeling deep ambivalence:

I just didn't know where I belonged. All the existential questions at once, all of them. It is two such different worlds and the idea that this life in Ethiopia carries on when I am not there. In this very moment they are still there and they are still walking there and they are still breathing that air and they are still eating that delicious food and they are still starving. And I go back there and I just—oh, I mean, of course when you come back here you appreciate things so much, I mean drinking tap water, what a crazy thing to do, it is so luxurious and so wonderful, and just taking a shower with so much water, and cleaning your clothes, all those things. . . . I have everything here, so why am I not completely happy? It's confusing. The first maybe two or three months I just wanted to be back. I just wanted to go back. I just wanted to leave, pack my suitcase and go back. Then later, I just felt like, "I belong nowhere."[21]

On my last visit to Stockholm in May 2006, I visited Sofia just after the birth of her first child, a daughter. As we sat in her comfortable apartment sipping raspberry soda and eating pastries from the shop on the first floor, her daughter slept, closely wrapped in a swaddling cloth that Sofia had wound carefully around her own body. She described her most recent trip to Addis Ababa, together with her partner, a few months before her baby was born. She went again to visit the hospital where her mother had died giving birth to her, and she described her fear as she gave birth to her own baby in Stockholm, three months later, that she too might not survive, and her joy that her daughter was born and she was alive. Sofia talked about how important it had been for her to make the trip, in spite of her parents' reservations, while she was carrying her child. The given child (Sofia) and the kept child (then in Sofia's womb) were metaphorically joined in that moment. The presence of her Swedish partner also contributed to making this family, a process in which the historical connection of Sweden to Ethiopia is reenacted in Sofia's return and transformed in her giving birth to a Swedish-Ethiopian child. The name she chose for her daughter— Viktoria Abeba Berzelius (Viktoria: victory; Abeba: from "Addis Abeba," where "abeba" means "flower"; Berzelius, the surname of Sofia's adoptive parents)—joins past with present. It links Sweden to Ethiopia in ways that emphasize the complex history that joins the two nations, and it embodies this history in Sofia's adoption, her baby's birth, and her acknowledgment of the woman who died giving birth to her.

For Anna ChuChu, who met her birth parents in 1997 and made four journeys to Ethiopia in the following five years, the experience of living between Sweden and Ethiopia meant that (in 2002) "the actual adoption no longer exists for me. It happened 25 years ago and what is it now? Now it's a constellation of two mothers and that is what I try to relate to." Chu-Chu continues to visit Ethiopia regularly, most recently (in spring 2008) together with her husband and their two-year-old daughter, Judit. After her marriage in Stockholm in 2005, she celebrated another wedding in Addis Ababa, with her birth mother, her birth father, and a large gathering of Ethiopian kin. In a brightly colored photo accompanying a recent e-mail, she is standing between her birth parents, their arms circling one another.

Amanda Fredriksson explains that for her, learning to relate to both countries and the constellation of kin that took shape around her

> has been a process. Now it has settled itself and I can relate myself to Ethiopia and to Sweden in a better way. Before it was either/or and I couldn't even say it for a while, that I was Swedish. I thought it was really hard. But when we were last in Ethiopia, it felt as though "Of course I am Swedish. I am very Swedish." I don't like everything in Ethiopia. There are lots of things that one gets completely frustrated and angry over. And I can even feel that I am glad I grew up here, in some ways. . . . Now I feel much more in the way it is—that I am Swedish and I am Ethiopian also, although in a different way.[22]

Contributing to the "settling" of the relationship of these women to Sweden and Ethiopia is what Amanda describes as the sense that "I can have Ethiopia here (in Stockholm), not as 'Ethiopia,' but I no longer have to feel that 'Ethiopia' exists only in Ethiopia." When she was growing up, by contrast, there was "nothing" of Ethiopia in Sweden.

AMANDA: When one comes here, one is a little lonely in this whole situation, but there—it is a little hard to put words to it—there is so much surrounding one, and so many things happening. To be adopted or to have been abandoned, it's no big thing there. But here in our society it's huge.

SARA: Friends and contacts we have there, there are many who live in big families, there are cousins and neighbors and many of them are not related by blood. So they say: "Jaha, that one there is also my brother, though not my real brother." But here, people are really careful about: "And who are you like, and who is yours?"—so that one is reminded the whole time that one actually is not biological. There, one has people, even if one isn't family, one is like them. But here, one is like very few.

AMANDA: Even if one feels one is very different there [in Ethiopia], in one way I felt safer, more relaxed. It's nothing, no one cares if I am black.

The relationship of these adoptees to Ethiopia is "not uncomplicated," Amanda noted, since it is inseparable from the fact that "of course I am

Swedish." The struggle to come to terms with this reality—and of whether the "Swedish" has been changed by the transnational adoptee—is a recurrent theme in interviews with adults whose sense of being "Swedish" is always constituted vis-à-vis a known or imagined Korean, Colombian, or Ethiopian "past"—a birth mother or father, "brothers" and "sisters" with whom they once lived in a children's home in Bogota, Addis, Pusan, or Santiago—and a present in Sweden where they are living their lives. As Mikael Jarnlo, who sat on the AC board for several years, observes, "Sweden is changing. Sweden has changed tremendously in the last 20, 25, 30 years that have passed since we were adopted, for the better from an adoption perspective, I think. So those who are adopted today have it much better." ChuChu Petersson adds: "But when we see the children—when I was in Addis the first time and one sees children who are on their way to Sweden, it's with mixed feelings, such incredibly mixed feelings, that one sees that child. Actually, one thinks, 'Oh, how sweet!' And then the adoptive parents are there. On the other hand, 'But, my God, is this little person going to be exposed to . . .' And they know nothing. And they are about to set off on their way."

Epilogue

When we went for the first time with our sons Dag and Finn to Bolinas, the small coastal town in California where Finn spent his first few months of life, Finn was five years old. His birth mother, Diana, had arranged for us to stay in a local bed-and-breakfast for two nights, and after settling in, we joined Diana and Shao, Finn's birth father, at The Shop, the restaurant where Shao worked waiting tables. Diana had left us gift packages at the B&B with special soaps, shampoos, and body lotion. Shao treated us to lunch. They had last seen Finn when he was four months old. I have pictures on my desk today from that weekend—Diana on the beach with Finn, examining a shell; Finn buried in the sand, with only his face showing; Dag, Finn, Shao, Diana's daughter Angela, and I, gathered around a picnic table.

On that first evening, we assembled at Shao's place for a barbecue. There were fifteen of us—siblings, "half" siblings, parents, birth parents, adoptive parents, stepparents—marking what became the first of several reunions, always in California, until Finn was in his midteens. At one point in what had been an intense, emotionally draining, but exhilarating day, the older children (mostly teenagers, including Dag, then fifteen, Shao's daughters Breath and Asia, and Diana's daughters DeeDee and Angela) stretched out on a blanket as the sky darkened above us, while Asia made up a list of the four mothers, three fathers, and nine children who together comprised our extended family.

Since that day twenty-two years ago, I (and to a lesser extent, Finn) have maintained fairly regular mail (and later e-mail) contact with his birth family, supplemented by occasional visits, mostly involving our traveling to California as Finn was growing up. His sister Asia came to visit us in Massachusetts when Finn was in Japan in 2005, and I spent some time in Seattle with Diana a few years ago, when she was caring for her father shortly before his death. The heady sense I had when Finn was a child that Diana and I were transgressing some invisible boundary that divided "real" from "unreal" mothers settled down as Finn grew older and as open adoption became a more familiar way of building families (Mundy 2007). But I also came to realize that this "invisible" boundary was no less powerful for its seeming porosity and that although Diana and I had been able to develop a relationship based on each recognizing the significance of the other in Finn's life, Finn's relationship to her and to his birth family was more complicated. Indeed, my sense today is that the relative ease with which I have been able to maintain my relationship to Diana is inseparable from Finn's unquestioning acceptance of the place that Sigfrid, Dag, and I have in his life.

After our last visit to Bolinas, in 1996, when Finn was fifteen and he and I went alone, it became clear that these visits, which had begun with such promise, were becoming increasingly fraught experiences for him. Much as I would have liked to believe I could mediate the emotionally and culturally complex relationship of adoptive to birth parent and of birth parent to adopted child, I realized that Finn's relationship to his birth family was *his* relationship. I could encourage or discourage such a connection, but it was not really my place to do so, especially as Finn grew older. Grasping this apparently straightforward truth might seem self-evident. But in my own experience—and to judge from my interviews with adoptive parents and adopted adults over the past decade and a half—it is not. It is a dimension of the advice that Swedish social worker Ingrid Stjerna gives to adoptive parents (chapter 5), that the adopted child must be "given his own life." Sara Nordin (chapter 6) phrases the idea somewhat differently, cautioning the parents of transnational adoptees in Sweden to remember, however much they may be committed to making their child their own, "I didn't give birth to this child, but the child had a history already and must have its history the whole time, without my attempting to transform this into our history. It is the child's and that is fine, it is something positive, not something tragic."

To allow the child its own history and not attempt to transform it into our history means respecting the difference of the child without insisting on the child's difference, and it means acknowledging our connection to our child without insisting on the child's sameness. This dynamic of sameness and difference goes on in any parent-child relationship, but it is complicated in adoptive families by social and economic circumstances that typically divide birth parent from adoptive parent and birth parent from adopted child in ways that are difficult, if not impossible, to transcend. It is further complicated by cultural assumptions in adopting nations about the potency of "blood," creating the expectation that birth parent and child are "like" one another in fundamental ways that adoptive parent and child

can only approximate.

Legal technologies that create a "clean break" between birth and adoptive families, while constituting the adoptive family "as if" it were the only family of the child, impose a truncated history on the parents and children involved in adoptive kinship. Such truncated histories are most fully represented in U.S. adoption law, where secrecy in the form of sealed records and altered birth certificates officially eradicates the birth family and constitutes the adoptive mother as the birth mother of her adopted child. Efforts to unseal adoption records and thus to recognize the multiple origins of adopted children have made inroads in some U.S. states over the past decade. But the gradual introduction of "strong" or "plenary" adoptions (adoptions that give the adopted child the same rights, including inheritance rights, as a legally acknowledged "natural" child, and that cancel all legal entitlements between birth parent and adopted child) in other Anglo-European nations over the course of the twentieth century have institutionalized the de facto erasure of the birth family in these nations, as well. With the approval (in 1993) and subsequent ratification of the Hague Convention on Intercountry Adoption by most sending and receiving nations (the United States was the seventy-fifth of the signatories to ratify the Convention in 2007), plenary adoptions have also come to be accepted as the norm in a transnational arena, although the Hague Convention mandates the preservation of records documenting the adopted child's parental, ethnic, and national identity, if such records are available.

Even as the legal erasure of the birth family has facilitated the making of adoptive families, while avoiding potentially complex ties to persons and places whose nonexistence made the "abandoned" child "free" for adoption (Yngvesson 2002, 2004), activism by domestic and increasingly, in the twenty-first century, by transnational adoptees underscores the ways that repressed histories have a way of returning to trouble adoptive families and nations. For transnational adoptees, many of whom are identified or have come to self-identify as ethnically or racially different from their adopting parents, the "as if" dimension of their relationship to the adoptive family and the adopting nation has had a particular potency. It emerges most notably in questions, as they are growing up, about where they are "from," whether they know or have met their birth parents, and whether they have ever been "back." Such questions work in tension with official representations of the adoptive family as the only family of the child and are especially complex in the context of a "back" that both does and does not exist. The questions may incite adoptees, their adoptive families, and sometimes their birth families toward risky, tentative, but compelling efforts to discover or recover this "back," efforts that serve to reveal the instabilities of "home," its dependence on the journeys required in an adopted world for its realization.

The transformative potential of return lies in the temporary (and inevitably fragile) identifications it enables in the spaces of "nonidentity" that open up between the adopted child and the child who was left behind—a child who "might have been me" but for the chance occurrence that placed him or her with a family in Sweden, Italy, or the United States—or between adoptive mother and birth mother. These moments of nonidentity introduce the "cutting edge" of negativity—a negativity that occurs "in the borderline of a past that did exist and a past that was not allowed to exist" (Santos 1999, 43)—"into the very interior" of adoptive identity (Kristeva 1986, 210). While these moments are unsettling, adoptees (and occasionally their mothers) are continually pulled back into them, motivated by the strange familiarity of the other child or the other mother and by the desire for a stable ground of belonging in a world where a coherent identity is just out of reach. This process is powerfully apparent in the narratives of Jaclyn Aronson and her mother (chapter 7), but it is also a central theme in the stories recounted by other adopted children and adults in chapters 5 and 7, as well as in my own recounting of our returns with Finn to visit his birth family.

As these stories suggest, entering a space of nonidentity and the double vision it produces can be excruciating, sometimes unbearable. It interrupts the myth that the legal transformation to an "other" was free—that the child simply came home to a site of love where he or she always belonged—revealing instead the cost of belonging (and of love), its inseparability from the birth mother, the orphanage, the courthouse, the agency, and from the histories linking nations that give children in adoption to those that receive them. What emerges in the openings these moments provide is both within us and outside us, simultaneously disruptive and confirming. It moves us away from familiar trajectories but provides no models. The subjects who take shape in narratives of return are not simply given in the biological connection of mother to child or made as a "code for conduct" in the legal family. Rather, they are discovered and reworked in journeys "back" and in entanglements that inevitably result in the need for one more journey.

I will travel home. I will travel home in both directions.
—Lovisa Sammarco

Appendix

Tables

TABLE 1. Countries sending the most children for transnational adoption, 1980–2007 (listed in descending order of number of children sent)

1980–89	1998	2003	2006	2007
Korea	China	China	China	China
India	Russia	Russia	Russia	Russia
Colombia	Vietnam	Guatemala	Guatemala	Guatemala
Brazil	Korea	Korea	Ethiopia	Ethiopia
Sri Lanka	Colombia	Ukraine	Korea	Vietnam
Chile	India	Colombia	Colombia	Colombia
Philippines	Guatemala	India	Vietnam	Ukraine
Guatemala	Romania	Haiti	Haiti	Korea
Peru	Brazil	Bulgaria	Ukraine	India
El Salvador	Ethiopia	Vietnam	**India**	Kazakhstan

Source: Selman n.d., table 7.

TABLE 2. Transnational adoption to selected receiving countries, 1980–2007, by rank in 2004 (peak year in bold)

Country[a]	1980–89 (average)	1993–97 (average)	1998	2001	2003	2004	2006	2007
USA	7,761	10,070	15,774	19,237	21,616	**22,884**	20,679	19,613
Spain	19	784	1,487	3,428	3,951	**5,541**	4.472	3,648
France	1,850	3,216	3,777	3,094	3,995	**4,079**	3,977	3,162
Italy	1,006	2,047	2,233	1,797	2,772	3,402	3,188	**3,420**
Canada	109	1,934	**2,222**	1,874	2,180	1,955	1,535	1,713
Subtotal for 5 top States	10,745	18,051	25,493	29,430	34,514	37,861	33,851	31,556
Netherlands	1,153	640	825	1,122	1,154	**1,307**	816	778
Sweden	**1,579**	906	928	1,044	1,046	1,109	879	800
Norway	464	531	643	713	**714**	706	448	426
Denmark	582	510	624	**631**	523	528	447	429
Australia	356	247	245	289	278	370	**421**	405
Total[a] (max 23)	16, 268 (14)	22,799 (14)	31,710 (21)	36,379 (23)	41,530 (23)	45,288 (23)	39,742 (22)	37,526 (23)
% to top 5	66	79	80	81	83	84	85	84
% to USA	48	44	50	53	52	51	52	52

Sources: Selman n.d., table 1; 2008, table 1.

[a] 12 other countries are included in the overall totals for 1998–2007. Averages for 1980–89 and 1993–97 are based on 14 countries reviewed by Kane (1993).

TABLE 3. Adoptions from Ethiopia, 1998–2006

Country[a]	1998	2002	2003	2004	2005	2002–5% increase	2006	Agencies[b]
USA	96	105	135	289	441	320	732	22
France	155	209	217	390	397	90	408	7
Spain	0	12	107	220	227	1,792	304	9
Italy	9	112	47	193	211	88	227	7
Belgium	46	41	52	62	112	173	88	3
Netherlands	18	25	39	72	72	188	48	2
Australia	37	36	39	45	59	64	70	1
Sweden	24	18	21	26	37	106	32	1
Norway	46	44	46	47	36	–18	27	1
Denmark	29	20	40	41	30	50	38	1
Total[c]	481	695	854	1,553	1,740	150	2,128	50+

Source: Selman 2008, table 17; 2007.

[a] Countries are listed by descending number of children received in 2005.

[b] The number of agencies licensed by the Ministry of Justice in 2007.

[c] Totals include other countries that received children from Ethiopia in this period, e.g., Austria, Finland, Ireland, Malta, Switzerland.

TABLE 4. Contribution of three key sending countries to 2004–7 decline in number of adoptions and counterinfluence of three countries sending more children; peak year in bold

Country	2004	2005	2007	Total Change 2004–7	% Change 2004–7
Total sent to 23 receiving countries	45,288	43,857	37,526	−7,762	−17
Countries sending fewer children					
China	13,048	**14,493**	8,757	−4,291	−33(−40)[a]
Russia	**9,425**	7,471	4,873	−4,552	−48
Korea	**2,258**	2,101	1,208	−1,050	−47
Total for 3 countries	24,371	24,065	14,838	−9,533	−39
Countries sending more children[b]					
Guatemala	3,424	3,857	**4,847**	+1,423	+42
Ethiopia	1,527	1,713	**3,031**	+1,504	+98
Vietnam	483	1,190	**1,692**	+1,209	+250
Total for 3 countries	5,434	6,760	9,570	+4,136	+76

Source: Selman n.d., table 5.

[a] Figure in parentheses is decline from 2005, when number of adoptions peaked.

[b] In FY 2008 the number of adoptions from Guatemala to the United States fell by 12% and those from Vietnam by 9%, but adoptions from Ethiopia rose by 37%.

TABLE 5. Crude transnational adoption rates (per 100,000 population), selected years, 1980–2007; highest rate for each year in bold

Country	1980	1985	1990	1998	2001	2004	2006	2007
Sweden	**22.7**	**18.8**	11.2	10.5	11.8	12.3	9.7	8.8
Norway	9.6	12.4	**11.9**	**14.6**	**15.9**	**15.4**	9.6	**9.1**
Spain	n/a	n/a	n/a	3.8	8.6	13.0	**10.2**	8.2
USA	2.2	4.1	2.8	5.8	7.6	7.8	6.8	6.4

Sources: Selman 1999, 238 (table 6); 2008, table 6.

TABLE 6. Arrivals of non-Nordic adoptive children (0–10 years) in Sweden, 1969–2008

Year of arrival	Africa	Asia	Europe	North & South America	Australia & Oceania[a]	Total	Cumulative total
1969	7	323	604	94	3	1,031	1,031
1970	31	497	527	93	2	1,150	2,181
1971	64	741	439	124	1	1,369	3,550
1972	66	860	296	135	7	1,364	4,914
1973	85	981	100	140	8[b]	1,314	6,228
1974	81	1,103	67	188	4[b]	1,443	7,671
1975	132	1,065	81	234	5[c]	1,517	9,188
1976	128	1,209	39	406	9[d]	1,791	10,979
1977	14	1,360	53	437	—	1,864	12,843
1978	8	1,075	62	474	6	1,625	14,468
1979	6	824	43	508	1	1,382	15,850
1980	18	1,085	48	551	1	1,703	17,553
1981	21	1,210	49	509	—	1,789	19,342
1982	13	1,020	32	409	—	1,474	20,816
1983	28	1,137	47	439	—	1,651	22,467
1984	30	973	63	427	—	1,493	23,960
1985	32	961	49	516	2	1,560	25,520
1986	30	1,000	68	444	—	1,542	27,062
1987	28	809	115	403	—	1,355	28,417
1988	41	597	76	361	—	1,075	29,492
1989	40	413	104	326	—	883	30,375
1990	60	371	174	360	—	965	31,340
1991	46	463	247	355	2	1,113	32,453
1992	54	478	201	382	—	1,115	33,568
1993	42	411	172	308	1	934	34,502
1994	32	466	207	253	1	959	35,461
1995	49	425	186	235	—	895	36,356
1996	44	451	220	192	1	908	37,264
1997	52	404	221	156	1	834	38,098
1998	52	535	208	133	—	928	39,026
1999	38	594	235	152	—	1,019	40,045
2000	33	559	248	140	1	981	41 026
2001	111	561	212	159	1	1,044	42,070
2002	100	634	228	144	1	1,107	43 177
2003	112	615	209	109	1	1,046	44,223
2004	95	740	179	95	—	1,109	45,332
2005	129	773	110	71	—	1,083	46,415
2006	121	579	103	74	2	879	47,294

Continued

TABLE 6. *continued*

Year of arrival	Africa	Asia	Europe	North & South America	Australia & Oceania[a]	Total	Cumulative total
2007	128	548	72	51	1	800	48,094
2008	178	479	77	58	1[b]	793	48,887
Total	2,379	29,329	6,471	10,645	63	48,887	

Source: Swedish Intercountry Adoptions Authority, www.mia.eu.
[a] Children whose birth location was unknown were included in this category.
[b] Birth location unknown.
[c] Three of the five were in the "unknown" category.
[d] Eight of the nine were in the "unknown" category.

TABLE 7. Arrivals in Sweden of non-Nordic adoptive children (0–10 years), by age, 1981–2008

Year of arrival	0–1 yr.		2–3 yrs.		4–5 yrs.		6 yrs. or older		Total
	No.	%	No.	%	No.	%	No.	%	
1981	1,209	67.6	333	18.6	112	6.3	135	7.5	1,789
1985	1,037	66.5	348	22.3	113	7.2	62	4.0	1,560
1990	573	59.4	200	20.7	87	9.0	105	10.9	965
1993	536	57.4	213	22.8	83	8.9	102	10.9	934
1994	560	58.4	225	23.5	101	10.5	73	7.6	959
1995	493	55.1	236	26.4	87	9.7	79	8.8	895
1996	547	60.2	203	22.4	80	8.8	78	8.6	908
1997	460	55.2	215	25.8	72	8.6	87	10.4	834
1998	611	65.8	164	17.7	71	7.6	83	8.9	929
1999	650	63.8	211	20.7	74	7.3	84	8.2	1,019
2000	619	63.1	228	23.2	65	6.6	69	7.0	981
2001	665	63.7	218	20.9	72	6.9	89	8.5	1,044
2002	762	68.8	183	16.5	84	7.6	78	7.0	1,107
2003	694	66.3	217	20.7	50	4.8	85	8.1	1,046
2004	727	65.6	250	22.5	64	5.8	68	6.1	1,109
2005	675	62.3	262	24.2	44	4.1	102	9.4	1,083
2006	543	61.8	197	22.4	46	5.2	93	10.6	879
2007	378	47.3	264	33.0	57	7.1	101	12.6	800
2008	388	48.9	191	24.1	73	9.2	141	17.8	793

Source: Swedish Intercountry Adoptions Authority, www.mia.eu.

TABLE 8. Arrivals of non-Nordic adoptive children in Sweden in 2002, by source continent, age, and sex

	America		Asia		Europe		Africa			
	No.	%	No.	%	No.	%	No.	%	Total	%
Age										
0–1 yr.	121	84	512	81	64	28	65	65	762	69
2–3 yrs.	12	8	79	12	88	39	4	4	183	17
4–5 yrs.	6	4	24	4	48	21	6	6	84	8
6 yrs. or older	5	3	20	3	28	12	25	25	78	7
Sex										
M	74	51.4	181	28.5	149	65.3	57	57.0	461	42.0
F	70	48.6	454	71.5	79	34.7	43	43.0	646	58.0
Total	144		635		228		100		1,107	

Source: Swedish Intercountry Adoptions Authority, www.mia.eu.

TABLE 9. Arrivals of non-Nordic adoptive children in Sweden in 2008, by source continent, age, and sex

	South & North America		Asia & Oceania		Europe		Africa			
	No.	%	No.	%	No.	%	No.	%	Total	%
Age										
0–1 yr.	40	69	274	57	14	18	59	34	388	49
2–3 yrs.	8	14	135	28	26	34	22	13	191	24
4–5 yrs.	5	9	38	8	11	14	19	11	73	9
6 yrs. or older	5	9	36	7	25	33	75	43	141	18
Sex										
M	29	50	214	44	53	70	85	49	382	48
F	29	50	269	56	23	30	90	51	411	52
Total	58		483		76		175		793[a]	

Source: Swedish Intercountry Adoptions Authority, www.mia.eu.
[a] This total includes 1 one-year-old boy whose country of origin is unknown.

Notes

Prologue

1. By "patriarchy," I mean a set of practices and assumptions, traceable at least to patriarchalism in the 17th century, that position women and children in the context of their relation to men and that deny them legitimacy (in both private and public life) unless they are officially connected to a man as wife or child. Patriarchalism extends beyond the family to include "a whole body of practices and expectations, over the whole of living" (to draw on Raymond Williams' (1977, 110) familiar definition of hegemony). As Linda Gordon (1988, 256) notes, however, patriarchy is expressed not as absolute right but as "custom and bargaining." As this implies, patriarchy is not ubiquitous and should not be reified as an unchangeable moral/legal code. Its hegemony is always incomplete, its manifestations are sometimes subtle and almost always appear in tension with competing practices and ideologies, and its dominance at any one point in time may give way to other forms (see also Shanley 1982; Grossberg 1985, 26; Fineman 1995; Hartog 2000).
2. Stjerna made this statement in an address to visiting Russian adoption co-workers at a meeting organized by the Swedish adoption organization Adoption Centre, in Stockholm, August 21, 1996.

Chapter 1

1. I was reminded of such blind spots as I listened to an interview conducted by Terry Gross on NPR's *Fresh Air* on February 3, 2009, with the singer Antony, whose new CD (*The Crying Light*, Antony and the Johnsons) had just been released. Antony, who is transgender, described his research at New York University into forty years of queer performance; his powerful experience as he engaged with those materials was that *this* was his narrative (Hegarty 2009).
2. All translations from non-English sources are my own unless indicated otherwise.
3. See Schneider 1968, 23–29, for a discussion of the order of nature and the order of law in American kinship. And see Collier, Rosaldo, and Yanagisako's discussion (1982, 33) of "The Family" as "a 'moral' unit, a way of organizing and thinking about human relationships in a world in which the domestic is perceived to be in opposition to a politics shaped outside the home, and individuals find themselves dependent on a set of relatively noncontingent ties in order to survive the dictates of an impersonal market and external political order."

4. David Schneider (1968, 39) makes a similar point, noting that "the child brings to-gether and unifies in one person the different biogenetic substances of both parents. The child thus affirms the oneness or unity of blood with each of his parents; this is a substantive affirmation of the unity of the child with each of his parents and with his siblings of those parents."

5. See Yngvesson and Coutin 2008 on the retroactive instantiation of meaning in law, and, more generally, Žižek's discussion (1989, 100–102) of the effect of retroversion.

6. For an elaboration of this theme, see Yngvesson (1997, 67–71); and Cussins's discus-sion (1998, 45) of the ways an egg recipient in an in-vitro fertilization with donor egg procedure explains her likeness to the egg donor. Orenstein's discussion (2007) of the use of donated eggs by prospective parents describes the search for a donor in which "it felt *familial*" (she notes that it involves "the grueling [and expensive] task of finding a stranger who feels like family" [2007, 38, emphasis in original]).

7. See Katherine O'Donovan's insightful discussion (2002, 373) of the power of discourse in England, France, and Germany, three nations with distinct legal approaches to the meaning of motherhood, to constitute a "real" mother as a mother who has given birth and to define the act of giving up a birth child as "unnatural for a 'real' mother."

8. My research, which began in 1995, was funded by two grants from the National Sci-ence Foundation (numbers SES-9113894 and SBR-9511937) and by faculty develop-ment grants from Hampshire College. Encompassing the period from the early 1960s to the present, it was focused initially on the transactions of individual parents and eventually of agency staff with orphanages and children's homes, and it involved ethnographic fieldwork in Sweden, India, Colombia, Ecuador, and Bolivia. With a base in Stockholm's Adoption Centre (AC), I conducted archival research on adop-tion and child welfare policy in Sweden; interviewed staff in charge of adoptions from different regions of the world; attended conferences and workshops with AC staff and local adoption professionals in La Paz (1995), Bangalore (1995), Quito (1996), New Delhi (1996), and Hong Kong (1996), as well as in Sweden; and accompanied AC representatives on trips to visit institutional children's homes in Asia and Latin America. I also interviewed children's home directors, social workers, legal profes-sionals, and others in sending nations who were involved in arranging for the place-ment of children in adoption overseas.

During a second phase, extending roughly from 1999 to 2006, I attended events and meetings organized by adopted adults in Sweden, read memoirs and watched videos or documentaries written or made by them or in which they were the sub-jects, and conducted interviews with twenty-four adopted young adults and adults between the ages of sixteen and thirty-six who were born in Ethiopia, Chile, Colom-bia, India, and Korea. In addition, two interviews were conducted with an adopted adult (one together with her adoptive mother) who was born in Korea and raised in the United States. All of the interviews were open-ended conversations that focused on experiences of growing up adopted in Sweden (or the United States) or on return-ing to visit a birth country or birth family, or on both types of experiences. Some interviews were carried out once with one person alone. Others involved conversa-tions with two, three, or four adopted adults together. A few were conducted with adopted teenagers or adults together with their adoptive parent or parents. A series

of interviews between 1999 and 2006 involved adopted adults born in Ethiopia who
had returned up to four times to visit their birth country or birth family. I also accompanied a group of twelve Swedish families with children adopted in Chile on a
two-week "roots trip" organized by AC. On that trip, I acted as interpreter at a meeting of an adoptee, her adopted mother, and her birth mother. Following the trip, I
conducted follow-up interviews in Sweden with the parents and the children and
with staff at AC who organized the trip.

9. See Bohman (n.d.) on orphanages, the foster-care industry, and baby-farming in
Sweden from the eighteenth to the early twentieth century.

10. Delegates to the conference included representatives from all of the most important "sending" and "receiving" nations in transnational adoption at the time (a total
of sixty-seven nations were represented). While members of the Hague Conference
on Private International Law consisted at the time primarily of Western developed
(adopting) nations, plus a handful of non-Western (sending) nations, special invi-
tations were extended to nonmember sending nations. The Republic of Korea, the
world's principal sending nation at the time, initially declined to participate but
joined as an invitee to the Seventeenth Session, at which the Convention was unani-
mously approved by delegations at the conference (Carlson 1994, 246). The full text of
the Hague Convention is available at www.hcch.net/index_en.php?act=conventions
.text&cid=69.

11. Hague Convention 1993, articles 26, 30. Note, however, that the Convention recognized that sending nations might have different perspectives on terminating birth
parent ties (articles 26c, 27).

12. Katherine O'Donovan (2002, 351–356) provides a helpful discussion of the history of
articles 7 and 8 of the UNCRC, which she suggests "were developed to deal with the
problems of children caught up in political struggles and armed conflict, and with
refugees" (351). At the same time, O'Donovan notes that the articles "may be read
more broadly to cover various aspects of identity" (351) and that "nowhere does the
Child Convention define 'identity,' leaving a wide margin for interpretation in domestic law" (353). She makes the important point that nations governed by a shared
international convention (e.g., the UNCRC or the 1993 Hague Convention) may nonetheless provide different accountings of the meanings of identity and of children's
rights to "know" their identity.

13. Grossberg (1985, 270–273), describing the rapid proliferation of adoption laws in the
United States in the mid-nineteenth century, cites Witmer et al. 1963 and Ben-Orr
1976 as key sources on the Massachusetts Act and other adoption statutes.

14. See Lawrence Hampton's overview (1989) of the effect of nonrelative adoptions on
inheritance rights in the United States and his conclusion that "the 'for all purposes'
language that permeates adoption legislation often stops short of a complete substitution. In-family adoptions, stepparent adoptions and adult adoptions may be
subject to separate rules which only partially intersect the rules governing nonrelative adoptions" (chap. 12, p. 92).

15. The expression in Swedish is "kan inte mer hävas" or "cannot be undone" (Agell and
Saldeen 1991, 80). Agell and Saldeen note an exception to this rule, in that "*an earlier
adoption can be replaced by another*, e.g. through the biological parents readopting the
child that has already been adopted by others" (80).

16. Matching according to ethnic origins, culture, language, and religion is recommended but not required by adoption policy in the United Kingdom, as well (www .adoptionpolicy.org/eu.html; eu-England.pdf).

17. Vinnerljung, Hjern, and Lindblad (2006, 729) note that "long-term foster care before adolescence constitutes the strongest and the longest-lasting child welfare intervention in Sweden, providing a child with a substitute home for the better part of the formative years." By contrast, "national adoption does not exist as a child welfare intervention in Sweden" (724).

18. The Colombian case involved a child who was abducted together with his mother and abandoned in another town after the mother was killed. When efforts by the Colombian child welfare authority to locate birth kin of the abandoned child failed, the child was placed in adoption with a Swedish family. The maternal grandparents, after discovering that the child had survived, went to court in Colombia to challenge Colombia's sealed-record policy and were eventually successful in locating the child's adoptive family and establishing contact with them, over the strong objections of Adoption Centre and the Swedish national adoption authority.

19. Adult adoptees wanting access to identifying information about their parents have succeeded in changing some U.S. state laws. By 2005 Alabama, Alaska, Delaware, Kansas, Oregon, and Tennessee permitted access to birth certificates upon request by an adult adoptee. In addition, numerous states have registries that allow access to confidential adoption records upon mutual consent of the birth parent and the adoptee, while others release identifying information upon mutual consent without registries (Hollinger 1993, 50–54). For a careful historical analysis of the shift from confidentiality to secrecy to openness in U.S. adoption policy, see Carp 1998, 102–137.

20. Howell (2006, 9) notes that "adoption is a practice that challenges those kinship ideologies that base themselves upon the constituting value of biological connectedness." Howell is less attentive, however, to the ways that adoption calls for those very ideologies (see discussion above at 13–15, 23).

21. The stratification of reproduction is most apparent in transnational adoption. But it is also documented in Swedish and British research into the risks for children of entry into (foster) care. In both countries, according to a recent study by Franzén, Vinnerljung, and Hjern, "having a single, a low-educated and an unemployed mother were all separately related to children having higher odds of entering care. . . . There is marked continuity when we compare our results for the younger children with historical findings on child welfare in the twentieth century. *One of the main components of child welfare is still the removal of children from poor, single women*" (2008, 1055).

22. See Coutin, Maurer, and Yngvesson (2002, 820–822) for a discussion of "laundering" adoptees and its resemblance to money laundering.

23. According to an online overview of Swedish adoption law, in 2000 there were 113 adoption cases involving children born in Sweden (Center for Adoption Policy, www .adoptionpolicy.org/eu.html; www.adoptionpolicy.org/pdf/eu-sweden.pdf).

24. Statistics on unrelated domestic adoptions in the United States are hard to come by (by contrast with the ease of obtaining statistical information online about international adoption). According to the Evan B. Donaldson Adoption Institute, unrelated domestic adoptions fell from the 1970 figure of 89,200 to 47,700 by 1975, and since that time no collective figures on unrelated domestic adoptions have been assembled

(www.adoptioninstitute.org/FactOverview/domestic.html). Several Web sites are devoted to challenging the "myth" that there are no infants available for adoption in the United States and provide figures regarding the number of infants adopted. For example, the Adoptive Families site, www.adoptivefamilies.com/domestic _adoption.php, estimates that 25,000–30,000 infants are adopted annually by non-relatives in the United States.

25. There is an extensive literature on open adoption, ranging from academic research (Modell 1994; Yngvesson 1997; Grotevant and McRoy 1998; Brodzinsky 2005; Grotevant, Perry, and McRoy 2005), to narrative accounts by journalists (Caplan 1990; Mundy 2007; Winerip 2008), to memoirs (Waldron 1995), to "how to" books by adoption professionals (Rappaport 1992; Melina and Roszia 1993).

26. See especially Peter Wade's discussion (2007a, 8) of "kinship as vital to grasping race because a key aspect of the discourse of race is ideas about inheritances, whether 'natural' or 'cultural,' for which a key medium of transmission is the family." He claims that "assignations to a given racial category or identity are ultimately grounded on reckonings of kinship, even if these are so obvious as to be tacit—i.e., in the case of a person who seems unproblematically 'black' or 'white,' the unspoken assumption is that his/her parents are likewise black or white."

27. Richard Carlson (1994, 256n47) notes that "an undetermined number of children are sent from the U.S. to other countries for adoption each year" and adds that one estimate sets the number at "'a few hundred' every year" (citing Special Commission on Intercountry Adoption 1991). While Carlson does not provide details, his comment is confirmed by verbal reports at a conference on transnational adoption hosted by Holt International in 1996. A conference participant from the Netherlands noted that some three hundred African American children were sent annually to the Netherlands and other northern European nations in adoption. According to demographer Peter Selman, although there is no data on adoptions out of the United States by ethnicity, all adoptions out between 2003 and 2007 ranged from 130 to 185 per year, mainly to Canada, the Netherlands, and the United Kingdom (Selman, personal communication, April 21, 2009).

28. See Gordon 1999 for a penetrating analysis of the ways race took shape in the "orphan incident" along the Mexico-Arizona border in the early twentieth century. Arguably, the effort to place forty Irish "orphans" with Mexican Catholic families in an Arizona mining camp constitutes an early (heatedly contested and ultimately failed) version of what is known today as transnational transracial adoption. See Hübinette 2006, 141, for a discussion of this incident as comparable to current transnational adoption practice.

29. For a careful consideration of what is at stake in this issue, see Roberts 2002, 147–172; and Fogg-Davis 2002. For a statement of NABSW policy on preservation of African American families, see www.nabsw.org/mserver/PreservingFamilies.aspx.

30. See Strong 2001 for a discussion of the complex historical, political, and cultural issues surrounding the adoption of Native American children by white families. There are parallels between the history of forced incorporation of Native American children in the early twentieth century and the adoption of these same children later in that century, on the one hand, and widespread criticism of the forced incorporation and elimination of Aboriginal populations (known as the Stolen Generation) in

Australia through intermarriage, adoption, and other forms of absorption, on the other (Human Rights and Equal Opportunity Commission 1997).

31. Ben Campbell (2007, 114–115) provides an insightful discussion of related processes of regularization in the domain of gamete matching as practiced in Spain, Norway, and the United Kingdom. Campbell notes differences between the ways ethnic boundaries are produced in kin constructivism (where reproductive technologies are deployed in ways that "naturalize" kinship by replicating parental physical characteristics) and the "constructive reinvention" of persons at the national level in the "posteugenic" nation. I suggest that transnational transracial adoption both operates as "constructive reinvention" of persons at the national level *and* naturalizes "origins" at the level of individual identity. Also see Foucault's discussion of racialization as "establishing a biological-type caesura within a population that appears to be a biological domain" (Foucault 2003, 255).

32. See David Theo Goldberg's analysis of the "liberal paradox" of modernity: that as "modernity commits itself progressively to idealized principles of liberty, equality and fraternity . . . there is a multiplication of racial identities and the sets of exclusions they prompt and rationalize, enable and sustain" (1993, quoted in Stoler 1995, 37n51).

33. Following Foucault, Steedman's use of "historicity" here refers to nineteenth-century Europeans' experience of themselves as "emptied" of history and as recovering this history "in the depths of [their] own being" (Foucault 1970, 369). Steedman suggests that "the self *within* . . . [was] created by the laying down and accretion of our own childhood experiences, our own history, in a place inside" (1995, 12).

34. Christine Gailey makes a related point in her discussion of the adoption of Korean infants in the 1950s by members of the U.S. armed forces as "a laboratory for assimilationist beliefs in the redemptive qualities of capitalist culture. These children were going to become 'real' American Asians, because they would be reared by 'real,' that is, middle class, conservative and patriotic (i.e. military), white Americans" (1999, 60).

35. For a discussion of these issues, see Pilotti 1993; Selman 2002; and more generally, the examination of stratified reproduction and the global production of gendered inequality in Ginsburg and Rapp 1995b.

36. See Selman 2002, 222; 2005a, 17–20. The figure for total Korean adoptions in 1958–2007 comes from combining material in Selman 2005b, 25; and Selman n.d., table 4. For more detailed information on Korean transnational adoptions over time, see Hübinette 2006; E. Kim 2005; and J. R. Kim 2006, 155.

37. Per capita gross income in South Korea in 1997 was $10,550 USD; in 2003 it was $12,030 USD, extraordinary figures in comparison to those of other major sending nations. South Korea's fertility rate in 1998 was 1.7; in 2003, it was 1.4, a lower rate than that in many of the nations to which Korea sends children in adoption (Selman 2005a, table 9).

38. Foucault (2003, 245) describes biopolitics as a technology of power that concerns "the population as a political problem, as a problem that is at once scientific and political." In Foucault's analysis, biopolitics is inseparable from processes that racialize a population, creating "breaks" or "caesuras" that determine who is allowed to live and who is made to die (both physically and politically speaking) (247–256). See also discussion in chapter 2, note 32.

39. The literature on China's one-child policy and on transnational adoptions from China is theoretically and empirically rich. It includes Susan Greenhalgh's research (1994, 2003) on China's population control policy; Ann Anagnost's analysis (1995, 2004) of the "corporeal politics of quality" in China; and research focused more specifically on adoptions from (and in) China by Kay Ann Johnson (2002, 2004, 2005); Johnson, Banghan, and Liyao (1998); Anagnost (2000); Toby Volkman (2005b); and Sara Dorow (2006).

40. For recent U.S. figures on adoptions from China, see statistics on immigrant visas issued to orphans coming to the United States, at www.travel.state.gov/family/adoption/stats/stats_451.html.

41. Kyazze is referring to Angelina Jolie's adoption of a baby girl from Ethiopia in 2005 and Madonna's adoption of a boy from Malawi in 2006.

42. A recent CBC-Radio Canada investigation, "Learning the Truth," aired on March 20, 2009, presents interviews with several adoptive parents of Ethiopian "orphans" who discovered from their children that they had living parents in Ethiopia (www.cbc.ca/national/blog/video/internationalus/learning_the_truth.html).

43. The quote is from an interview with the celebrated Icelandic artist Olafur Eliasson in a profile featured in the *New Yorker* (Zarin 2006, 78).

44. The name "Kunta Kinte" is taken from the main character of Alex Haley's novel *Roots* and is intended by Wallensteen to be emblematic of a stereotyped representation of an African immigrant.

45. See the discussion by Brooks et al. (2005, 12) of psychological issues related to identification and "double consciousness" that are particularly complex for transnational transracial adoptees.

46. See Carsten 2001 and Weston 2001 for a nuanced discussion of what "blood" "*does*" in American culture, and specifically the links between blood and race in American culture.

47. See, for example, Stuart Hall's observation about the importance of the tension implied in Derrida's notion of "the trace of something which still retains its roots in one meaning while it is, as it were, moving to another, encapsulating another" (1997, 50).

48. See Povinelli 2002 for a discussion of the global circulation of a genealogical grid and its colonization of social and geographical space.

49. The phrase "safehouse of identity" was used by Anna Deavere Smith in her address at Smith College upon receipt of an honorary doctorate in 2003.

50. See also Elizabeth Grosz's discussion (1995, 131, citing Massumi 1993a, 27–31) of boundaries as "only produced and set in the process of passage. Boundaries do not so much define the routes of passage: it is movement that defines and constitutes boundaries." And see Balibar 1991; Gupta and Ferguson 1997a; Coutin, Maurer, and Yngvesson 2002; and Coutin 2005 for discussions of related issues.

Chapter 2

1. Pilotti, in an analysis of trends in intercountry adoption between 1979 and 1991 that focuses on Sweden and the United States, lists India as the principal sending nation for Sweden during those years, with a total of 3,867 children adopted; Colombia was

next, with 2,995 children adopted; Korea was a close third (2,863). For U.S. adoptions in the same period, Korea was by far the largest sending nation, with 51,062 children placed; Colombia was second, with 8,127 children adopted; India, with 6,225 children adopted by U.S. parents, was third (Pilotti 1993, 176–177). For Swedish adoption statistics, see www.mia.eu. See table 1, appendix, for variations in sending nations over the period 1980–2007.

2. Table 5, appendix. Sweden's adoption rate (adoptions per 100,000 population) peaked in 1980 at 22.7, equivalent to a rise of 0.2 in the birthrate. The adoption rate in the United States at that time was only 3.3, in spite of the large numbers of children involved. The adoption ratio in Sweden in number of transnational adoptions per 1,000 live births was 17.4 in 1978 (Selman 2002, 212). Sweden's adoption rate remains high: at 12.3 in 2004, 9.7 in 2006, and 8.8 in 2007, it ranked either second or third among adopting nations. See Selman 2002, 211–212, for a discussion of problems of standardization in measuring transnational adoptions.

3. Emphasis added. The interviews in this chapter took place in the mid-to-late 1990s: Gunilla Andersson, May 26, 1997, and August 21, 1999 (with Maria Brunn), both in Stockholm; Anne-Charlotte Gudmundsson, November 11, 1995, Bangalore, India; Margareta Blomqvist, August 6, 1995, Stockholm; Rama Ananth, November 10, 1995, Bangalore; Nomita Chandy, November 11, 1995, and October 4, 1997, Bangalore; Nina Nayak, November 13, 1995, Bangalore; Andal Damodaran, November 6, 1995, Chennai, India.

4. See Anagnost 2000, 407: "The substitutability of the infant constitutes a violation of the bond between mother and child, suggesting that the mother will not 'know' her own child. *But for her a substitute can never be merely an abstract equivalent of the infant she has already bonded with. In such moments, the shadow of the commodity once again lurks over the child and is refused*" (emphasis added).

5. The quotations here are from Slavoj Žižek's discussion (1989, 18) of the sublime object that is produced during the act of exchange, when "individuals proceed *as if* the commodity is not submitted to physical, material exchanges; *as if* it is excluded from the natural cycle of generation and corruption"; and from Carolyn Steedman's discussion (1995, 5) of the difference between "the ideational and figurative force" of a child as "true thing," on the one hand, and "real children, living in the time and space of particular societies," on the other. See also pp. 28–29.

6. I am grateful to Nina Payne for this perceptive observation about the value of th child.

7. See Jean-Luc Nancy's discussion (1993, 44–45) of abandonment as "abandonment to respect of the law," a respect that is "in the first place, a look back (*re-spicere*): turned toward the *before* of abandonment, where there is nothing to see, which is not to be seen. It is not a regard for the invisible, it is not an ideal or ideational regard. It is the *consideration* of abandonment."

8. Campbell (2007) discusses related issues as they affect Norway, the U.K., and Spain. He notes that more generally, "a common conundrum faces all European welfare states," where "significant numbers of people who lie territorially within, but are legally and economically marginal, challenge the idea of the nation as a set of primordial ties of collectivity prior to, or beyond, social contract. In this context, multi-

cultural 'integration' can be seen as a 'choice of rhetoric designed explicitly to rescue the nation-state'" (115, citing Favell 2003, 37).

9. In 1969 alone, the year when Sweden's National Board for Intercountry Adoptions (NIA) began official record-keeping, 1,031 children were admitted to the country so they could be adopted, more than a fourfold increase over all adoptions during the earlier sixteen-year period.

10. This Swedish-Korean agreement, in turn, was made possible by the passage in Korea, in 1961, of the Law of Special Application for Adoption of Orphans. See discussion in chapter 1, p. 30. There is a growing literature on the phenomenon of Korean transnational adoptions. See generally Hübinette 2004; E. Kim 2005, 2007; and Trenka, Oparah, and Shin 2006.

11. Figures are from *Adoption av utländska barn* (1967, 22–23). Between 1969 and 2008, 8,725 South Korean children were adopted by Swedish parents (*Adoption—till vilket pris?* 2003, 108; MIA Web site at www.mia.eu).

12. Adoption of children from within the Nordic Union (Sweden, Norway, Denmark, Finland, and Iceland) was treated in the same way as a domestic Swedish adoption, beginning with a 1931 agreement among the five Nordic Union nations (*Adoptionsfrågor* 1989, 174). Adoptions from outside the Nordic Union were regarded as "foreign adoptions" and treated differently, beginning in 1971 (51, citing Swedish statute SFS 1971:796 om internationella rättsförhållande rörande adoption [on international judicial processes relating to adoption]). The term "non-Nordic children" is used in *Internationella adoptionsfrågor* 1994, 10.

13. The term *neger* (Negro) was used at various points in the 1967 report in discussion of adoptees of African descent. It was also used by Ethiopian and Colombian-born adoptees with whom I conducted interviews in the 1990s and early 2000s to describe derogatory terms used by others (for example in school) to refer to them as they were growing up. At the time of my research, a popular round black candy sold in Sweden was still referred to as a *negerboll* (literally, Negro ball).

14. A plenary adoption is one in which all ties to the preadoptive family of the child are cut off. See discussion in chapter 1, p. 22.

15. See Hanna Markusson Winkvist's discussion (2006) of tensions between the state-appointed commission's sense of responsibility toward children in need of care, on the one hand, and the commission's willingness to set aside the concerns of sending nations regarding the well-being of children placed in adoption in other nations, on the other. I am grateful for Winkvist's willingness to share her paper with me.

16. For a discussion of Swedish population policy in the 1930s, see Hatje 1974; Kälvemark 1980; Hirdman 1989; Carlson 1990; and Freiburg 1993. See Grönwall, Holgersson, and Nasenius 1991, 31–35, for a discussion of the emergence of a welfare state in Sweden in the post-1930 period.

17. Births to unmarried parents in Sweden rose from 15 percent of all births in 1966 to 52 percent in 1989 (Agell and Saldeen 1991, 15). The Swedish Adoption Act of 1917 (and an accompanying law affecting the rights of illegitimate children) made adoption of Swedish children possible and began a long-needed reform process to improve the care of abandoned and neglected children. After passage of the Adoption Act and until the middle of the 1960s, approximately 50,000 Swedish children were adopted

by unrelated parents (a rate approximately equivalent to 1 adopted child for every 100 children born). After 1960, domestic Swedish adoptions "where the mother or both parents chose to have a new-born child adopted" by strangers have been rare (Åkerman and Lindblad 1995, 213). See also discussion in chapter 1, pp. 21–23; 188n17.

18. Francisco Pilotti (1993, 169), in a widely cited early analysis of issues and policy in transnational adoption, notes that "trends exhibited by these two countries [Sweden and the United States] are indicative of broader, global tendencies, since Sweden and the US are often considered 'pioneer' countries where intercountry adoption on a large scale, originated several decades ago."

19. While U.S. ratification took place in December 2007, the treaty was not fully put into place in the United States until April 2008 (Gross 2007, A25). See discussion of the Hague Convention in chapter 1.

20. See table 5, appendix; and note 2 above.

21. See discussion above, pp. 19–20; 187n12.

22. See the discussion of the Hague Convention in chapter 1 and the discussion of efforts to regulate transnational adoption in chapter 3.

23. See Howell's discussion (2006, 9–11) of the role of the "psy" professions in contributing to policies that promote the importance of a family environment as a response to the abandonment of children. Howell draws on the discourse of "governmentality" deployed by Foucauldian theorists in her critique of the psy professions. But her descriptions of the ways Norwegian adoptive families "transubstantiate" foreign-born children into members of Norwegian society by "kinning" them seems to pull back from a consideration of "kinning" and "transubstantiation" as dimensions of governmentality. Likewise, Howell's critique of the role of the psy professions in provoking adoptees to return to their birth nations in search of information about "roots" stops short of an examination of the complex forces (including efforts to transubstantiate the adoptee) provoking such journeys and their potential consequences for the adoptee and the adoptive family (130). Such an examination might illuminate the broader implications of kinning, as a strategy deployed not only by adoptive parents but by adoptees who may seek to "kin" the potential immigrant (the birth parent or sibling) who was left behind with the child's adoption and is denied access to belonging in Norway.

24. See United Nations 1989, article 8; and Hague Convention 1993, preamble.

25. See especially Etienne Balibar's discussion (1991, 101–102) of this issue, which includes these comments:

> The modern family circle is quite the opposite of an autonomous sphere at the frontiers of which the structures of the state would halt. It is the sphere in which the relations between individuals are immediately charged with a "civic" function and made possible by constant state assistance. . . . Thus, as lineal kinship, solidarity between the generations and the economic functions of the extended family dissolve, what takes their place is neither a natural micro-society nor a purely "individualistic" contractual relation, but a nationalization of the family, which has as its counterpart the identification of the national community with a symbolic kinship, circumscribed by the rules of pseudo-endogamy, and with a tendency not so much to project itself

into a sense of having common antecedents as a feeling of having common descendants. . . . That is why the idea of eugenics is always latent in the reciprocal relation between the "bourgeois" family and a society which takes the nation form.

26. Also see Peter Wade's discussion (2007b, 15) of Marre's research (2007) on the relationship of transnational adoption to Spanish immigration practices. Referring to Spanish benevolence regarding the incorporation of nonwhite babies (as versus nonwhite immigrants), Wade notes: "It is tempting to interpret this benevolence as being motivated by the desire to achieve a multicultural nation, with all the apparent difficulties and conflicts that multicultural immigration involves seemingly conveniently defused by the work of benign family relations that retain apparently only superficial racialized difference, while creating culturalized citizens." See chapter 4 of the present volume for an analysis of the complications that accompany a similar policy in Sweden.

27. See note 3 for the dates of several interviews, which are the sources of numerous quotations in the final sections of the chapter.

28. The UN Declaration (United Nations 1986) includes several articles relevant to transnational adoption, including preference for in-country rather than intercountry foster care or adoption (article 17), prohibition of "improper financial gain" (article 20), the importance of establishing that the child is "legally free" for adoption (article 22), and the importance of giving "due regard . . . to the child's cultural and religious background and interests" in intercountry placements (article 24).

29. I am indebted to Solveig Johansson for details on the founding of SICW.

30. Adoptions from India to Sweden remained at or above 245 children a year from 1975 to 1988, after which there was a relatively steady decline that lasted through the 1990s. Annual adoptions from India to Sweden from 2000 to 2008 have ranged from a low of 37 in 2003 to a high of 75 in 2001. Adoptions from India to the United States had risen to 807 in 1987 but fell off by the end of the decade. Between 1993 and 2008, adoptions from India to the United States ranged from a low of 307 in 2008 to a high of 543 in 2001 (see www.mia.cu for Swedish statistics and www.travel.state.gov/family/adoption/stats/stats_451.html for U.S statistics).

31. Veena Das (1995) provides an insightful discussion of related processes of inclusion and exclusion of women and children during the violence accompanying partition in the new nation-states of India and Pakistan in 1947. Recovery of women "came to be defined as a state responsibility, [and] the identity of women was firmly fixed as either Muslim or Hindu" (229). At that time, when children were not yet considered strategic resources for the state, "'undesirable' children concerned the state only as they impinged upon the identity of the women" (231).

32. See Foucault's discussion (2003, 243) of biopower as an "anatomo-politics of the human body" or a "'biopolitics' of the human race" (the population as a political problem), in which such things as birthrate, mortality rate, longevity, and associated economic and political problems become objects of knowledge in the second half of the eighteenth century. This biopower establishes the right of sovereignty to "make" live and "let" die (241). Also see Rajeswari Sunder Rajan's discussion (2003, 194) of female infanticide regulation in India as a technology of rule, in the Foucaul-

dian sense. Transnational adoption is likewise a dimension of biopolitics, in which certain categories of children are privileged as belonging (or not belonging) to the national body (e.g., as entitled to a family in India or in Sweden) and certain adults are entitled to become parents and raise children, while others are discouraged or prohibited from doing so. See Fonseca 2002 for an insightful discussion of the ways that state policy labeling certain households as "disorganized" (400) contributes to this dynamic and the alternative measures engaged in by residents of a Brazilian favela that allow poor families to care for their children.

33. Sunder Rajan's analysis is based on an insightful interpretation of the process by which a Muslim child bride, Ameena, came to be hailed as "Indian" after widespread media coverage of her sale by her parents to a sixty-year-old Saudi Arabian national in 1991.

34. Opposition to transnational adoption and efforts to bring it to a halt have shadowed the practice almost from the beginning. In chapter 3, I discuss a lawsuit brought to the Indian Supreme Court in 1981 by opponents. More recently, the state of Andra Pradesh in India became the focus of a baby-selling scandal in which activists led by Gita Ramaswamy brought a lawsuit and successfully shut down transnational adoptions from that state for a period of months (chapter 3). In the 1990s, as adoptions from nations that had been part of the former Soviet Union soared, repeated efforts were made to stop them; these attempts occurred notably in Georgia, where foreign adoption was described by Nanuli Shevardnadze as depleting the nation's gene pool (Stanley 1997, 1). During the Olympic Games held in Seoul in 1988, opponents to transnational adoption from South Korea made public the extent of their nation's involvement in placing children in other nations, leading to a commitment by the Korean government to decrease the number of annual adoptions and eventually to phase out the practice.

Chapter 3

1. Gunilla Andersson, interview by author, May 26, 1997, Stockholm.

2. For an example of such a reunification, see Yngvesson 2004, 211–212.

3. *Lakshmi Kant Pandey v. Union of India* 1985, 15. The only adoption law in India at the time of the judgment (and the only one today) was the same one that existed when the first foreign adoptions took place in the 1960s, the Hindu Adoption Act of 1956. This act was framed so as to facilitate adoptions "among known people" (Damodaran, interview by author, November 6, 1995) but did not allow for adoption by non-Hindus.

4. Aloma Lobo, personal communication, October 1, 2005.

5. A recent *New York Times* article discussing caste discrimination in India notes that "across the caste ladder, fair complexion is still preferred over dark" (Sengupta 2008, A7).

6. My interview with Nomita Chandy was carried out at Ashraya Children's Home in Bangalore, India, on October 4, 1997. Chandy repeated this observation to me on other occasions, most recently at a conference on transnational adoption in Amherst, Massachusetts, in 2002. MIA (*Myndighet för Internationella Adoptionsfrågor*, the Swedish Intercountry Adoption Authority) reports that between 1981 and 2008, the

percentage of children age six and over adopted transnationally by Swedish parents ranged from 4.0 percent in 1985 (the lowest) to 17.8 percent in 2008 (table 7, appendix). The average percentage of children age six and over adopted in the years 1993–2006 is 8.58, with small variations around this figure. As table 7 indicates, adoptions of children age six and over increased between 2006 and 2008. In 2007 adopted children in this age group rose to 12.6 percent, while in 2008, when Sweden had its lowest number of transnational adoptions since official record-keeping began in 1969, 17.8 percent of adopted children were age six and over. There is a significant variation in the age distribution of transnational adoptions in Sweden by source continent, but with an overall shift upward in age, as indicated in tables 8 and 9 (appendix). Online figures on age distribution are available for 2002–2008 only at www.mia.eu.

7. Although in this case the parents appear to have had no doubts about this choice, in other cases such decisions can be wrenching. During an interview in March 1996 with a representative for Holt International Children's Services, in Quito, Ecuador, the representative burst into tears shortly after we began speaking. She apologized, explaining that she had just come from a meeting between American parents and the severely disabled child they had come to Ecuador to adopt. After months of planning for this adoption, during which time the parents (who had previously adopted disabled children) were fully informed of the child's condition, they found once they met the child that they could not proceed with the adoption. She acknowledged both how difficult the decision had been for them and how complicated it would be to find other parents for the child.

8. Lamellar ichthyosis is a rare inherited skin condition of the newborn in which scaly, plate like layers of skin are shed. The disease continues throughout life and, while not life-threatening, is quite disfiguring, causing considerable psychological stress to affected patients (www.emedicine.com/DERM/topic190.htm).

9. Aloma Lobo, personal communication, October 1, 2005.

10. This "sense," of course, derives from a creative reading of both Marx on use and exchange value (1971, 1973) and Simmel on the philosophy of money (1978). Simmel, in particular, notes the capacity of money to "set people and things into motion," in this way both enabling their acquisition of "uniqueness" or "distinction" and jeopardizing it. "Distinction represents a quite unique combination of senses of differences *that are based upon and yet reject any comparison at all*" (390, emphasis added). See also Appadurai's discussion of commodities and the politics of value (1986). As Kopytoff suggests, in state societies, the process of stopping (or starting) the work of commodification is typically "the handwork of the state," which may either prevent or authorize the commodification of certain things. Indeed, "power often asserts itself symbolically precisely by insisting on its right to singularize an object or a set or class of objects" (1986, 73).

11. As Callon, Méadel, and Raberharisoa argue, "the notion of quality has the advantage of closely binding [intrinsic and extrinsic] meanings and of including the classical question in both economics and economic sociology of the hierarchy of comparable goods (as when one talks of the quality of a service or second-hand car). Talking of quality means raising the question of the controversial processes of qualification, processes through which qualities are attributed, stabilized, objectified and arranged" (2002, 199).

12. The Hague Convention is less explicit than the Indian Supreme Court decision about measures for securing domestic adoption or other alternatives to adoption overseas, but it mandates that "each State should take, as a matter of priority, appropriate measures to enable the child to remain in the care of his or her family of origin" (preamble) and that intercountry adoption is acceptable only if "competent authorities of the State of origin have determined, after possibilities for placement of the child within the State of origin have been given due consideration, that an intercountry adoption is in the child's best interests" (article 4). See the discussion of the Hague Convention on pp. 18–20 above.

13. See, for example, Marilyn Strathern's discussion (1988) of "commodity thinking" and its assumption that persons and things have "properties" that "belong" to them in a definitional sense, constituting them as unitary social entities ("individuals") (104). In commodity thinking, persons "'are' what they 'have' or 'do.' Any interference with this one-to-one relationship is regarded as the intrusion of an 'other'" (158). See also Lisa Cartwright's discussion (2003, 91–92) of the marketing of Russian children at "Precious in His Sight," a Web-based, non-password-protected site "that allows users to sort children by age, gender, and 'country.'"

14. The terminology here is that of the Colombian AC co-worker with whom I spoke in 1996 and 1997.

15. While I was unable to confirm the report that Colombian children's homes avoided placement of children of African origin in the United States, a young American couple I met at Pension Stein, a hotel frequented by foreign couples waiting for adoptions from Cali to be approved, provided corroborating evidence. The couple described the concern of their social worker at a well-known New York–based adoption agency, when they expressed interest in a child of African origin from Colombia, and the social worker's ambivalence about the fact that the father of the light-skinned baby who was ultimately placed with them was possibly black (the implication being that the child might ultimately "become" black). The wife told me how upsetting it was to discover when she arrived in Colombia that European adoptive parents (including two Swedish couples) who were staying in the same hotel all had dark-skinned babies, while their own adoption had been restricted to a "white" child.

16. Internal memo, February 18, 1980, emphasis in original.

17. The quotes in this sentence are from Marilyn Strathern (1992, 178–179 and 181).

18. See, for example, Viviana Zelizer's discussion (1985, 14) of the complex relationship of children's economic and sentimental value in the late nineteenth and early twentieth centuries in the United States: "How could value be assigned if price were absent?" Likewise, Zelizer notes that a shift toward an exclusively emotional valuation of children "had a profoundly paradoxical and poignant consequence: the increasing monetization and commercialization of children's lives" (15).

19. The Hague Convention, which was drafted as a consequence of concerns about child trafficking in the context of transnational adoptive placements, prohibits any form of payment in exchange for the relinquishment of a child. The preamble to the Convention states that one of its goals is "to prevent the abduction, the sale of, or traffic in children" and article 1 reiterates this phrase. The same issue—prevention of "improper or other financial gain," pursuit solely of "non-profit objectives,"

and prohibition of payments other than those for allowable costs, expenses, and services—is a recurrent theme throughout the document (Hague Convention 1993, preamble, articles 1, 4, 11, 32). See discussion of the Hague Convention in chapter 1, pp. 18–20. See chapter 2, note 28, for a brief discussion of the UN Declaration on Social and Legal Principles Relating to the Protection and Welfare of Children, with Special Reference to Foster Placement and Adoption, Nationally and Internationally (United Nations 1986).

20. See Yngvesson 2002 for a discussion of a contested Colombian adoption in Sweden; and see *Dokument Inifrån* 2002.

21. See Pilotti 1993, 171, for a discussion of children as "at risk" for intercountry adoption. And see discussion of "paper" or manufactured orphans in Graff 2008.

22. As an example of the symbolic importance with which "giving" is viewed in the adoption industry and of the strategies for implementing "cleanness" in adoption, I provide the following instance from a prominent children's home in Colombia that supplies children to the United States, Sweden, and several other European nations. At the time when I was visiting Colombian orphanages in the late 1990s in conjunction with my research, officials at some institutions began expressing concern about the ways in which donations were being handled. At a time when U.S. per-child donations were estimated at $5,000 (exclusive of lawyer's fees) and Swedish per-child donations were set at $4,000 (inclusive of lawyers fees), at least one well-known home proposed annual, rather than per-child, donations from foreign agencies to avoid the appearance of impropriety. Impropriety is inevitably associated with what a *New York Times* article described as "piec[ing] together deals" for children (Mansnerus 1998, A14). The director of one of the best-known Colombian adoption homes, FANA, told a *Time* magazine reporter in 1991, her organization "is not a business; it's total devotion to children" (Serrill 1991, 46).

23. Similar arguments about the donation or sale of organs can be found in the literature on traffic in body parts (Scheper-Hughes n.d., 2008).

24. Nina Nayak, personal communication, September 1997.

25. Andal Damodaran, interview by author, Chennai, November 1995.

26. Monica Lind, "Notes from Workshop Adoptionscentrum-India Partners at Angsana Resort," Bangalore, March 26–29, 2006.

27. Reports of infanticide in the area appeared in the Indian media in 1986, and by the early 1990s empirical evidence derived from birth records in Primary Health Centres led to "the reasonably certain conclusion that the killing of female children at birth is a widespread practice in these regions" (Sunder Rajan 2003, 179).

28. Indian Council for Child Welfare–Tamil Nadu, Annual Report (1995–96, 10). Female infanticide has been a crime equivalent to murder in India since 1870, when the British colonial administration passed the Female Infanticide Act. But as Sunder Rajan (2003, 177) notes, the criminal status of the practice is in tension with its popular acceptance in certain areas of India. Acceptance is explained in the context of widespread preference for sons and an accompanying discrimination against girl children, the degree of which varies by region. "Neither the preference nor the discrimination is much camouflaged," however, and "the abhorrence of female children is intense enough to affect their chances and rates of survival" (177). An article in the *New York Times* (Gentleman 2006, A13) describes the jailing of a doctor in the north-

ern Indian state of Haryana for telling a woman the sex of her fetus and offering to abort it. Noting that a 1994 law in India "bars doctors from using ultrasound tests to determine the sex of a fetus," the article points out that "the law is widely flouted" in the context of "Indian cultural preference for sons [which] has distorted the sex ratio across the nation."

29. Officials at AC were so disturbed when the report was published that the director sent a letter to the membership suggesting that the curtailment of aid programs in sending countries would likely mark the beginning of the end of transnational adoptions in Sweden. This issue has shadowed the project of international adoption in Sweden from the outset. An article in *AC Rapport* in 1973 quoted AC treasurer Jan Nygren as saying that the aid-adoption connection should be viewed as a "purely ethical" matter. "We should not provide aid in such a way that it can be misunderstood, so people think we are helping in order to obtain children for adoption" (Biståndsverksamheten igång 1973, 17). Gunilla Andersson, in charge of Indian adoptions for AC, noted, however, that there was an "unavoidable connection" between aid projects and adoption, in that the latter often inspired the former (16). Madeleine Kats, the incoming president of AC in 1973, pointed out: "When one sees that help is needed, it is natural that one tries to help." She added, "In India, for example, they accept help quite naturally and would more likely respond negatively if we didn't provide it: 'You just want to have and have, but what about all the children who are left? Don't you care about them?'" (17).

30. See discussion in chapter 2.

31. O'Donovan's distinction (2002) between "maternity" and "motherhood" in French law and her discussion of the potential insights this may provide into Anglo-American biases regarding the biological bias that underpins assumptions about what makes a "mother" are helpful in gaining some purchase on this complex issue, at least in a Euro-American context. O'Donovan's discussion points to the importance of developing a more nuanced analysis that is not restricted to either condemning or idealizing the birth mother. See also Colen 1995 on stratified reproduction and discussion above, chapter 1.

32. The quote is from Maria Brunn, a woman who was adopted from India as an infant and returned when she was twelve years old to visit the orphanage from which her parents adopted her. See chapter 5.

Chapter 4

1. This interview was conducted in Swedish with AE and MA on August 30, 1996, in Gothenburg, Sweden. Translation by the author.

2. The quote is taken from the title of Betty Jean Lifton's children's book *Tell Me a Real Adoption Story* (1993).

3. NIA n.d., 21–22, freely translated.

4. See Viviana Zelizer 1985 on the circumstances (including adoption) in which a sentimentalized discourse of childhood took shape in late-nineteenth- and early-twentieth-century America; and see Carolyn Steedman 1995 on changing attitudes toward childhood in Europe between 1780 and 1930 and the connection of these attitudes to social and cultural understandings of the self. Sharon Stephens (1995b)

takes up related issues in her discussion of the tensions and contradictions that mark modern notions of childhood and that influence perceptions of the "needs" of Third World children as expressed in documents such as the 1989 UN Convention on the Rights of the Child. See also chapter 1 for a discussion of these issues.

5. I am indebted here to Diana Fuss's discussion (1995, 141–172) of Fanon.

6. Quotes are from Nordin 1999, 13. The issue of potential problems in moving children adopted from Ethiopia to Sweden in the 1960s was explicitly raised as a concern by Ethiopian officials and the Ethiopian Women's Welfare Association, when questioned by the members of a Swedish commission charged with investigating Ethiopian attitudes toward intercountry adoption (see chapter 2 and *Adoption av utländska barn* 1967, 49–50).

7. Between 1969 and 2008, a total of 1,091 children from Ethiopia were adopted by Swedish parents (calculation based on figures from NIA 1996; also see the MIA [formerly NIA] Web site at www.mia.eu). Adoptions from Ethiopia to Euro-American nations increased significantly between 2001 and 2007 (complete figures for 2008 were not available when this book went to press); the increase was related to a dramatic rise in the number of children orphaned as a result of drought and HIV/AIDS, as well as to decreases in adoptions from major sending nations, such as Korea, Russia, and China. See tables 3 and 4 (appendix) and discussion in chapter 1.

8. My interviews with Margareta Blomqvist took place on August 16, 1995, and on May 27, 1997, in Stockholm. The interview with the adopted adult (AP) who comments on Blomqvist's attitude toward Ethiopian adoptees took place on August 22, 1999, also in Stockholm.

9. Quoted in Kats 1984b, 37–38; this is a reprinted 1982 article.

10. As a powerful testimony to the symbolic importance of this mission in the twenty-first century, the August 2003 issue of AC's magazine *Att Adoptera* (To adopt) featured a story about the twenty-thousandth child, named Adina, whose adoption was mediated by AC. A picture of Adina's face fills an entire page at the beginning of the article, which describes her arrival from Ethiopia in April 2003, when she was eight months old, accompanied by her parents, Sophie and Tore Kleist, who live just outside Stockholm (Adre-Isaksson 2003, 8–10).

11. Other authorized adoption organizations in Sweden include Adoptionsföreningen La Casa (organized in 1992), Barnen Framför Allt—Adoptioner (organized 1979), Barnens Vänner Internationell—adoptionsförmedling (organized 1979), Familjeföreningen för Internationell Adoption (organized 1980), and Stiftelsen Frösunda Solidaritet (organized 1998).

12. The most prominent of such scholars was David Schwartz, editor of the journal *Invandrare och Minoriteter* in the mid-1970s and author of several books on identity and minority issues. See Schwartz 1977, 1980; and see Regnér 1978; Abrahamsson 1978; and Andersson 1980.

13. Cederblad and colleagues (1994, 32–33) note the difference between European and U.S. literature in that the former avoids the term *racial* in describing adoptee identity, in favor of *ethnic*, which Cederblad and colleagues suggest is a "broader" concept that includes cultural belonging and interest in cultural origins, rather than "only appearance, language and ethnic group belonging." They suggest that the U.S. literature focuses more narrowly on whether a child has taken on "a black identity." Al-

though this is surely an accurate representation of literature on domestic transracial adoption in the United States in the mid-twentieth century, substitution of the term *ethnic* or *cultural* for the (discriminatory) term *racial* or *racism* where the adoptee of African or Asian provenance is concerned is arguably a mechanism for avoiding engagement (by professionals, by parents) with practices of racial discrimination that affect adopted children (see further development of this point in chapter 5).

14. Escobar's discussion here builds on the work of Ashis Nandy (1987). Sweden's centrality in promoting and practicing transnational adoption in the second half of the twentieth century was closely linked to its role in the modernization of nations in Africa (as the example of the Svedbergs suggested) and Asia, through SIDA (the Swedish Agency for International Development). Indeed, Swedish nationals involved with SIDA in Ethiopia and elsewhere in the Third World became some of the earliest international adopters, underscoring the inseparability of the relationship between importing experts and exporting resources of various kinds (some of which, like the adoptee, may provide unexpected returns, a topic to which I turn in chapter 7).

15. The term "familialist discourse" is used by Balibar (1991, 101), who is concerned with the penetration of family relations by the nation-state, both at the discursive (which he considers a "superficial" level) and at a deeper level, in which the emergence of "private life" coincides with the emergence of family policy of the state. This coincidence of the emergence of a "private" sphere with state family policy points to "a nationalization of the family, which has as its counterpart the identification of the national community with a symbolic kinship, circumscribed by rules of pseudo-endogamy, and with a tendency not so much to project itself into a sense of having common antecedents as a feeling of having common descendants" (101–102; see also Wade 2007b for a discussion of kinship and nationalism).

16 See Carolyn Steedman's discussion (1995, 5) of the child figure as representing "the core of an individual's psychic identity," as contained in "his or her lost past, or childhood"; and see discussion above, chapter 1.

17. See also Elizabeth Povinelli's discussion (2002, 230) of intimate love as simultaneously a way of describing sympathy with the intimate stirrings of an "other" *and* a lifting up of the dialectic of the intimate I and thou into nationalism, in the form of We-the-People: "Love of persons and love of country are the twin contracts of modernity" (233).

18. The "immigrant-ness" of the adopted child was underpinned, or at least reinforced, by the child's status, in many cases, as a citizen of his or her native land, by virtue of birth there. This issue remains a complex dimension of adopted identity, since adopted children were not granted automatic Swedish citizenship upon their adoption by Swedish parents until July 1, 1992. Double citizenship is now officially permitted by Swedish law, but as late as 1989 it was discouraged (*Adoptionsfrågor* 1989, 76), making the de facto double citizenship of children whose birth nations continued (and continue today) to recognize them as citizens (e.g., Ethiopia, Chile, Ecuador, Colombia, and India) a potentially tricky issue in terms of their official belonging in one nation or the other. The Hague Convention (1993) comments only on the permanent residence of the adopted child as shifting to the receiving state (articles 17 and 18).

19. Rojas (1995, 92), citing Proposition 1975:26, the state's proposition on guidelines for immigrant and minority policy.

20. And see Stuart Hall (1997, 55–56): "Nobody would talk about racism but they were perfectly prepared to have 'International Evenings,' when we would all come and cook our native dishes, sing our own native songs and appear in our own native costume. It is true that some people, some ethnic minorities in Britain, do have indigenous, very beautiful indigenous forms of dress. I didn't. I had to rummage in the dressing-up box to find mine. I have been de-racinated for four hundred years. The last thing I am going to do is to dress up in some native Jamaican costume and appear in the spectacle of multi-culturalism."

21. Caldwell (2006, 56) notes that "Swedes have begun to use a word—'segregation'—that they used to employ only when lecturing other countries."

22. And see Campbell's discussion (2007, 108) of shifts in the representation of "Norwegianness" from contrasts with other Scandinavian countries to "a white Europeanness in contrast to people of non-European descent" and its implications for "'an ethnically defined nationalism'" (quoting Gullestad 2004, 192).

23. Ann Anagnost (2000, 407) makes a similar point in her discussion of the construction of a Chinese "culture" by American adoptive parents for their adopted children; she notes that there is "a curious split . . . in which 'culture' or 'ethnicity' signifies an aestheticized difference, displacing race and class, which register as more unbridgeable frames of difference."

Chapter 5

1. Cederblad et al. (1994, 6) note that in the first half of the 1970s, reports in Sweden and other Nordic countries about how transnational adoptees were faring were generally positive. But as a large cohort of these children reached adolescence, "alarming reports" began to come in from teachers, school administrators, and child psychology clinics that "one saw many problems with adopted teenagers." In two Swedish studies in the mid-1980s and early 1990s, "foreign-born adopted children in their teens were overrepresented in [child psychiatry] patient materials compared with their representation in the surrounding population." The main reason for contact with psychiatric professionals was "asocial or acting-out behavior," and problems in relations with parents and others, as well as in school, were common.

2. A recent report by the Evan B. Donaldson Adoption Institute regarding the effects of a federal law in the United States that downplayed race and culture in domestic adoptions of minority children makes a similar point. The report "points out that transracial adoption itself does not produce psychological or other social problems in children, but that these children often face major challenges as the only person of color in an all-white environment, trying to cope with being different" (Nixon 2008, A15).

3. These quotations are from a manuscript by Kats, obtained from files at AC, Stockholm, and cited under conditions stated by the author as permissible; also see Kats 1990a, 15–16. There is an extensive literature on transnational adoption (most notably literature by psychologists) that focuses on developmental problems among

adopted children. For overviews, see Bohman and Sigvardsson 1990; Brodzinsky and Schechter 1990; Silverman and Feigelman 1990; Brodzinsky and Palácios 2005; Juffer 2005; Carey 2007; Juffer and Van IJzendoorn 2007; and Van IJzendoorn and Juffer 2006. While this research has been productive in stimulating debate about the existence and sources of developmental and social "disturbances" among transnationally adopted children, the fact that the transnationally (and transracially) adopted child has been subject to such extensive psychological scrutiny is arguably a reflection of (parental, professional, societal) attitudes that themselves create a "disturbance" for the adoptee. Also see Howell's discussion (2006, 88–93) of the "psy" professions and shifting psychological models for understanding issues of adoptee development.

4. See Hochsbergen and ter Laak 2005 for a discussion of shifting expectations among adoptive parents in different "generational" cohorts (pre-1970, 1971–81, 1982–92, and post-1993).

5. Lindqvist and Ohlén's film *En gång var jag korean: En dokumentär film för Sveriges Television* (2003) focused on the negative experiences of Korean-born adoptees in Sweden, and specifically on the suicide of one young adult. It was aired on Swedish public television.

6. See note 3.

7. In a later study, Hjern et al. cite research in Canada as indicating that racism may be a "causal mechanism" that explains the high risk of suicide among intercountry adoptees (2004, 414).

8. The study included control groups of 2,343 Swedish-born siblings of the transnational adoptees, 4,006 immigrant children, and a general population of 853,419 Swedish-born residents. In subsequent research comparing transnational adoptees to children in foster care, using a large national sample, Hjern and his colleagues note that the adoptees fare better on mental health indicators than do children in foster care (Vinnerljung, Hjern, and Lindblad 2006, 730).

9. In a recent review of the literature on risk and resilience among transnational adoptees, Michael Rutter (2005, 67) points to the evidence for "relatively good psychological outcome," even among higher-risk adoptees from deprived backgrounds. See also Juffer and Van IJzendoorn (2005), who report similar results based on an examination of adoption studies between 1950 and 2005 involving a total of 25,281 international and native adoptees. These authors, who compared international adoptees with children who had not been adopted as well as with native adoptees, concluded that international adoptees fared better than domestic adoptees.

10. See also Janet Carsten's discussion (2001, 32) of "the image of a baby born without feelings because it was never connected to maternal emotion, never received the effects of maternal cravings" (citing Edwards 1992).

11. See Christine Gailey's critique of "the myth that genetic connection makes attachment expected or even automatic" and of the related premise that adoptive mothers should "be held most accountable for their children's attachment or lack of bonding" (2000, 23).

12. The issue of the adoptee's difference and how to handle it has been a long-standing concern of adoption law (see discussion in chapter 1, pp. 21–26. Research by psychologists and other "psy" professionals has also tended to focus on this issue.

One of the most influential early works addressing difference in the adoptee and its implications for the adoptive family is David Kirk's *Shared Fate* (1964). Kirk (who focused primarily on domestic, same-race, adoptions) developed the concepts "rejection of differences" and "acknowledgment of differences" as frameworks for coming to grips with the ways adoptive parents and adopted children avoid or engage with the fact that the adopted child is not a biological child. As the work of Triseliotis and Russell (1984) suggests, this can be particularly problematic in invisible ("same race") adoptions (see Cederblad et al. 1994, 95).

13. And see Jessica Benjamin 1998, 79, for discussion of the place of the "not me" in identity formation.

14. See Yngvesson 2005 for a discussion of adoptive parents' encounters with the birth-place of their child.

15. Fuss's original sentence reads, "If psychoanalysis is right to claim that 'I is an Other,' then otherness constitutes the very entry into subjectivity; subjectivity names the detour through the Other that provides access to a fictive sense of self" (1995, 143).

16. Winnicott (1971, 110) defines "potential space" as "a third area of human living, one neither inside the individual nor outside in the world of shared reality."

17. Lisa Cartwright (2003, 96), with reference to the "special needs" classification of a child. And see Gunnar and Kertes's observation (2005, 63) that "stereotypes exist both in the professional adoption community and among adoptive parents regarding the impact of early adversity on children's development, and parents often have unrealistic beliefs (both positive and negative) regarding the possibilities of ameliorating the effects of early adversity." In a related analysis, Palacios and Sanchez-Sandoval (2005, 138), commenting on bias in adoption research, argue that "the more the investigation is based on a hypothesis of adoption as a mild psychopathological condition and the more clinically biased the sample and the measurement methods are, the more likely it is that the results will show deficiencies and clinical problems in adopted children."

18. Anagnost, whose research involved Internet postings by U.S. parents adopting children from China, is here describing parental responses to photographs received of the child they are scheduled to adopt: "One mother wrote that she could already imagine her child's ethnicity. . . . We see the workings of the imaginary dimensions of subjectivity in which the parent projects him or herself into the ego-ideal of the 'educative parent' who must replicate her or his class subjectivity in the child through modern regimes of child nurture. Yet here the project is expanded by the addition of the successful negotiation of ethnicity as one of the duties of the responsible parent, an added bonus on which parental worthiness can be evaluated and appraised" (2000, 406). Anagnost adds that "the problem of naming" involves both anxiety about anchoring the child's identity to its place of origin and marking its difference, or about "the violence of renaming as the erasure of a difference that will eventually reassert itself with a vengeance" (408). For a discussion of the issue of naming among adult adoptees, see chapter 7.

19. Femmie Juffer and her colleagues at the University of Leiden provide video-feedback sessions for adoptive parents, building on attachment theory and with the goal of developing a more secure parent-child relationship (Juffer 2005; Juffer, Bakermans-Kranenburg, and Van IJzendoorn 2005). The Center for Adoption Services in Utrecht

has made the video-feedback service available to all new adoptive families since 2000.

20. See Edward Said's discussion (1979, 54–55) of the relationship of identity to "imaginative geography."

21. Gunilla Andersson, interview by author, Stockholm, August 21, 1999.

22. For a discussion of the mutual process of making parent and child, see Erikson 1959, 59; Urwin 1984; Fonagy 2001, 57–62; and Mahoney and Yngvesson 1992, especially 52.

23. For a moving account of very different circumstances in which the history of an adopted child is imagined, see Kendall 2005, 162–181.

24. This interview was recorded in Stockholm on August 22, 1999, in Swedish and was translated by the author.

25. The second interview with Sara Nordin was recorded in Stockholm on August 25, 2002.

26. This interview was recorded in English in Stockholm on August 26, 2002. The name of the interviewee has been changed.

27. Anne Anlin Cheng (2001, 11), quoting Toni Morrison's words from *Playing in the Dark* (1992, 17), emphasis in original.

28. Triseliotis and Hill (1990, 116), citing Triseliotis 1973, argue that "a vital part in the jigsaw of identity formation is knowledge about one's background and forebears, including the history of one's family and by extension of one's race and ethnic group." Erik Erikson's definition of identity as a "sense of psychological well-being, *a feeling of being at home in one's body*, of knowing where one is going, of inner assuredness of anticipated recognition from those who count" (1968,165, emphasis added), is particularly relevant to the experience of transracially adopted children and adults. See also Cederblad et al. 1999; and Irhammar 1997.

29. Cederblad et al. (1994, 45) note that earlier Swedish studies described fear on the part of adoptive parents that to discuss their child's origin would make the child feel "different." In their own research, they note that parents were divided on whether they should downplay their child's "Asian/African" appearance or celebrate it (71) and that adoptees, in response to the question "Do you feel that you are mostly Swedish or mostly Asian, African, Latin American, etc. when you are in Sweden, in your country of birth, or abroad more generally," tended to identify themselves as Swedish, wherever they were (72). Moreover, they evidenced only a "weak" interest in their preadoptive origins (74). Three-quarters of the younger adoptees in their sample and two-thirds of the older group had not read their adoption records (66). While Cederblad et al. hint at the connection between adoptees' and their families' "weak" interest in origins and the public erasure of race as a topic of discussion in conjunction with Sweden's "immigrant problem," they tend to come at the topic obliquely, in discussions of adoptees' "appearance" or "foreign-bornness" (77).

30. See Callon, Méadel, and Rabeharisoa (2002) for a discussion of the concept of "good" as used here, and see my discussion in chapter 3.

Chapter 6

1. The flag is ubiquitous in Swedish life. It appears at all celebrations, is used (in miniature versions) to decorate Christmas trees, and is regularly displayed on public

buildings and in private homes. It is also commonly found on the price stickers of Swedish products such as glass, linen, and handicrafts, or on the bumper stickers of Volvos or Saabs (before the take-over of these companies by GM and Ford in the 1990s). The flag proclaims the uniquely "Swedish" character of these things.

2. This woman spoke with me in Stockholm on August 22, 1999. Our conversation was in Swedish; the translation is mine.

3. Interestingly, staff of Adoption Center expressed concern about the popularity of adoptees from Russia among new adoptive parents in the 1990s, considering this an indication of a shift both in the social class of the parents and in the ideals that they themselves had espoused—a multicultural society in Sweden—in the period between the early 1960s and the early 1990s.

4. My interviews of Sara Nordin and Daniel Rosenlind were conducted in Stockholm on August 22, 1999, in Swedish. The translation from Swedish to English is mine, and italicized sections indicate my added emphasis.

5. Greta Svedberg's role in placing Ethiopian children in Swedish homes is described in chapter 4.

6. See Nordin's more detailed discussion of this issue in chapter 5.

7. Emphasis in original. All foundlings from the Haile Selassie orphanage during this period were given the last name Haile Selassie.

8. "Nice and friendly" is the closest I can get to the Swedish phrase "*så här mysig,*" which implies some combination of friendly, nice, and comfortable.

9. This interview was conducted by me in Stockholm on May 11, 1999, in Swedish. The name of the interviewee has been changed. The translation from Swedish to English is mine. Italicized phrases indicate my added emphasis.

10. In Swedish, the words are "*Jävla neger!*"

11. The word "*Nja*" expresses an ambiguous "yes": a "yes"—*ja*—that begins with an *n* for *nej* (no).

12. The words Mattias used for being split were "*den här kluvenheten.*"

13. My interview of this woman, KC, occurred in Stockholm on May 20, 1998, in Swedish. The translation is mine.

14. My interviews of Anna ChuChu Petersson were conducted in Stockholm on August 22, 1999 (together with Mikael Jarnlo and Amanda Fredriksson), and on August 26, 2002. The translation is mine. Italicized phrases indicate my added emphasis.

15. The phrase used by Amanda here was "*Jag föraktar det!*"

16. Mikael's words were "*Det ställer jag inte upp på.*"

17. Amanda's words in Swedish were "*Jo, men det är så fint med mulattbarn!*"

18. Carsten, in an article that examines the complex relationship of adopted adults with their "past," a past that is made "present" in reunion narratives (2000, 689), notes that her interviews with the adopted "in many respects . . . can be read as accounts of a kind of retrospective bereavement process" (694); also see Carsten 2007a.

19. Freud's essay appears in Freud 1955, 239–260.

20. Sara Nordin, interview by author, Stockholm, August 25, 2002.

21. The words are Astrid Trotzig's, taken from her memoir, *Blod är tjockare än vatten* (Blood is thicker than water). The full sentence, from a paragraph describing how her passport picture was "cut away" (*skurit bort*) from a photograph in which she

is held in the arms of her foster mother, is particularly evocative of the meaning of incorporation for the Swedish transnational adoptee: "Only my face shows. The picture is in my passport, my permission to enter 'The Kingdom of Sweden,' signed by the then foreign minister of Korea" (1996, 23, freely translated).

22. Nordin interview, August 25, 2002.

23. Interview by author, Stockholm, August 26, 2002, in English.

24. The phrase is from Ingrid Stjerna 1976, 101; also see discussion in chapter 5. For a theoretical discussion of the child's potential for psychic agency, see Mahoney and Yngvesson 1992.

25. The words are Amanda Fredriksson's, from my interview in Stockholm, August 25, 2002. The emphasis is mine.

26. The phrase is Astrid Trotzig's, in her memoir, *Blod är tjockare än vatten* (1996). Trotzig, who was adopted from Korea in 1971, returned on her own to visit Pusan, where she was born, in her early twenties. She spoke no Korean. At one point she wanted to find a pharmacy and got help from a salesman in a shoe store. He wrote on a piece of paper, in Korean characters, a brief statement of what she was looking for, in case she became lost and needed to ask someone else for help. Explaining what he had written, he translated for her verbally: "'Hello, I am looking for a pharmacy.' And then: 'I am from Sweden,' but in his English this [became]: 'I am Swedish people'" (241).

Chapter 7

1. Interviews in this chapter were conducted by the author in Stockholm on the following dates: Sara Nordin, August 25, 2002, in Swedish; Sofia Berzelius, August 26, 2002, in English; Anna ChuChu Petersson (together with Mikael Jarnlo and Amanda Fredriksson), August 22, 1999, in Swedish; and a second interview with Anna Chu-Chu Petersson on August 26, 2002. Translation of the Swedish interviews is mine.

2. Borshay Liem was born Kang Ok Jin but placed in adoption as another child (Cha Jung Hee) after the father of Cha Jung Hee removed his daughter from the Korean orphanage where both girls were staying. Cha Jung Hee had been scheduled for adoptive placement with the Borshay family in California. Kang Ok Jin was sent in her place.

3. Also see Benjamin 1998, 79: "The ego is not really independent and self-constituting . . . because it is always incorporating the other, demanding that the other be like the self. From these points follow two distinct interpretations of the idea that the self is nonidentical. First, the self is constituted by the identifications with the other that it deploys in an ongoing way, in particular to deny the loss and uncontrollability that otherness necessarily brings. Second, it is reciprocally constituted in relation to the other, depending on the other's recognition, which it cannot have without being negated, acted on by the other, in a way that changes the self, making it nonidentical."

4. See Slavoj Žižek's illuminating discussion (1989, 169) of Lacan's concept of the real as both "hard, impenetrable kernel" and "product, remainder, leftover, scraps of [the] . . . process of symbolization."

5. These last two sentences are taken from Yngvesson and Mahoney 2000, 81–82.

6. A similar point is made by Janet Carsten in her discussion (2000, 698) of the signifi-

cance of reunions of adult adoptees with birth parents as a way of asserting "one's own creative control over events shaped by others." In an article that focuses on reunions in domestic adoptions, Carsten also points to the role of the ethnographer who listens to the narratives, arguing that "both telling these stories and having them listened to is constitutive of the process of rearranging the past" (698).

7. Amanda Fredriksson was interviewed in Stockholm on August 22, 1999, and on August 25, 2002, in Swedish; my translation.

8. Janet Carsten (2000, 690) notes the recurrence of death as a theme in adoptee narratives of searching for birth kin.

9. Interviews with Jaclyn Aronson were conducted in Amherst, Massachusetts, on November 27, 1995, and, together with her mother, Barbara Rall, in New York, on March 31, 2001. I was the supervisor of Aronson's senior thesis at Hampshire College in 1997 and have drawn on that document as well in the pages that follow. I remain in contact with both Aronson and Rall, and they kindly provided me with an audio tape of a workshop on search and reunion that they conducted in 2005.

10. See especially the insightful observations of Cederblad and colleagues on this issue, based on a series of empirical studies carried out in the 1980s and 1990s among Swedish transnational adoptees (Cederblad et al. 1994; 1999). And see discussion in chapter 4, pp. 97–100.

11. Joyce Maguire Pavao is an adoption consultant and author of *The Family of Adoption* (1998). She is a strong advocate of open adoption and holds regular workshops for adoptive parents, adoptees, and adoption professionals.

12. This sentence is adapted from Yngvesson and Mahoney 2000, 103.

13. Interview conducted in Stockholm on August 22, 1999, in Swedish; my translation.

14. Interviews conducted in Stockholm on August 25, 2002, in Swedish; my translation.

15. For a discussion of this difficulty, see Yngvesson 2004.

16. Interview conducted in Stockholm, May 11, 1999, in Swedish; my translation.

17. E-mail communication with Daniel Rosenlind, March 2, 2009.

18. See Janet Carsten's perceptive observation (2000, 698) that "assertion of agency over one's own past may perhaps explain the disjuncture between the often problematic relations which adoptees establish with birth kin and the positive terms in which they speak about the results of conducting searches." In Nordin's case, since there were no kin to be found, there were no problematic relationships, a situation she described as "a kind of luxury, even though it has a price" (see p. 148 and note 6, above).

19. In Swedish, Sara's words for this last sentence, which is finely tuned and difficult to translate well, read as follows: *"Dessa kontakter är viktiga för mig för det gör landet mer verkligt och mer levande och jag har också genom dessa personer fått en chans att närma mig någon form av vardag vilket kanske är ett tecken på att man kommit något . . . närmare något."*

20. E-mail communication with Sara Nordin, March 9, 2009.

21. Interview conducted in Stockholm, August 26, 2002, in English.

22. Interview conducted in Stockholm, August 25, 2002, in Swedish; my translation.

References

Abrahamsson, Ulla B. 1978. Adoptivbarn och invandrarbarn (Adoptive children and immigrant children). *Att Adoptera* 8 (1): 124.

Adoption av utländska barn (Adoption of foreign children). 1967. SOU, vol. 57. Betänkande avgivet av tillkallade utredningsmän. Stockholm: Statens Offentliga Utredningar.

Adoptionsfrågor (Adoption questions). 1989. SOU, vol. 100. Slutbetänkande av förmynderskapsutredningen. Stockholm: Statens Offentliga Utredningar.

Adoption—till vilket pris? (Adoption—at what price?). 2003. SOU, vol. 49. Betänkande av Utredningen om internationella adoptioner. Stockholm: Statens Offentliga Utredningar.

Adre-Isaksson, Anne. 2003. Adina: Det tjugotusende barnet (Adina: The twenty-thousandth child). *Att Adoptera* 34 (3): 8–10.

Agell, Anders, and Åke Saldeen. 1991. *Faderskap, vårdnad, adoption* (Paternity, custody, adoption). Stockholm: Iustus Förlag.

Åkerman, Ingrid, and Frank Lindblad. 1995. Nationella adoptioner i Sverige (National adoptions in Sweden). *Social medicinsk Tidskrift* 4–5:213–216.

Anagnost, Ann. 1995. A surfeit of bodies: Population and the rationality of the state in post-Mao China. In Ginsburg and Rapp 1995a.

———. 2000. Scenes of misrecognition: Maternal citizenship in the age of transnational adoption. *Positions* 8 (2): 389–421.

———. 2004. The corporeal politics of quality. *Public Culture* 16 (2): 189–208.

Anderfelt, Lena. 1982. Föräldrar förnekar att barnen särbehandlas (Adults deny that children are treated differently). *Att Adoptera* 13 (5): 10–11.

Anderson, Benedict. 1983. *Imagined communities.* New York: Verso.

Andersson, Gunilla. 1980. Vi är medvetna om fördomarna—men barnens situation innehåller mer" (We are aware of the prejudices—but the children's situation involves more). *Att Adoptera* 11 (2): 16.

———. 1986. The adopting and adopted Swedes and their contemporary society. In *Adoption in worldwide perspective*, edited by René Hochsbergen. Lisse: Swets & Zeitliger.

———. 1991. Intercountry adoption in Sweden: The experience of 25 years and 32,000 placements. Adoption Centre, Sundbyberg, Sweden.

Andersson, Gunvor. 1990. Barnförhållande till föräldrar och fosterföräldrar (Children's relationship to parents and foster parents). *Nordisk Psykologi* 42 (1): 59–74.

Andersson, Maria. 1984. Maria skriver (Maria writes). Originally published in *Att Adoptera* 1 (1981). Reprinted in *Ur Att Adoptera* (1979–1983): 35–36.

Antze, Paul. 1996. Telling stories, making selves: Memory and identity in multiple personality disorder. In Antze and Lambek 1996.

Antze, Paul, and Michael Lambek, eds. 1996. *Tense past: Cultural essays in trauma and memory*. New York: Routledge.

Appadurai, Arjun. 1986. Introduction: Commodities and the politics of value. In *The social life of things: Commodities in cultural perspective*, edited by Arjun Appadurai. Cambridge: Cambridge University Press.

Aronson, Jaclyn C. 1997. "Not my homeland": A critique of the current culture of Korean international adoption. Senior thesis, Hampshire College, Amherst, MA.

Balibar, Etienne. 1991. Racism and nationalism. In Balibar and Wallerstein 1991.

Balibar, Etienne, and Immanuel Wallerstein. 1991. *Race, nation, class: Ambiguous identities*. London: Verso.

Baran, Annette, Reuben Pannor, and Arthur D. Sorosky. 1976. Open adoptions. *Social Work* 21: 97–100.

Barth, Richard P. 1992. Child welfare services in the United States and Sweden: Different assumptions, laws, and outcomes. *Scandinavian Journal of Social Welfare* 1:36–42.

———. 1998. Death rates among California's foster care and former foster care populations. *Children and Youth Services Review* 20:577–604.

Bartholet, Elizabeth. 1993. *Family bonds: Adoption and the politics of parenting*. Boston: Houghton Mifflin.

Bates, J. Douglas. 1993. *Gift children: A story of race, family, and adoption in a divided America*. New York: Ticknor & Fields.

Benjamin, Jessica. 1988. *The bonds of love: Psychoanalysis, feminism, and the problem of domination*. New York: Pantheon.

———. 1998. *Shadow of the other: Intersubjectivity and gender in psychoanalysis*. New York: Routledge.

Ben-Orr, Joseph. 1976. The law of adoption in the United States: Its Massachusetts origins and the statute of 1851. *NEHGR* 130:265–267.

Berlant, Lauren. 1998. Intimacy. *Critical Inquiry* 24 (2): 281–288.

Bhabha, Homi. 1994. *The location of culture*. London: Routledge.

Biståndsverksamheten igång trots delade meningar inom adoptionscentrum [Aid projects under way in spite of divided opinions at Adoption Centre]. 1973. *AC Rapport* 1:16–17.

Blomqvist, Lise. 1981. Delta i kampen för ett Sverige för alla! (Participate in the struggle for a Sweden for everyone!). *Att Adoptera* 12 (2): 16.

Blustein, Jeffrey. 1982. *Parents and children: The ethics of the family*. New York: Oxford University Press.

Bohman, Michael. n.d. The Swedish adopted child: Social heredity from an historical perspective. In Yngvesson's collection.

Bohman, Michael, and Sören Sigvardsson. 1990. Outcome in adoption: Lessons from longitudinal studies. In Brodzinsky and Schechter 1990.

Boholm, Åsa. 1983. *Swedish kinship: An exploration into cultural processes of belonging and continuity*. Gothenburg Studies in Social Anthropology, 5. Gothenburg, Sweden: Acta Universitatis Gothoburgensis.

Bonner, Raymond. 2003a. A challenge in India snarls foreign adoptions. *New York Times*, June 23, A3.

———. 2003b. For poor families, selling babies was economic boom. *New York Times*, June 23, A3.

Borshay Liem, Deann. 2000. *First person plural*. Ho-He-Kus, NJ: Mu Films.

Bowie, Fiona, ed. 2004. *Cross-cultural approaches to adoption*. New York: Routledge.

Broberg, Gunnar, and Mattias Tydén. 1991. *Oönskade i folkhemmet: Rashygien och sterilisering i Sverige* (Undesired in the home of the people: Race hygiene and sterilization in Sweden). Stockholm: Gidlunds.

Brodzinsky, David M. 2005. Reconceptualizing openness in adoption: Implications for theory, research, and practice. In Brodzinsky and Palacios 2005.

Brodzinsky, David M., and Jesús Palacios, eds. 2005. *Psychological issues in adoption: Research and practice*. Westport, CT: Praeger.

Brodzinsky, David M., and Marshall D. Schechter, eds. 1990. *The psychology of adoption*. New York: Oxford University Press.

Brooks, Devon, Cassandra Simmel, Leslie Wind, and Richard P. Barth. 2005. Contemporary adoption in the United States: Implications for the next wave of adoption theory, research, and practice. In Brodzinsky and Palacios 2005.

Brown, Jane. 2000. Abandonment: What do we tell them? *Adoption Today* 2 (5): 32–34.

Butler, Judith. 1993. *Bodies that matter: On the discursive limits of "sex."* New York: Routledge.

Caldwell, Christopher. 2006. Islam on the outskirts of the welfare state. *New York Times Magazine*, February 5, 54–59.

Callon, Michel, Cécile Méadel, and Vololona Rabeharisoa. 2002. The economy of qualities. *Economy and Society* 31 (2): 194–217.

Campbell, Ben. 2007. Racialization, genes, and the reinventions of nation in Europe. In Wade 2007b.

Caplan, Lincoln. 1990. *An open adoption*. New York: Farrar, Straus & Giroux.

Carey, Benedict. 2007. Study quantifies orphanage link to I.Q. *New York Times*, December 21, A30.

Carlson, Allan. 1990. *The Swedish experiment in family politics: The Myrdals and the interwar population crisis*. New Brunswick, NJ: Transaction.

Carlson, Richard R. 1994. The emerging law of intercountry adoptions: An analysis of the Hague Conference on Intercountry Adoption. *Tulsa Law Journal* 30:243–304.

Carp, E. Wayne. 1998. *Family matters: Secrecy and disclosure in the history of adoption*. Cambridge, MA: Harvard University Press.

Carsten, Janet. 2000. "Knowing where you've come from": Ruptures and continuities of time and kinship in narratives of adoption reunions. *Journal of the Royal Anthropological Institute* 6 (4): 687–703.

———. 2001. Substantivism, antisubstantivism, and anti-antisubstantivism. In Franklin and McKinnon 2001.

———. 2007a. Connections and disconnections of memory and kinship. In Carsten 2007b.

———, ed. 2007b. *Ghosts of memory*. New York: Blackwell.

Cartwright, Lisa. 2003. Photographs of waiting children: The transnational adoption market. *Social Text* 21 (74): 83–109.

Cederblad, Marianne. 1984. Följde sin pappa som en skugga (Followed his father like a shadow). Originally published in *Att Adoptera* 3 (1983). Reprinted in *Ur Att Adoptera* (1979–1983): 31–34.

Cederblad, Marianne, Börje Höök, Malin Irhammar, and Ann Mari Mercke. 1999. Mental health in international adoptees as teenagers and young adults: An epidemiological study. *Journal of Child Psychology and Psychiatry* 40 (8): 1239–1248.

Cederblad, Marianne, Malin Irhammar, Ann Mari Mercke, and Eva Norlander. 1994. *Identitet och anpassning hos utlandsfödda adopterade ungdomar* (Identity and adjustment among foreign-born adopted youth). Lund, Sweden: Forskning om barn och familj, Avdelning för barn och ungdomspsykiatri, Lund University.

Cheng, Anne Anlin. 2001. *The melancholy of race: Psychoanalysis, assimilation, and hidden grief.* New York: Oxford University Press.

Colen, Shellee. 1995. "Like a mother to them": Stratified reproduction and West Indian childcare workers and employers in New York. In Ginsburg and Rapp 1995a.

Collier, Jane, Michelle Z. Rosaldo, and Sylvia Yanagisako. 1982. Is there a family? New anthropological views. In *Rethinking the family: Some feminist questions*, edited by Barrie Thorne. New York: Longman.

Coutin, Susan. 2003. Cultural logics of belonging and movement: Transnationalism, naturalization, and U.S. immigration politics. *American Ethnologist* 30 (4): 508–526.

———. 2005. Being en route. *American Anthropologist* 107 (2): 195–206.

Coutin, Susan, Bill Maurer, and Barbara Yngvesson. 2002. In the mirror: The legitimation work of globalization. *Law and Social Inquiry* 27 (4): 801–843.

Crossette, Barbara. 1999a. In days, India, chasing China, will have a billion people. *New York Times*, August 5, A10.

———. 1999b. Rethinking population at a global milestone. *New York Times*, September 19, 1.

Cussins, Charis M. 1998. Quit sniveling, cryo-baby. We'll work out which one's your mamma! In Davis-Floyd and Dumit 1998.

Das, Veena. 1995. National honor and practical kinship: Unwanted women and children. In Ginsburg and Rapp 1995a.

Davis-Floyd, Robbie, and Joseph Dumit, eds. 1998. *Cyborg babies: From techno-sex to techno-tots.* New York: Routledge.

Dokument Inifrån (An inside document). 2002. (I) Sveket mot de adopterade (Treachery against the adopted); (II) Barn till varje pris (A child for every price). Sveriges Television, Nordisk Film, A.B.

Donzelot, Jacques. 1979. *The policing of families.* New York: Pantheon.

Dorow, Sara K. 2006. *Transnational adoption: A cultural economy of race, gender, and kinship.* New York: New York University Press.

Duncan, William. 1993. Regulating intercountry adoption: An international perspective. In *Frontiers of family law*, edited by Andrew Bainham and David S. Pearl. New York: Wiley.

Edwards, Jeanette. 1992. Explicit connections: Ethnographic enquiry in North-West England. In *Technologies of procreation: Kinship in the age of assisted conception*, edited by Jeanette Edwards, Sarah Franklin, Eric Hirsch, and Frances Price. Manchester, UK: Manchester University Press.

Elshtain, Jean Bethke, ed. 1982. *The family in political thought.* Amherst: University of Massachusetts Press.

Erikson, Erik H. 1959. *Identity and the life cycle: Selected papers by Erik H. Erikson.* Vol. 1, *Psychological issues.* New York: International Universities Press.

————. 1968. *Identity: Youth and crisis.* New York: Norton.

Escobar, Arturo. 1995. *Encountering development: The making and unmaking of the Third World.* Princeton, NJ: Princeton University Press.

Fanon, Frantz. 1967. *Black skin, white masks.* Translated by Charles Lam Markmann. New York: Grove Press.

Favell, A. 2003. Integration nations: The nation state and research on immigrants in western Europe. In *The multicultural challenge*, edited by Georg Brochmann. Amsterdam: JAI.

Fein, Esther. 1998. Secrecy and stigma no longer clouding adoptions. *New York Times*, October 25, 1.

Fineman, Martha A. 1995. *The neutered mother, the sexual family, and other twentieth century tragedies.* New York: Routledge.

Fogg-Davis, Hawley. 2002. *The ethics of transracial adoption.* Ithaca, NY: Cornell University Press.

Fonagy, Peter. 2001. *Attachment theory and psychoanalysis.* New York: Other Press.

Fonseca, Claudia. 2002. Inequality near and far: Adoption as seen from the Brazilian favelas. *Law and Society Review* 36 (2): 397–431.

Foucault, Michel. 1970. *The order of things: An archaeology of the human sciences.* New York: Random House.

————. 2003. *Society must be defended: Lectures at the Collège de France:1975–1976.* Translated by David Macey. New York: Picador. Originally published in 1997.

Franklin, Sarah, and Susan McKinnon. 2001. *Relative values: Reconfiguring kinship studies.* Durham, NC: Duke University Press.

Franzén, Eva, Bo Vinnerljung, and Anders Hjern. 2008. The epidemiology of out-of-home care for children and youth: A national cohort study. *British Journal of Social Work* 38 (6): 1043–1059.

Freiburg, Jeanne. 1993. Counting bodies: The politics of reproduction in the Swedish welfare state. *Scandinavian Studies* 65 (2): 226–235.

Freud, Sigmund. 1955. *The standard edition of the complete psychological works of Sigmund Freud.* Translated by James Strachey. London: Hogarth Press.

Fuss, Diana. 1995. *Identification papers.* New York: Routledge.

Gailey, Christine Ward. 1999. Seeking "Baby Right": Race, class, and gender in US international adoption. In Rygvold, Dalen, and Saetersdal 1999.

————. 2000. Ideologies of motherhood and kinship in U.S. adoption. In Ragoné and Twine 2000.

Gentleman, Amelia. 2006. Doctor in India jailed for telling sex of a fetus. *New York Times*, March 30, A13.

————. 2008. India nurtures business of surrogate motherhood. *New York Times*, March 10, A9.

Ginsburg, Faye, and Rayna Rapp, eds. 1995a. *Conceiving the new world order: The global politics of reproduction.* Berkeley: University of California Press.

———. 1995b. Introduction: Conceiving the new world order. In Ginsburg and Rapp 1995a.

Goldberg, David. 1993. *Racist culture: Philosophy and the politics of meaning*. Oxford: Blackwell.

Goodman, Peter S. 2006. Stealing infants for adoption. *Washington Post*, March 12, A1.

Gordon, Linda. 1988. *Heroes of their own lives: The politics and history of family violence*. New York: Viking.

———. 1999. *The great Arizona orphan abduction*. Cambridge, MA: Harvard University Press.

Graff, E. J. 2008. The lie we love. *Foreign Policy*, November–December, 58–66.

Greenhalgh, Susan. 1994. Controlling births and bodies in village China. *American Ethnologist* 21 (1): 3–30.

———. 2003. Planned births, unplanned persons: "Population" in the making of Chinese modernity. *American Ethnologist* 30 (2): 196–215.

Grönwall, Lars, Leif Holgersson, and Jan Nasenius. 1991. *Socialtjänstens mål och medel* (The goals and methods of social service). Stockholm: Förlagshuset Gothia.

Gross, Jane. 2007. U.S. joins overseas adoption overhaul plan. *New York Times*, December 11, A25.

Gross, Jane, and Will Connors. 2007. In Ethiopia, open doors for foreign adoptions. *New York Times*, June 4, A1.

Grossberg, Michael. 1985. *Governing the hearth: Law and family in nineteenth century America*. Chapel Hill: University of North Carolina Press.

Grosz, Elizabeth. 1995. *Space, time, and perversion*. New York: Routledge.

Grotevant, Harold D., and Ruth G. McRoy. 1998. *Openness in adoption: Exploring family connections*. Newbury Park, CA: Sage.

Grotevant, Harold, Yvette V. Perry, and Ruth G. McRoy. 2005. Openness in adoption: Outcomes for adolescents within their kinship networks. In Brodzinsky and Palacios 2005.

Grünewald, Annika. 1980. Resan tillbaka till Indien (Journey back to India). *Att Adoptera* 11 (2): 3–5.

Gullestad, Marianne. 2004. Blind slaves of our prejudices: Debating "culture" and "race" in Norway. *Ethnos* 69 (2): 177–203.

Gunnar, Megan R., and Darlene A. Kertes. 2005. Prenatal and postnatal risks to neurobiological development in internationally adopted children. In Brodzinsky and Palacios 2005.

Gupta, Akhil, and James Ferguson. 1997a. Beyond "culture": Space, identity, and the politics of difference. In Gupta and Ferguson 1997b.

———, eds. 1997b. *Culture, Power, Place: Explorations in Critical Anthropology*. Durham, NC: Duke University Press.

Hague Convention. 1993. Hague conference on private international law, final act of the seventeenth session, May 29, 32 I.L.M. 1134, www.hcch.net/index_en.php?act =conventions.text&cid=69.

Hall, Stuart. 1997. Old and new identities, old and new ethnicities. In *Culture, globalization, and the world-system*, edited by Anthony D. King. Minneapolis: University of Minnesota Press.

Hampton, Lawrence P. 1989. The aftermath of adoption: The economic consequences— support, inheritances, and taxes. In Hollinger 1989.

Hartog, Hendrik. 2000. *Man and wife in America: A history.* Cambridge, MA: Harvard University Press.

Hatje, Ann-Katrin. 1974. *Befolkningsfrågan och välfärden* (Population policy and the welfare state). Stockholm: Allmänna Förlaget.

Hegarty, Antony. 2009. Interview by Terry Gross on *Fresh Air,* February 3, WHYY, www .npr.org/Templates/story/story.php?storyId=100162285.

Henningson, Margret. 1999. The need to know about roots. Talk presented at workshop for adoptees organized by the Adoption Centre, Stockholm, April 27.

Hirdman, Yvonne. 1989. *Att lägga livet till rätta: Studier i svensk folkhemspolitik* (To put one's life in order: Studies in Swedish "folkhem" politics). Stockholm: Carlsson Bokförlag.

Hjern, Anders, and Peter Allbeck. 2002. Suicide in first- and second-generation immigrants in Sweden: A comparative study. *Social Psychiatry and Psychiatric Epidemiology* 37:423–429.

Hjern, Anders, Frank Lindblad, and Bo Vinnerljung. 2002. Suicide, psychiatric illness, and social maladjustment in intercountry adoptees in Sweden: A cohort study. *Lancet* 360:443–448.

Hjern, Anders, Bo Vinnerljung, and Frank Lindblad. 2004. Avoidable mortality among child welfare recipients and intercountry adoptees: A national cohort study. *Journal of Epidemiology and Community Health* 58:412–417.

Hochsbergen, René, and Jan ter Laak. 2005. Changing attitudes of adoptive parents in northern European countries. In Brodzinsky and Palacios 2005.

Hollinger, Joan, ed. 1989. *Adoption law and practice.* New York: Matthew Bender.

———. 1993. Adoption law. *Future of Children* 3 (1): 43–61.

Howell, Signe. 2006. *The kinning of foreigners.* Oxford: Berghahn Books.

Hübinette, Tobias. 2004. Adopted Koreans and the development of identity in the "third space." *Adoption and Fostering* 28 (1): 16–24.

———. 2006. From orphan trains to babylifts: Colonial trafficking, empire building, and social engineering. In Trenka, Oparah, and Chin 2006.

Human Rights and Equal Opportunity Commission. 1997. *Bringing them home: Report of the national inquiry into the separation of Aboriginal and Torres Strait Islander children from their families.* Sydney, Australia: Human Rights and Equal Opportunity Commission.

Humphrey, Carolyn, and Stephen Hugh-Jones, eds. 1992. *Barter, exchange, and value: An anthropological approach.* Cambridge: Cambridge University Press.

Indian Child Welfare Act. 1978. P.L. 95–608.

Indian Council for Child Welfare—Tamil Nadu. 1995–96. Annual Report, ICCW-TN, Madras.

Internationella adoptionsfrågor: 1993 års Haagkonvention m.m. (International adoption questions: 1993 Hague Convention, etc.). 1994. SOU, vol. 137 Betänkande av Adoptionslagstifningsutredningen. Stockholm: Statens Offentliga Utredningar.

Irhammar, Malin. 1997. *Att utforska sitt ursprung: Identitetsformande under adolescensen hos utlandsfödda adopterade. Betydelsen av biologiskt och etniskt ursprung* (To search for one's origin: Identity formation during adolescence among foreign-born adoptees: The meaning of biological and ethnic origin). Lund, Sweden: Avdelning för barn-och ungdomspsykiatri, Lund University.

Irigaray, Luce. 1985. *Speculum of the other woman*. Ithaca, NY: Cornell University Press.

Jenson, Jane, and Boaventura de Sousa Santos, eds. 2000. *Globalizing institutions: Case studies in regulation and innovation*. Aldershot, UK: Ashgate.

Johnson, Kay Ann. 2002. Politics of international and domestic adoption in China. *Law and Society Review* 36 (2): 379–396.

———. 2004. *Wanting a daughter, needing a son: Abandonment, adoption, and orphanage care in China*. St. Paul, Minnesota: Yeong & Yeong.

———. 2005. Chaobao: The plight of Chinese adoptive parents in the era of the one-child policy. In Volkman 2005a.

Johnson, Kay Ann, Huang Banghan, and Wang Liyao. 1998. Infant abandonment and adoption in China. *Population and Development Review* 24 (3): 469–510.

Juffer, Femmie. 2005. Post-adoption services with video-feedback: Evidence from re-search and practice in the Netherlands. Paper presented at the 1st Global Adoption Research Conference, Copenhagen, Denmark, September 8–10.

Juffer, Femmie, Marian J. Bakermans-Kranenburg, and Marinus H. Van IJzendoorn. 2005. The importance of parenting in the development of disorganized attachment: Evidence from a preventive intervention study in adoptive families. *Journal of Child Psychology and Psychiatry* 46:263–274.

Juffer, Femmie, and Marinus H. Van IJzendoorn. 2007. Adoptees do not lack self-esteem: A meta-analysis of studies on self-esteem of transracial, international, and domestic adoptees. *Psychological Bulletin* 133 (6): 1067–1083.

Juffer, Femmie, and Rien Van IJzendoorn. 2005. Behavioral problems and mental health referrals of international adoptees: A meta-analysis. *Journal of the American Medical Association* 293 (20): 2501–2515.

Kälvemark, Anne-Sofie. 1980. *More children of better quality? Aspects of Swedish population policy in the 1930's*. Stockholm: Almqvist & Wiksell International.

Kane, Saralee. 1993. The movement of children for international adoption: An epidemio-logical perspective. *Social Science Journal* 30 (4): 323–339.

Kats, Madeleine. 1975. Är adoptivbarn invandrarbarn? (Are adoptive children immigrant children?). *Att Adoptera* 6 (2): 124.

———. 1984a. Alla våra barn har en historia (All our children have a history). Originally published in *Att Adoptera* 4 (1981), reprinted in *Ur Att Adoptera* (1979–1983): 17.

———. 1984b. Mamma till två svarta pojkar i tonåren (Mamma to two black boys in their teens). Originally published in *Att Adoptera* 2 (1982), reprinted in *Ur Att Adoptera* (1979–1983): 37–38.

———. 1985. Oroliga barn oroar oss (Unsettled children unsettle us). *Att Adoptera* 16 (5): 12–13.

———. 1990a. *Adoptiv barn växer upp* (Adopted children grow up). Stockholm: Bon-niers.

———. 1990b. Babies without human support will develop problems. Unpublished translation of article published in *Dagens Nyheter*, 1990. In Yngvesson's collection.

Kendall, Laurel. 2005. Birth mothers and imaginary lives. In Volkman 2005a.

Kim, Dae Jung. 1999. President Kim Dae Jung's speech: October 23, 1998 at the Blue House. *Chosen Child* 1 (5): 15–16.

Kim, Eleana. 2003. Wedding citizenship and culture: Korean adoptees and the global family of Korea. *Social Text* 74 21 (1): 57–81.

———. 2005. Wedding citizenship and culture: Korean adoptees and the global family of Korea. In Volkman 2005a.

———. 2007. Our adoptee, our alien: Transnational adoptees as specters of foreignness and family in Korea. *Anthropological Quarterly* 80 (2): 497–531.

Kim, Jae Ran. 2006. Scattered seeds: The Christian influence on Korean adoption. In Trenka, Oparah, and Shin 2006.

Kirk, David. 1964. *Shared fate: A theory of adoption and mental health.* New York: Free Press.

Kopytoff, Igor. 1986. The cultural biography of things: Commoditization as process. In *The Social Life of Things*, edited by Arjun Appadurai. Cambridge, MA: Harvard University Press.

Kramer, Jane. 2005. Comment: Difference. *New Yorker*, November 21, 41–42.

Kristeva, Julia. 1986. *The Kristeva Reader*, edited by Toril Moi. New York: Columbia University Press.

Kunzel, Regina G. 1993. *Fallen women, problem girls: Unmarried mothers and the professionalization of social work, 1890–1940.* New Haven, CT: Yale University Press.

Kyazze, Simwogerere. 2006. What is this Hollywood clamor to adopt "darkies"? *Daily Nation*, Kenya, http://watchingamerica.com/dailynationka000001.shtml, October 15.

Lakshmi Kant Pandey v. Union of India. 1985. Writ Petition Cil. No. 1171 of 1982. Decided on September 27, 1985.

Lewis, Jane, and Gertrude Åström. 1992. Equality, difference, and state welfare: Labor market and family policies in Sweden. *Feminist Studies* 18 (1): 59–87.

Lifton, Betty Jean. 1993. *Tell me a real adoption story.* New York: Alfred A. Knopf.

———. 1994. *Journey of the adopted self: A quest for wholeness.* New York: Basic Books.

Lind, Johan. 1985. Svenskheten är inte alltings mått (Swedishness is not the measure of everything). *Att Adoptera* 16 (2): 3.

Lindqvist, Bosse, and Bo Ohlén. 2003. *En gång var jag korean: En dokumantär film för Sveriges Television* (Once I was Korean: A documentary film for Swedish Television). Swedish Television, Channel 2.

Loving v. Virginia. 388 U.S. 1 (1967).

Mahoney, Maureen A., and Barbara Yngvesson. 1992. The construction of subjectivity and the paradox of resistance: Reintegrating feminist anthropology and psychology. *Signs* 18 (1): 44–73.

Mansnerus, Laura. 1998. Market puts price tags on priceless. *New York Times*, October 26, A1.

Marre, Diana. 2007. "I want her to learn her language and maintain her culture": Transnational adoptive families' views of "cultural origins." In Wade 2007b.

Marx, Karl. 1971. *Capital.* Vol. 1, *A critical analysis of capitalist production.* Moscow: Progress Publishers. Original publication in 1887.

———. 1973. *Grundrisse: Foundations of the critique of political economy.* New York: Vintage Books.

Massumi, Brian. 1993a. Everywhere you want to be: Introduction to fear. In Massumi 1993b.

———, ed. 1993b. *The politics of everyday fear.* Cambridge, MA: MIT Press.

Matwejeff, Susanna. 2004. *Svenskfödda adopterades sökprocess* (The Swedish-born adoptees' search process). Linköping, Sweden: Institution for Behavioral Science, Linköping University.

Melina, Lois Ruskai, and Sharon Kaplan Roszia. 1993. *The open adoption experience.* New York: Harper Collins.

Modell, Judith S. 1994. *Kinship with strangers: Adoption and interpretations of kinship in American culture.* Berkeley: University of California Press.

Morrison, Toni. 1992. *Playing in the dark: Whiteness and the literary imagination.* Cambridge, MA: Harvard University Press.

Mundy, Liza. 2007. Open (secret). *Washington Post Magazine*, May 6, 18–36.

Nancy, Jean-Luc. 1993. Abandoned being. In *The birth to presence*, by Jean-Luc Nancy, translated by Brian Holmes and others. Stanford, CA: Stanford University Press.

Nandy, Ashis. 1987. *Traditions, tyranny, and utopias.* Delhi: Oxford University Press.

National Association of Black Social Workers (NABSW). 1972. Position paper, approved at Fourth Annual Conference, April 1972. Published in *Transracial adoption*, edited by Rita J. Simon and Howard Altstein (New York: Wiley, 1977).

National Board for Intercountry Adoptions (NIA). 1996. Barn som 1969–1996 invandrat till Sverige och adopterats senare, fördelat på år, världsdelar och länder (Children who immigrated to Sweden and were later adopted, divided by year, world region and nation). NIA, Stockholm.

———. n.d. *Gruppsamtal om adoption* (Group conversations about adoption). Stockholm: Statens nämnd för internationella adoptionsfrågor.

Nixon, Ron. 2008. De-emphasis on race in adoption is criticized. *New York Times*, May 27, A15.

Norberg, Viveca Halldin. 1977. *Swedes in Hailie Selassie's Ethiopia, 1924–1952.* Stockholm: Almqvist and Wiksell International.

Nordin, Sara. 1996. Mer eller mindre svart (More or less black). *SvartVitt* 1:4–6.

———. 1999. Hämtade 61 barn från "världens ände" (Brought 61 children from "the end of the world"). *Tenaestelin* 40 (1): 12–14.

O'Donovan, Katherine. 2002. "Real" mothers for abandoned children. *Law and Society Review* 36 (2): 347–377.

Ong, Aihwa. 1999. *Flexible citizenship: The cultural logics of transnationality.* Durham, NC: Duke University Press.

Orenstein, Peggy. 2007. Your gamete, myself. *New York Times Magazine*, July 15, 34.

Palacios, Jesús, and Yolanda Sánchez-Sandoval. 2005. Beyond adopted/non-adopted comparisons. In Brodzinsky and Palacios 2005.

Park-Edström, Eleonore. 1993. Tar vi vårt ansvar som invandrarfamilj? (Do we accept our responsibility as an immigrant family?). *Att Adoptera* 24 (1): 6–7.

Pavao, Joyce Maguire. 1998. *The family of adoption.* Boston: Beacon Press.

Pilotti, Francisco. 1993. Intercountry adoption: Trends, issues, and policy implications for the 1990s. *Childhood* 1:165–177.

Povinelli, Elizabeth A. 2002. Notes on gridlock: Genealogy, intimacy, sexuality. *Public Culture* 14 (1): 215–238.

Pred, Allan. 2000. *Even in Sweden*. Berkeley: University of California Press.

Presser, Stephen B. 1971–72. The historical background of the American law of adoption. *Journal of Family Law* 11:443–516.

Probyn, Elspeth. 1996. *Outside belongings*. New York: Routledge.

Rädda Barnen. 1992. *Barnets rättigheter . . . och samhällets skyldigheter: Lagar och regler* (The child's rights . . . and society's obligations: Laws and rules). Stockholm: Wahlström & Widstrand.

Radin, Margaret Jane. 1996. *Contested commodities*. Cambridge, MA: Harvard University Press.

Ragoné, Heléna, and France Winddance Twine, eds. 2000. *Ideologies and Technologies of Motherhood: Race, Class, Sexuality, Nationalism*. New York: Routledge.

Rappaport, Bruce M. 1992. *The open adoption book: A guide to adoption without fears*. New York: Macmillan.

Rastas, Anna. 2005. Adoptive families and racism. Paper presented at the First Global Adoption Research Conference, September 9–10, Copenhagen.

Regnér, Anders. 1978. Ökas motsättningarna? Drabbas barnen? (Is the antagonism growing? Are our children being affected?). *Att Adoptera* 9 (1): 127.

Report on archaeological discovery in Ethiopia. 2007. Living on earth series, *All things considered*, National Public Radio, May 22.

Ricoeur, Paul. 1991. Life in quest of narrative. In *On Paul Ricoeur: Narrative and interpretation*, edited by David Woods. New York: Routledge.

———. 1992. *Oneself as another*. Chicago: University of Chicago Press.

Riles, Annelise. n.d. Is law hopeful? In Hope in the economy, edited by Hirokazu Miyazaki and Richard Swedberg. In Yngvesson's collection.

Roberts, Dorothy. 2002. *Shattered bonds: The color of child welfare*. New York: Basic Books.

Rojas, Mauricio. 1995. *Sveriges oälskade barn: Att vara svensk men ändå inte* (Sweden's unloved children: To be Swedish but yet not Swedish). Stockholm: Brombergs.

Rutter, Michael. 2005. Adverse preadoption experiences and psychological outcomes. In Brodzinsky and Palacios 2005.

Rygvold, Anne-Lise, Monica Dalen, and Barbro Saetersdal, eds. 1999. *Mine yours—ours and theirs: Adoption, changing kinship and family patterns*. Oslo, Norway: Department of Special Needs Education.

Said, Edward. 1979. *Orientalism*. New York: Vintage Books.

Sammarco, Lovisa. 2003. The Bright Star—en kulturbrygga (The Bright Star—a cultural bridge). *NIA Informerar* 2:6–7.

Santos, Boaventura de Sousa. 1999. The fall of Angelus Novus: Beyond the modern game of roots and options. *Revista Mexicana de Sociologia* 2:35–58.

Scheper-Hughes, Nancy. 2008. Illegal organ trade: Global justice and the traffic in human organs. In *Living donor organ transplants*, edited by Rainer Grussner and Enrico Bedeti. New York: McGraw-Hill.

———. n.d. *The world cut in two: The global traffic in organs*. Berkeley: University of California Press. Forthcoming.

Schneider, David M. 1968. *American kinship: A cultural account*. Chicago: University of Chicago Press.

Schwartz, David. 1977. Motsättningar ökas—barnen drabbas! (Conflicts increase—children suffer!) *Att Adoptera* 7 (4): 126.

————. 1980. Adoptivbarn—invandrarbarn: Får de samma framtid? (Adoptive children—immigrant children: Will they have the same future?) *Att Adoptera* 11 (1): 2.

Sciolino, Elaine. 2007. Plan to test DNA of some immigrants divides France. *New York Times*, October 11, A3.

Selman, Peter. 1989. Inter-country adoption: What can Britain learn from the experiences of other European countries? In *Towards a European welfare state*, edited by G. Room. Bristol, UK: SAUS.

————. 1999. The demography of intercountry adoption. In Rygvold, Dalen, and Saetersdal 1999.

————. 2002. Intercountry adoption in the new millennium: The "quiet migration" revisited. *Population Research and Policy Review* 21:205–225.

————. 2005a. The "quiet migration" in the new millennium: Trends in intercountry adoption, 1998–2003. Paper presented at the 8th Global Conference, Manila, August 10–12.

————. 2005b. Trends in intercountry adoption, 1998–2003: A demographic analysis. PowerPoint presentation from 8th Global Conference, Manila, August 10–12.

————. 2006. The movement of children for international adoption: Developments and trends in receiving states and states of origin, 1998–2004. Paper presented at the First International Forum on Childhood and Families, "On philia and phobias," Barcelona, Spain, September 29–October 3.

————. 2007. Ethiopia: 1998–2006 (table with figures for Ethiopian adoptions to 22 adopting nations). Personal communication, July 16, 2007.

————. 2008. The movement of children for transnational adoption: Paper presented at the Globalization of Motherhood Symposium, Institute of Commonwealth Studies, London. October 14–16.

————. n.d. The rise and fall of intercountry adoption. In International social work: Special edition on intercountry adoption, edited by Karen Rotabi and Judith Gibbons. In Peter Selman's possession.

Sengupta, Somini. 2008. Crusader sees wealth as cure for caste bias. *New York Times*, 30 August, A1.

————. 2009. As Indian growth soars, child hunger persists. *New York Times*, March 13, A1.

Serrill, Michael S. 1991. "Wrapping the earth in family ties." *Time International*, November 4, 40–46.

Shanley, Mary Lyndon. 1982. Marriage contract and social contract in seventeenth century political thought. In Elshtain 1982.

Silverman, Arnold R., and William Feigelman. 1990. Adjustment in interracial adoptees: An overview. In Brodzinsky and Schechter 1990.

Simmel, Georg. 1978. *The philosophy of money.* Edited by David Frisby, translated by Tom Bottomore and David Frisby. New York: Routledge. Original publication in 1907.

Simon, Rita J., Howard Altstein, and Marygold S. Melli. 1994. *The case for transracial adoption.* Washington, DC: American University Press.

Smith, Anna Deavere. 2003. Address given at Smith College, Northampton, MA, upon receipt of honorary doctorate, May.

Society for Indian Children's Welfare. 1996. Life book. SICW, Kolkata, India.

Solinger, Ricky. 1992. *Wake up little Susie: Single pregnancy and race before Roe v. Wade.* New York: Routledge.

Special Commission on Intercountry Adoption. 1991. Report of meeting. The Hague Conference on Private International Law, Doc. 17, p. 3 (April 24).

Stanley, Alessandra. 1997. Hands off our babies, a Georgian tells America. *New York Times*, June 29, 1.

Steedman, Carolyn. 1986. *Landscape for a good woman: A story of two lives.* New Brunswick, NJ: Rutgers University Press.

———. 1995. *Strange dislocations: Childhood and the idea of human interiority, 1780–1930.* Cambridge, MA: Harvard University Press.

Steichen, Edward. 2003. *The family of man.* New York: Museum of Modern Art. Originally published in 1955.

Stephens, Sharon, ed. 1995a. *Children and the politics of culture.* Princeton, NJ: Princeton University Press.

Stephens, Sharon. 1995b. Children and the politics of culture in "late capitalism." In Stephens 1995a.

Stjerna, Ingrid. 1976. Biologiska mamman—ett hot? (The biological mother—a threat?). *Att Adoptera* 7 (3): 100–101.

Stoler, Ann Laura. 1995. *Race and the education of desire: Foucault's history of sexuality and the colonial order of things.* Durham, NC: Duke University Press.

Strathern, Marilyn. 1988. *The gender of the gift.* Berkeley: University of California Press.

———. 1992. Qualified value: The perspective of gift exchange. In Humphrey and Hugh-Jones 1992.

———. 1995. Displacing knowledge: Technology and the consequences for kinship. In Ginsburg and Rapp 1995a.

Strong, Pauline Turner. 2001. To forget their tongue, their name, and their whole relation: Captivity, extra-tribal adoption, and the Indian Child Welfare Act. In Franklin and McKinnon 2001.

Sunder Rajan, Rajeswari. 2003. *The scandal of the state: Women, law, and citizenship in postcolonial India.* Durham, NC: Duke University Press.

Therborn, Göran. 1996. Child politics: Dimensions and perspectives. *Childhood* 3:29–44.

Trenka, Jane Jeong, Julia Chinyere Oparah, and Sun Yung Shin, eds. 2006. *Outsiders within: Writing on transracial adoption.* Cambridge, MA: South End Press.

Triseliotis, John. 1973. *In search of origins.* London: Routledge and Kegan Paul.

Triseliotis, John, and Malcolm Hill. 1990. Contrasting adoption, foster care, and residential rearing. In Brodzinsky and Schechter 1990.

Triseliotis, John, and James Russell. 1984. *Hard to place: The outcome of adoption and residential care.* London: Heinemann.

Trotzig, Astrid. 1996. *Blod är tjockare än vatten* (Blood is thicker than water). Stockholm: Albert Bonniers Förlag.

United Nations. 1986. Declaration on social and legal principles relating to the protection and welfare of children, with special reference to foster placement and adoption, nationally and internationally. G. A. Res. 41/85, U.N. GAOR, 41st sess., annex at art. 5.

———. 1989. *Convention on the Rights of the Child.* G. A. Res. 44/25, U.N. GAOR, 61st plen. mtg., annex at art. 21.

Urwin, Cathy. 1984. Power relations and the emergence of language. In *Changing the subject*, edited by Julian Henriques, Wendy Holloway, Cathy Urwin, Couze Venn, and Valerie Walkerdine. New York: Methuen.

Vaihinger, Hans. 2001. *The philosophy of "as if": A system of the theoretical, practical and religious fictions of mankind.* Translated by Charles K. Ogden. London: Routledge. Originally published in 1924.

Van IJzendoorn, Marinus H., and Femmie Juffer. 2006. The Emanuel Miller Memorial Lecture 2006: Adoption as intervention: Meta-analytic evidence for massive catch-up and plasticity in physical, socio-emotional, and cognitive development. *Journal of Child Psychiatry* 47 (12): 1228–1245.

Vård i familjehem: Ovisshetens barn (Out-of-home care: Children of uncertainty). 1995. SOS-rapport, vol. 8. Stockholm: Socialstyrelsen.

Vinnerljung, Bo, Anders Hjern, and Frank Lindblad. 2006. Suicide attempts and severe psychiatric morbidity among former child welfare clients—a national cohort study. *Journal of Child Psychology and Psychiatry* 47 (7): 723–733.

Volkman, Toby Alice, ed. 2005a. *Cultures of transnational adoption.* Durham, NC: Duke University Press.

———. 2005b. Embodying Chinese culture: Transnational adoption in North America. In Volkman 2005a.

von Melen, Anna. 1998. *Samtal med vuxna adopterade* (Conversations with adult adoptees). Stockholm: Rabén Prisma.

Wade, Peter. 2007a. Race, ethnicity, and nation: Perspectives from kinship and genetics. In Wade 2007b.

———, ed. 2007b. *Race, ethnicity, and nation: Perspectives from kinship and genetics.* New York: Berghahn Books.

Wadia-Ells, Susan, ed. 1995a. *The adoption reader: Birth mothers, adoptive mothers, and adoptive daughters tell their stories.* Seattle: Seal Press.

———. 1995b. The Anil journals." In Wadia-Ells 1995a.

Waldron, Jan L. 1995. *Giving away Simone: A memoir.* New York: Random House.

Wallensteen, Hanna. 2000. Veta sin plats (Know your place). Monologue in one act. In Yngvesson's collection.

Wegar, Katarina. 1997. *Adoption, identity, and kinship: The debate over sealed birth records.* New Haven, CT: Yale University Press.

Weigl, Kerstin. 1997. *Längtansbarnen: Adoptivföräldrar berättar* (Children of longing: Adoptive parents tell their stories). Stockholm: Norstedts.

Weston, Kath. 2001. Kinship, controversy, and the sharing of substance: The race/class politics of blood transfusion. In Franklin and McKinnon 2001.

White, Hayden. 1980. The value of narrativity in the representation of reality. In *On narrative*, edited by W. J. J. Mitchell. Chicago: University of Chicago Press.

Williams, Raymond. 1977. *Marxism and literature.* New York: Oxford.

Winerip, Michael. 2008. With open adoption, a new kind of family. *New York Times*, February 24, LI4.

Winkvist, Hanna Markusson. 2006. Defining a new family: The Swedish approach to intercountry adoption. Paper presented at Sixth European Social Science History Conference, Amsterdam, March 22–25.

Winnicott, D. W. 1971. *Playing and reality*. London: Tavistock.

Winterson, Jeanette. 1997. *Oranges are not the only fruit*. New York: Grove Press. Original publication in 1985.

Witmer, Helen L., E. Hertzog, E. Weinstein, and M. Sullivan. 1963. *Independent adoptions: A follow-up study*. New York: Russell-Sage Foundation.

Yngvesson, Barbara. 1997. Negotiating motherhood: Identity and difference in "open" adoptions. *Law and Society Review* 31 (1): 31–80.

———. 2000. "Un niño de cualquier color": Race and nation in inter-country adoption. In Jenson and de Sousa Santos 2000.

———. 2002. Placing the "gift child" in transnational adoption. *Law and Society Review* 36 (2): 227–256.

———. 2004. National bodies and the body of the child: "Completing" families through international adoption. In Bowie 2004.

———. 2005. Going "home": Adoption, loss of bearings, and the mythology of roots. In Volkman 2005a.

Yngvesson, Barbara, and Susan Bibler Coutin. 2006. Backed by papers: Undoing persons, histories, and return. *American Ethnologist* 33 (2): 177–190.

———. 2008. Schrödinger's cat and the ethnography of law. *PoLAR* 31 (1): 61–78.

Yngvesson, Barbara, and Maureen Mahoney. 2000. "As one should, ought, and wants to be": Belonging and authenticity in identity narratives. *Theory, Culture, and Society* 17 (6): 77–110.

Zarin, Cynthia. 2006. Seeing things: The art of Olafur Eliasson. *New Yorker*, November 13, 76–83.

Zelizer, Viviana. 1985. *Pricing the priceless child*. Princeton, NJ: Princeton University Press.

Zhao, Yilu. 2002. Immersed in 2 worlds, new and old: Adoptees exploring their foreign roots. *New York Times*, April 9, A27.

Žižek, Slavoj. 1989. *The sublime object of ideology*. London: Verso.

Index

The Chicago Series in Law and Society
Edited by John M. Conley and Lynn Mather